AF766798

The Financial Trilemma and Cross-border Bank Crisis Management in ASEAN

Wassamon Kun-amornpong

The Financial Trilemma and Cross-border Bank Crisis Management in ASEAN

palgrave
macmillan

Wassamon Kun-amornpong
Thammasat University
Lampang, Thailand

ISBN 978-981-95-0511-1 ISBN 978-981-95-0512-8 (eBook)
https://doi.org/10.1007/978-981-95-0512-8

© The Editor(s) (if applicable) and The Author(s), under exclusive license to Springer Nature Singapore Pte Ltd. 2025

This work is subject to copyright. All rights are solely and exclusively licensed by the Publisher, whether the whole or part of the material is concerned, specifically the rights of translation, reprinting, reuse of illustrations, recitation, broadcasting, reproduction on microfilms or in any other physical way, and transmission or information storage and retrieval, electronic adaptation, computer software, or by similar or dissimilar methodology now known or hereafter developed.
The use of general descriptive names, registered names, trademarks, service marks, etc. in this publication does not imply, even in the absence of a specific statement, that such names are exempt from the relevant protective laws and regulations and therefore free for general use.
The publisher, the authors and the editors are safe to assume that the advice and information in this book are believed to be true and accurate at the date of publication. Neither the publisher nor the authors or the editors give a warranty, expressed or implied, with respect to the material contained herein or for any errors or omissions that may have been made. The publisher remains neutral with regard to jurisdictional claims in published maps and institutional affiliations.

This Palgrave Macmillan imprint is published by the registered company Springer Nature Singapore Pte Ltd.
The registered company address is: 152 Beach Road, #21-01/04 Gateway East, Singapore 189721, Singapore

If disposing of this product, please recycle the paper.

Preface

This monograph is the product of many years of academic inquiry, professional development, and personal growth during my doctoral journey. At its core, the research explores the complex intersection between legal frameworks and financial integration in Southeast Asia, with a particular focus on cross-border bank crisis management—an area in which the existing literature remains limited. The monograph is framed in light of the financial trilemma model proposed by Dirk Schoenmaker.

The idea for this monograph grew out of my curiosity about the causes of financial crises and the measures used to mitigate them, as well as my observation of the increasing internationalisation of banking operations in ASEAN. Upon closer examination, it becomes evident that ASEAN still lacks a robust and unified legal mechanism to effectively address cross-border financial instability. Recognising the limitations of existing literature—much of which focuses on developed regions such as the European Union—I was motivated to examine the ASEAN context more closely. This monograph is therefore intended to fill a significant gap in legal scholarship by offering a comprehensive analysis of bank crisis management mechanisms in Southeast Asia, covering key aspects such as bank supervision, bank resolution, deposit insurance, fiscal backstops, and state supports.

Although legal in nature, this monograph is interdisciplinary in its outlook. It draws on a range of sources, including empirical data, policy documents, and regional legal instruments, in order to assess both theoretical frameworks and practical realities. It also reflects on the broader question of whether ASEAN's preference for soft law and informal governance—rooted in the 'ASEAN Way'—could offer a more viable path forward than the hard-law solutions typically advocated in Western models.

I hope this work will be of use not only to academics and students, but also to policymakers, regulators, and practitioners engaged in shaping the financial landscape of Southeast Asia. By highlighting the region's unique challenges and proposing context-sensitive solutions, it aims to stimulate further debate on cross-border bank crisis management and to contribute meaningfully to the discourse on regional financial integration and legal reform.

Lampang, Thailand Wassamon Kun-amornpong

Acknowledgements In completing this monograph, I am greatly indebted to the support from many people, to whom I would like to express my sincere gratitude here. I would like to thank Warwick Law School, an incredible community of which I am proud to be a part. I am grateful for the kind support from faculty members and staff of the Law School, especially my supervisor, Professor Dalvinder Singh, who dedicated his valuable time and efforts to provide academic guidance and advice throughout my Ph.D. studies.

I extend my gratitude to Thammasat University for their continued support, including the scholarship that enabled me to pursue advanced studies abroad. In addition, I would like to thank my Ph.D. colleagues and friends for their generous help throughout my doctoral journey. Moreover, I am particularly thankful to the legal, economic, and finance professionals I had the opportunity to meet during my doctoral years, whose invaluable practical insights have enriched this monograph.

Last but not least, I would like to dedicate this monograph to my beloved family, Mongkol, Siriwan, and Supasima Kun-amornpong, whose unwavering faith and sacrifices have made this achievement possible. Their love and support continue to inspire me.

Competing Interests The author has no competing interests to declare that are relevant to the content of this manuscript.

Contents

Abbreviations

ABIF	ASEAN Banking Integration Framework
ADB	Asian Development Bank
AEC	ASEAN Economic Community
AFAS	ASEAN Framework Agreement on Services
AFC	Asian Financial Crisis
AMC	Asset Management Company
AMRO	ASEAN +3 Macroeconomic Research Office
ASEAN	Association of Southeast Asian Nations
ASF	Available Stable Funding
AUD	Australian Dollar
BCBS	Basel Committee on Banking Supervision
BCLMV	Brunei, Cambodia, Lao PDR, Myanmar and Vietnam
BCP	Basel Core Principles
BERI	Business Environment Risk Intelligence
BIS	Bank for International Settlements
BNM	Bank Negara Malaysia
BOT	Bank of Thailand
BRRD	Bank Recovery and Resolution Directive
BRRD I	Bank Recovery and Resolution Directive 2014
BRRD II	Bank Recovery and Resolution Directive 2019
BSP	Banko Sentral ng Philopinas
BTA	Bank of Thailand Act, B.E. 2551 (2008)
CBS	Consolidated Banking Statistics
CDS	Credit Default Swap
CET1	Common Equity Tier 1
CJEU	Court of Justice of the European Union

CMI	Chiang Mai Initiative
CMIM	Chiang Mai Initiative Multilateralisation
CMIM-PL	CMIM Precautionary Line
CMIM-SF	CMIM Stability Facility
CRD IV	Capital Requirements Directive 2013
CRD V	Capital Requirements Directive 2019
CRR	Capital Requirements Regulation 2013
CRR II	Capital Requirements Regulation 2019
DGS	Deposit Guarantee Scheme
DGSD	Deposit Guarantee Schemes Directive 2014
DIS	Deposit Insurance System
DLI	Disbursement Linked Indicators
DMC	Developing Member Country
DPA	Deposit Protection Agency Act, B.E. 2551 (2008)
DPF	Development Policy Financing
DPO	Deposit Protection Office
D-SIB	Domestic Systemically Important Bank
EBA	European Banking Authority
ECB	European Central Bank
ECHR	European Convention on Human Rights
ECJ	European Court of Justice
EDSM	Enhanced Dispute Settlement Mechanism
EEA	European Economic Area
EFDI	European Forum of Deposit Insurers
EFTA	European Free Trade Association
EGAT	Electricity Generating Authority of Thailand
EIOPA	European Insurance and Occupational Pensions Authority
ELA	Emergency Liquidity Assistance
ELDMB	Executive Level Decision Making Body
EMV	Estimated Market Value
ESA	European Supervisory Authority
ESFS	European System of Financial Supervision
ESMA	European Securities and Markets Authority
ESRB	European Systemic Risk Board
EU	European Union
FDIC	Federal Deposit Insurance Corporation
FIBA	Financial Institutions Businesses Act, B.E. 2551 (2008)
FITD	Fondo Interbancario di Tutela dei Depositi
FOLTF	Failing or Likely to Fail
FRA	Financial Sector Restructuring Agency
FSAP	Financial Sector Assessment Programme
FSB	Financial Stability Board
FSCC	Financial Stability Coordination Council

FSCS	Financial Services Compensation Scheme
FSEC	Financial Stability Executive Committee
FSF	Financial Stability Forum
FSMA	Financial Services and Markets Act 2022 (Number 18 of 2022)
GDP	Gross Domestic Product
GFC	Global Financial Crisis
GFDD	Global Financial Development database
G-SIB	Global Systemically Important Bank
HLA	Higher Loss Absorbency
HQLA	High Quality Liquid Asset
IADI	International Association of Deposit Insurers
IAIS	International Association of Insurance Supervisors
IBRA	Indonesian Bank Restructuring Agency
IBRD	International Bank for Reconstruction and Development
ICRG	International Country Risk Guide
IFI	International Financial Institution
ILOLR	International Lenders of Last Resort
IMF	International Monetary Fund
IN-LAW	Informal International Lawmaking
IOSCO	International Organisation of Securities Commission
IPF	Investment Project Financing
ISDA	International Swaps and Derivative Association, Inc.
JMP	Jurisdictional Modular Protocol
JST	Joint Supervisory Team
LCR	Liquidity Coverage Ratio
LGD	Loss Given Default
LOI	Letter of Intent
LOLR	Lender of Last Resort
MA	Master Agreement
MAS	Monetary Authority of Singapore
MASA	Monetary Authority of Singapore Act
MDIC	Malaysian Deposit Insurance Corporate
MiFID	Markets in Financial Instruments Directive
MLDMB	Ministerial Level Decision Making Body
MOF	Minister of Finance
MOU	Memorandum of Understanding
MREL	Minimum Requirement for own funds and Eligible Liabilities
NCA	National Competent Authority
NCWO	No Creditor Worse Off
NGO	Non-Governmental Organisation
NIE	New Institutional Economics
NIM	Net Interest Margin
NIP	National Insolvency Proceedings

NOD	National Option And Discretion
NPA	Non-Performing Asset
NPL	Non-Performing Loan
NRA	National Resolution Authority
NRFA	National Resolution Funding Arrangement
NSFR	Net Stable Funding Ratio
OCR	Ordinary Capital Resources
OECD	Organisation for Economic Co-operation and Development
OJK	Otoritas Jasa Keuangan
OLA	Orderly Liquidation Authority
PCA	Prompt Corrective Action
PCSCC	Payment, Cash, Settlement, Clearing and Custody
PD	Probability of Default
PforR	Program-for-Results Financing
PIA	Public Interest Assessment
PIDM	Perbadanam Insurans Deposit Malaysia
PIU	Project Implementation Unit
PTT	Petroleum Authority of Thailand
PWC	Post-Washington Consensus
QAB	Qualified ASEAN Banks
QE	Quantitative Easing
RA	Republic Act
REV	Real Economic Value
RFA	Regional Financing Arrangement
RFF	Rapid Financing Facility
ROA	Return on Assets
ROE	Return on Equity
ROSC	Report on Observance of Standards and Codes
RSF	Required Stable Funding
RTC	Resolution Trust Corporation
RTS	Regulatory Technical Standards
RWA	Risk-Weighted Assets
SBV	State Bank of Vietnam
SIBOR	Singapore Interbank Offered Rate
SIFI	Systemically important financial institution
SME	Small and Medium-Sized Enterprises
SPV	Special Purpose Vehicle
SRB	Single Resolution Board
SREP	Supervisory Review and Evaluation Process
SRF	Single Resolution Fund
SRM	Single Resolution Mechanism
SRMR I	Single Resolution Mechanism Regulation 2014
SRMR II	Single Resolution Mechanism Regulation 2019

SSM	Single Supervisory Mechanism
SSMR	Single Supervisory Mechanism Regulation
TFEU	Treaty on the Functioning of the European Union
UNCITRAL	United Nations Commission of International Trade Law
UOB	United Oversea Bank Limited
UP	Universal Resolution Stay Protocol
VAMC	Vietnam Asset Management Company
VAR	Value-at-Risk
WGI	Worldwide Governance Indicators
WTO	World Trade Organisation

List of Figures

List of Tables

CHAPTER 1

Financial Trilemma and the Role of Law—The Case of ASEAN Financial Integration

1.1 Introduction

Banks have increasingly taken cross-border activities in order to reap the benefits of internationalisation (e.g., economies of scale, synergies among business lines and diversification of risks). However, their overseas expansion could pose regulatory challenges to national authorities. One of those challenges would be problems relating to conflicts of interest between the home and host states. In this monograph, a 'home country' refers to the country in which the parent bank is headquartered and incorporated. Meanwhile, a 'host country' is the country where the parent bank operates an establishment.

According to Richard J Herring, the main source of home-host conflicts would be the fact that national supervisors often give priority to their domestic policies in the event of an insolvency.[1] In addition, supervisory measures taken by national authorities towards foreign banks could result in conflicts of interest with foreign authorities. The approach

[1] Richard Herring, 'Conflicts between Home and Host Country Prudential Supervisors' in Douglas Evanoff et al. (eds), *International Financial Stability: Global Banking and National Regulation* (World Scientific 2007), 211.

© The Author(s), under exclusive license to Springer Nature Singapore Pte Ltd. 2025

W. Kun-amornpong, *The Financial Trilemma and Cross-border Bank Crisis Management in ASEAN*,
https://doi.org/10.1007/978-981-95-0512-8_1

of national authorities would depend upon whether or not the financial institution concerned is considered systemically important to their country.[2]

For instance, in the case in which the overseas office is not systemically important to either the home or host country, it would be unlikely to be a problem of conflicts of interest: the home and host authorities would lack an incentive to conduct intensive and thorough supervision. In contrast, a problem of home-host conflicts could occur where an entity is significantly important to both the home and host country. In this case, the home and host supervisors would have a high stake in assiduously supervising the financial institution.[3]

Herring's idea has been developed further by Dirk Schoenmaker, who has put forward a model of the 'financial trilemma'. This model is influenced by the classical monetary trilemma, which states that policy makers cannot pursue exchange rate stability, free flows of capital and national monetary policy simultaneously.[4] The 'financial trilemma' model demonstrates that an increase in financial integration, which exceeds some basic level, will come at the cost of financial instability. This is due to the fact that national policymakers are likely to pursue their national interest, rather than preserve the common good of international financial stability. In other words, it is impossible to combine together the three main policy goals of financial integration, financial stability and national financial policies. It is only possible to have two of the three objectives.

According to Schoenmaker, financial stability could go together with national financial policies. The combination of these policy goals would result in national banking. In the case that the policies regarding financial stability and financial integration are pursued together, states would not be able to deliver international financial stability by themselves. Hence,

[2] Ibid., 212–214.

[3] Ibid.

[4] Dirk Schoenmaker, 'The Financial Trilemma' (2011) 111(1) Economics Letters 57, 57. Not surprisingly, some authors utilise the term the 'financial trilemma' in order to state the idea of the monetary or macroeconomic trilemma rather than that of the 'financial trilemma' used in this monograph (e.g., Lucas K. Njoroge, Joshua Aizenman and Rajeswari Sengupta). Lucas K. Njoroge, 'The Financial Trilemma and Macroeconomic Instability: Empirical Evidence from Kenya' (2015) 2(2) American Journal of Trade and Policy. Joshua Aizenman and Rajeswari Sengupta, 'The Financial Trilemma in China and a Comparative Analysis with India' (2013) 18(2) Pacific Economic Review 123–146.

there would be a need to use international governance in so doing.[5] Meanwhile, the pursuance of financial integration and national financial policies is a risky strategy. National authorities might not take into account cross-border externalities; hence, international financial stability could be jeopardised. Schoenmaker utilises the prisoner's dilemma in order to elaborate this concern as a game of cooperation between national authorities. Each state authority would contribute to international financial stability only to the extent that it is 'individually rational' (i.e., 'each country's payoff is as large as it would be by acting independently'). As a result, there would be an inadequate provision of funds for recapitalising a troubled bank with cross-border operation.[6]

With respect to a 'non-cooperative Nash equilibrium' resulting from an insufficient contribution of states, Jerome Mathis has argued that there is always an equilibrium in which countries would contribute sufficient funds to rescue an ailing bank.[7] His Proposition demonstrates that the best response of states is to contribute as little as possible, rather than provide nothing at all.[8] This circumstance could occur regardless of the level of financial integration or social benefits in the home country. According to Mathis, it would be reasonable for states to contribute funds in order to avoid bailing out the bank entirely if two conditions are met: an assistance is given at minimal cost and relevant states make a contribution in proportion to the benefits they receive. Consequently, national financial policies, financial stability and financial integration could be pursued simultaneously.[9] Nevertheless, it is doubtful whether countries could comply with the conditions of Mathis's Proposition. For example, a state might not be in a position to contribute funds proportionately to the benefits it receives due to the fact that its economy is much smaller than its financial system.

Applying Schoenmaker's model to ASEAN, increasing financial integration in this sub-region, with a high degree of the utilisation of national

[5] Dirk Schoenmaker, *Governance of International Banking: The Financial Trilemma* (Oxford Scholarship Online 2013), 91.

[6] Ibid., 18.

[7] Jerome Mathis, 'Corrigendum to "The Financial Trilemma" [Economic Letters 111 (2011) 57–59]' (2023) 224 Economics Letters, 1.

[8] Ibid., 2.

[9] Ibid., 1.

approach, could exacerbate international financial instability.[10] According to Nardo et al., there is no universally accepted definition of financial integration.[11] The term could mean an integration of markets in the banking, insurance or securities sectors. In this monograph, financial integration focuses only on cross-border banking market integration in terms of the opening of domestic banking markets to foreign banks.

This monograph seeks to test the hypothesis taken from the model of the financial trilemma in the context of cross-border bank crisis management in Southeast Asia. In so doing, it aims to answer three main questions:

(1) does financial integration in ASEAN warrant a creation of an ASEAN bank crisis management framework?
(2) what are possible options for an ASEAN bank crisis management framework?
(3) what are obstacles or idiosyncratic factors that should be taken into account when creating an ASEAN bank crisis management framework?

In this chapter, I will discuss the role of law in relation to each objective of the financial trilemma by using ASEAN financial integration as an illustration. The chapter proceeds in two parts. Part I will provide an analysis regarding the accelerating factors of the financial trilemma in ASEAN region. In Part II, the interplay between the role of law and the increase in financial integration will be analysed. In addition, the relationship between law and financial stability will be considered. Moreover, this part will explore the role that law could play in alleviating home-host conflicts. These conflicts could occur in the case that national financial policies are prioritised over international financial stability. The chapter will conclude with a summary of the subsequent chapters of the monograph.

[10] Currently, ASEAN has ten member states. Timor-Leste is expected to officially join ASEAN in October 2025. https://timor-leste.gov.tl/?p=43601&lang=en&n=1, accessed 4 June 2025.

[11] Michela Nardo et al., 'Financial Integration in the EU28 Equity Markets: Measures and Drivers' (2022) 57 Journal of Financial Markets, 1.

1.2 Part I: ASEAN and the Existence of the Financial Trilemma

The financial trilemma exists when there is a sufficient degree of financial integration. According to Niels Thygesen (2003) and Schoenmaker (2005), financial integration which causes the development of the financial trilemma can occur at both global and regional levels.[12] Given this condition, I argue that the progress of financial integration among ASEAN member states, and the integration of ASEAN states with non-ASEAN countries, would exacerbate the financial trilemma for two main reasons.[13]

First, ASEAN has made a progress in a partial financial integration through the Qualified ASEAN Banks scheme (QAB scheme) which could help accelerate banking integration in this sub-region.[14] There are two phases for the QAB scheme. The first phase will proceed in accordance with the 'ASEAN minus x' approach in which the bilateral agreements will be made among the ASEAN-5 states (i.e., Indonesia, Malaysia, the Philippines, Thailand and Singapore). During this phase, capacity-building programmes will be provided for the rest of ASEAN states in order to prepare them for participating in the integration process. As for the second phase, non-QABs will gain access to the market through the integration process.[15]

However, the QAB programme does not specify mechanisms of supervisory and regulatory integration.[16] This could create conflicts and

[12] Schoenmaker (n 5).

[13] This argument will be supported by data from the banking industry which is the most developed part of the financial sectors for most ASEAN states.

[14] The notion of partial integration could be contrasted with the concept of full economic integration. The latter, according to Spaak Report (1956), would only be achieved when the member states jettison their autonomous budgetary, relinquish national financial and social policies, and adopt a single currency. Pedro Teixeira, 'The Legal History of the Banking Union' (2017) Eur Bus Org Law Rev 18, 536.

[15] Angus Chan et al., 'Depositor Preference and Deposit Insurance Schemes – Challenges for Regulatory Convergence and Regulatory Coordination in Asia' (2018) Law and Financial Markets Review 12 (2), 18–19, https://papers.ssrn.com/sol3/papers.cfm?abstract_id=3216357&download=yes, accessed 4 June 2025.

[16] Federico Lupo-Pasini, 'Banking Integration in ASEAN and the Challenges of Regulatory Cooperation', in Pasha L. Hsieh and Bryan Mercurio (eds), *ASEAN Law in the New Regional Economic Order: Global Trends and Shifting Paradigm* (Cambridge University Press 2019), 140.

uncertainty regarding the responsibility of the home and host authorities. Secondly, the data of international bank lending has shown a possibility of a contagion risk among ASEAN member states, as they are connected not only with banks in Southeast Asia, but also those outside the region. I will elaborate these two concerns in detail in the following sections.

1.2.1 Subsidiaries and Branches of ASEAN Banks and the Qualified ASEAN Banks Scheme

Cross-border expansion of ASEAN banks through subsidiaries and branches could help increase ASEAN financial integration. Nevertheless, it could also contribute to financial instability under the financial trilemma. The notion of financial stability has not been well defined. Financial instability can create either systemic risk, or risk which affects individual market participants. Financial instability may or may not lead to systemic risk depending on whether it generates a widespread contagion. Goodhart (2006) has stated that assessing financial stability of the banking sector is an 'intractable task because of cross-border spillovers, lack of a clear demarcation line between banks and shadow banks, financial vulnerabilities in sectors that are connected to the banking sector.' Nevertheless, Schinasi has argued that efficient allocation of capital, a forward-looking approach to assess financial risk, and the ability to absorb financial and real economic shocks should be considered as elements of financial stability.[17]

Home-host supervisory conflicts could occur in various scenarios during a financial crisis. For example, the host authority could ringfence assets of a troubled bank to the detriment of financial stability in the home state. In addition, there might be problems regarding burden-sharing, in the case of a large foreign bank failure.[18] A closure of a foreign branch means the depositors could recover deposits in other branch of the banking group (*Vishipco Line v. Chase Manhattan Bank*).[19] In turn,

[17] Garry J. Schinasi, *Safeguarding Financial Stability: Theory and Practice* (International Monetary Fund 2005).

[18] Jonathan Fiechter et al., 'Subsidiaries or Branches: Does One Size Fit All?' (7 March 2011) IMF Staff Discussion Note, 5, https://www.imf.org/external/pubs/ft/sdn/2011/sdn1104.pdf, accessed 4 June 2025.

[19] Vishipco Line v. Chase Manhattan Bank 660 F 2d 854 (1981). The New York court held that deposits placed with the Saigon branch of Chase Manhanttan Bank could be recovered in New York. This is the case when the Saigon branch was closed in order to

this can create tensions regarding national deposit insurance, as taxpayers might have to pay the debts to foreigners.

In order to analyse the significance of overseas expansion of ASEAN banks and the potential risk of home-host conflicts in this region, I have collected data regarding the number of branches and subsidiaries of the five largest commercial banks, by assets of each ASEAN member states.[20] In Fig. 1.1, the horizontal axis represents host states, while the vertical axis shows the percentage of the total number of foreign branches and subsidiaries of banks of the home states. Figure 1.1 illustrates that the five largest banks headquartered in Thailand, Malaysia, Indonesia, the Philippines, Singapore and Vietnam have subsidiaries and/or branches in other ASEAN member states. Among these banks, banks headquartered in Malaysia and Singapore have the highest numbers of branches and subsidiaries in ASEAN states. Meanwhile, the five largest commercial banks headquartered in Lao PDR, Brunei, Myanmar and Cambodia have neither branch nor subsidiary overseas.[21]

According to the data, the mean value of the number of ASEAN banks' branches and subsidiaries in other member states is 183.3. However, there is a significant gap between the number of overseas branches and subsidiaries of banks headquartered in Singapore (473 branches/subsidiaries) and Malaysia (1308 branches/subsidiaries), and those of banks headquartered in the rest of ASEAN states (e.g., Thailand has 28 overseas branches/subsidiaries and Vietnam has 17 overseas branches/subsidiaries).[22] The number of overseas branches and subsidiaries could

escape the Communist insurgents in Vietnam. The court held that deposits were liabilities of the bank as a whole.

[20] Sub-branch, representative office and agency are excluded. Subsidiaries and branches of non-ASEAN states are not included in the list of the five largest commercial banks. For example, Bank of Ayudhya Public Company Limited is the fifth largest commercial bank by asset in Thailand. However, it is a subsidiary of MUFG Bank, Ltd. which is the largest bank in Japan. Therefore, it is excluded from the list. The data includes the sixth largest commercial bank in Thailand, Thanachart Bank Public Company Limited, instead of Bank of Ayudhya Public Company Limited.

[21] Many banks in these countries are state-owned. Some of them are a joint venture between a national government and foreign entities.

[22] United Oversea Bank Limited (UOB) acquired Citigroup's consumer banking in Thailand, Malaysia, Indonesia and Vietnam in order to expand its retail business in ASEAN. Citigroup's consumer banking businesses in Thailand and Malaysia were acquired by UOB in 2022, while the acquisition of Citigroup's business in Indonesia and Vietnam was completed in 2023. UOB, 'UOB Completes Acquisition of Citigroup's

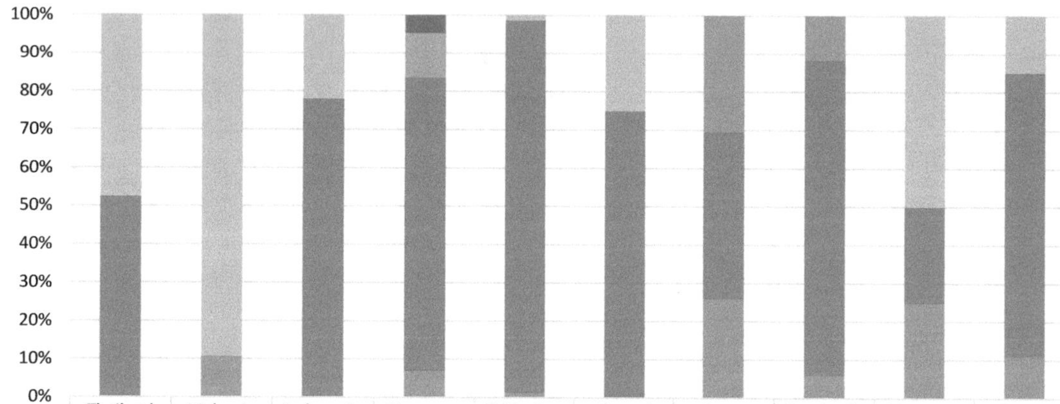

	Thailand	Malaysia	Indonesia	Singapore	Philippines	Brunei	Laos	Cambodia	Myanmar	Vietnam
Brunei	0	0	0	0	0	0	0	0	0	0
Myanmar	0	0	0	0	0	0	0	0	0	0
Cambodia	0	0	0	0	0	0	0	0	0	0
Laos	0	0	0	0	0	0	0	0	0	0
Vietnam	0	0	0	0	0	0	7	10	0	0
Philippines	0	0	0	2	0	0	0	0	0	0
Singapore	156	50	259	0	1	1	0	0	2	4
Indonesia	0	0	0	5	0	0	0	0	0	0
Malaysia	172	0	920	33	74	3	10	70	1	20
Thailand	0	6	3	3	1	0	6	5	1	3

Fig. 1.1 Number of foreign branches and subsidiaries of banks headquartered in ASEAN (share in %) (*Source* Author's calculations based on Orbis Bank Focus and commercial banks' websites)

increase as a result of the QAB scheme. The scheme could potentially accelerate financial integration as well as exacerbate the financial trilemma in this sub-region. The next section will provide some details about the progress of the QAB programme, as well as criticise it.

1.2.1.1 The ASEAN Banking Integration Framework and the QAB Scheme

The financial and capital markets integration of ASEAN became concrete when the ASEAN Economic Community (AEC) Blueprint was created in 2007.[23] Currently, ASEAN financial integration has the highest degree of convergence in Asia, when compared with other sub-regional markets.[24] This is especially the case for ASEAN-5, where financial interconnectivity has increased significantly in recent years.[25] In addition, in 2014, as part of the AEC Blueprint, the central bank governors of ASEAN Member States adopted the ASEAN Banking Integration Framework (ABIF) as well as its attendant Guidelines. The provision in the Protocol to Implement the 6th Package of Commitments on Financial Services, which was

Consumer Banking Businesses in Malaysia and Thailand' (*UOB*, 1 November 2022), https://www.uobgroup.com/uobgroup/newsroom/2022/uob-completes-acquisition-of-citigroups-consumer-banking-businesses-in-malaysia-and-thailand.page?path=data/uobgroup/2022/254&cr=segment, accessed 4 June 2025. UOB was expected to become top 5 bank for retail banking in Malaysia; it had been the seventh largest bank in Malaysia before the acquisition of Citigroup's business. Eukeik.ee, 'What Would Happen in the Retail Business When UOB Acquire Citigroup?' (*Marketeer*, 14 January 2022) (in Thai), https://www.uobgroup.com/uobgroup/newsroom/2022/uob-completes-acquisition-of-citigroups-consumer-banking-businesses-in-malaysia-and-thailand.page?path=data/uobgroup/2022/254&cr=segment, accessed 4 June 2025.

[23] Maria Monica Wihardja, 'Financial Integration Challenges in ASEAN beyond 2015' (November 2013) ERIA Discussion Paper Series, http://www.eria.org/ERIA-DP-2013-27.pdf, accessed 4 June 2025. At the Bali Summit in October 2003, ASEAN Leaders declared the AEC to be the goal of regional economic integration (Bali Concord II) by 2020. 'ASEAN Economic Community Blueprint', 7, https://asean.org/wp-content/uploads/archive/5187-10.pdf, accessed 4 June 2025.

[24] Aladdin D. Rillo, 'ASEAN Financial Integration: Opportunities, Risks, and Challenges' (2018) Public Policy Review 14 (5), 905. However, ASEAN financial markets are still more integrated with the global markets than with the region.

[25] Pablo Lopez Murphy, 'Systemic Risks and Financial Stability Frameworks' in Ana Corbacho and Shanaka J. Peiris (eds), *The ASEAN Way: Sustaining Growth and Stability* (International Monetary Fund 2018), 193.

created under the ASEAN Framework Agreement on Services (AFAS), has enabled the implementation of the ABIF.[26]

The ABIF was heavily influenced by a study of Park et al. in 2011,[27] in which a set of foundations for ABIF comprised the harmonisation of principles of prudential regulations, financial stability infrastructure, capacity building and a set of criteria for QABs.[28] The ABIF aims to achieve a free flow of financial services within ASEAN sub-regional banking market by 2020. Under the ABIF, member countries have adopted the scheme of QABs, in which a bank qualified in one jurisdiction will receive equal treatment in other ASEAN jurisdictions.[29] The idea is similar to that of the 'single bank passports' of the EU.[30] According to the Banko Sentral ng Philopinas (BSP), the ABIF aimed for all the member states to have concluded or be finalising at least one bilateral arrangement per member state by 2020.[31]

The QAB scheme has been welcomed by the member states. Their attitude towards the scheme can be explained by the push and pull factors models. According to Eduardo Fernandez-Arias, the determinants of capital inflows into developing countries could be considered into the 'push' and 'pull' factors.[32] The push factors occur outside the emerging

[26] Asian Development Bank, 'ASEAN Banking Integration Framework (ABIF)', https://aric.adb.org/initiative/asean-banking-integration-framework-abif, accessed 4 June 2025.

[27] Wihardja (n 23) 4.

[28] ibid. According to Park et. al., there are five regulatory areas to harmonize: (i) Bank accounting standards and disclosure requirements; (ii) Minimum capital requirements; (iii) Prompt Corrective Action (PCA) and methodologies for the resolution of failed banks; (iv) Restrictions on large exposures; (v) Anti-money laundering and consumer protection regulation. ibid 5.

[29] 'ASEAN Banking Integration and Lessons from Europe' (13 September 2015) BIS Quarterly Review, https://www.bis.org/publ/qtrpdf/r_qt1509z.htm, accessed 4 June 2025.

[30] Evgeny Vinokurov, 'Regional Financial Integration in ASEAN in the Comparative Perspective' (4 December 2017) MPRA Paper No. 83022, 19, https://mpra.ub.uni-muenchen.de/83022/1/MPRA_paper_83022.pdf, accessed 4 June 2025.

[31] Bangko Sentral ng Pilipinas, Working Committee on ASEAN Banking Integration Framework (WC-ABIF), http://www.bsp.gov.ph/asean/wc_abif.asp, accessed 4 June 2025.

[32] Eduardo Fernandez-Arias, 'The New Wave of Private Capital Inflows: Push or Pull?' (1994) World Bank Policy Research Working Paper 1312, 1, http://documents.worldbank.org/curated/en/832831468765600401/pdf/multi-page.pdf, accessed 4 June 2025.

country and push capital into the state (e.g., a low return on capital and an excessive supply of liquidity for distribution in developed countries). Meanwhile, the latter are determinants specific to the emerging country which pull capital into the country (e.g., an undersupply of liquidity and high yields on capital in a borrowing country).[33]

In the case of the QAB scheme, increasingly saturated domestic markets in some member states are a push factor for banks to expand overseas.[34] For example, Malaysia has a highly developed financial system; however, its domestic market is small. Hence, it would benefit in a significant way from financial integration.[35] In addition, the potential for a higher return on capital in some member states could act as a pull factor, in the case that entry barriers are eliminated. For instance, Singapore has a low lending interest rate at 1.96038 per cent for the cost of twelve-month SIBOR,[36] whereas short-term lending interest rate in Laos is 10 per cent.[37] Hence, the pull factor in Laos would attract overseas expansion of banks in Singapore into the country.

Moreover, the interplay between push and pull factors can be considered using a decision of Bangkok Bank, the third-largest bank by assets in Thailand, to acquire PT Bank Permata Tbk (Permata), the twelfth largest Indonesian bank by total assets.[38] In December 2019, Bangkok Bank issued a press release announcing that it has agreed with Standard

[33] Sophi.e.,Brana and Delphine Lahet, 'The Push–Pull Determinants of Cross-border Bank Claims on Emerging Countries: The Role of Parent Banks and their Subsidiaries' (2015), 5, https://gdrenice2015.sciencesconf.org/54125/document, accessed 4 June 2025.

[34] Handriyanto Wijaya et al., 'ASEAN Banking Integration and Its Impact on the Banking Industry in Indonesia', 3rd International Conference on Globalization of Law and Local Wisdom (October 2019), 96, https://www.atlantis-press.com/proceedings/icglow-19/125920772, accessed 4 June 2025.

[35] Satoshi Shimizu, 'ASEAN Financial and Capital Markets—Policies and Prospects of Regional Integration' (2014) RIM Pacific Business and Industries Vol. XIV, No. 54, 16, https://www.jri.co.jp/MediaLibrary/file/english/periodical/rim/2014/54.pdf, accessed 4 June 2025.

[36] As of 21 February 2020. The Association of Banks in Singapore, https://www.abs.org.sg/benchmark-rates/rates-sibor, accessed 4 June 2025. SIBOR stands for Singapore Interbank Offered Rate.

[37] Bank of the Lao P.D.R Interest Rate (2 weeks–1 year). Bank of the Lao P.D.R, https://www.bol.gov.la/en/index, accessed 4 June 2025.

[38] The deal is the largest acquisition of a foreign financial institution by a Thai bank.

Chartered Bank and PT Astra International Tbk to make a 'conditional share purchase' contract in order to acquire 89.12 per cent shareholding in Permata.[39] With regards to push factors, 'an economic slowdown, elevated household debt, deteriorating asset quality and low interest rates' in Thailand have caused Thai banks to seek opportunities overseas.[40]

Concerning pull factors, the Indonesian economy has expanded faster than those of many Asian countries. For example, the economy of Thailand has grown at less than twice the growth rate of Indonesia's.[41] In addition, Indonesia has the largest population in ASEAN (273 million people) with only 49 per cent of adults having access to basic consumer financial products and services.[42] In contrast, 82 per cent of Thai adults have access to banking services.[43] Hence, the Indonesian market is highly attractive for Thai banks. Moreover, this deal supports a regionalisation strategy as Bangkok Bank has aimed to become a leading regional bank in Asia and ASEAN.[44]

Currently, the bilateral agreements in the form of the 'Heads of Agreement' have been signed between Malaysia and Indonesia in 2014, Malaysia and the Philippines in 2016, and Malaysia and Thailand in 2016. In addition, a Letter of Intent has been made between Indonesia and Thailand in 2016.[45] There are some QABs operating in ASEAN member states. For example, Malaysia has two QABs operating in

[39] Bangkok Bank, 'Bangkok Bank to Strengthen Regional Position through Acquisition of Permata in Indonesia from Standard Chartered Bank and Astra International' (*Press Release*, 12 December 2019), https://www.bangkokbank.com/en/Investor-Relations/-/media/52611f5257d3488ea623e81817912a69.ashx, accessed 4 June 2025.

[40] 'Bangkok Bank Buys Standard Chartered's Indonesian Bank for $3.65 Billion' *The Straits Times* (Singapore, 13 December 2019), https://www.straitstimes.com/business/banking/bangkok-bank-buys-standard-chartereds-indonesian-bank-for-365-billion, accessed 4 June 2025.

[41] Ibid.

[42] Asli Demirguc-Kunt et al., *The Global Findex Database 2017: Measuring Financial Inclusion and the Fintech Revolution* (The World Bank 2018), 124, https://globalfindex.worldbank.org/sites/globalfindex/files/2018-04/2017%20Findex%20full%20report_0.pdf, accessed 4 June 2025.

[43] Ibid., 126.

[44] Supattha, 'Examining Five Issues Leading to the Permata Bank Deal of BBL' (*Marketeer*, 13 December 2019) (in Thai), https://marketeeronline.co/archives/135732, accessed 4 June 2025.

[45] Chan et al. (n 15) 246.

Indonesia. According to Wijaya et al., Malaysia is allowed to add a third QAB in Indonesia, after three Indonesian QABs are fully operational in Malaysia.[46]

In addition, Thailand and Malaysia have agreed to allow the establishment of QABs in accordance with the principle of reciprocity. Each country can issue a license of up to three commercial banks headquartered in the other party's country. Currently, there are two Malaysian commercial banks operating in Thailand: CIMB Thai Bank and RHB Bank. Meanwhile, Bangkok Bank Berhad is the only Thai QAB in Malaysia.[47]

However, ASEAN has not harmonised regulation in parallel with its efforts to increase financial integration in this sub-region. Besides, there is neither ASEAN crisis management, nor other safety nets in place. The experience of Europe has shown that the absence of these measures could lead to international financial instability as well as systemic risk. Prior to the unfolding of the global financial crisis (GFC), the EU increased financial integration in the region by utilising three main legal principles: 'the mutual recognition of national laws, the minimum harmonisation of national laws, and freedom of capital movement'. These principles laid down the basis for the 'single passport'.[48] In addition, national authorities were responsible for the prevention and management of financial crises on the ground that there would be no burden-sharing of costs of a crisis among the Member States.[49]

The 2008 crisis has turned the tide, as the minimum harmonisation of laws could not contain the impact of the crisis within national boundaries. Besides, the retention of national competences constrained cooperation among the national authorities.[50] For example, Swedish banks (i.e.,

[46] Wijaya et al. (n 34) 98.

[47] Bank of Thailand, 'A Cooperation of the Banking Sectors in ASEAN (Qualified ASEAN Bank) between Thailand and Malaysia' (Bank of Thailand News, 14 September 2021) (in Thai), https://www.bot.or.th/th/news-and-media/news/news-20210914-1.html, accessed 31 March 2025.

[48] Teixeira (n 14) 540.

[49] Ibid., 542.

[50] Ibid., 543.

Swedbank and SEB) possessed a market share of 80 per cent in the Estonian banking market.[51] Before the crisis broke out, the host and home supervisors lacked extensive cross-border coordination. As a result, there were gaps in supervisory attention for branches of the Swedish banks in Estonia.

Those branches were not subject to the capital adequacy requirements determined by the host state. In addition, the Swedish supervisors did not increase the requirements for them.[52] Moreover, the Swedish supervisors did not pay careful attention to the warnings from the Estonian authorities, regarding the risk taking of their banks in Estonia.[53] When Estonia was hit by the crisis, this inevitably affected the financial stability of Sweden, as their banks had extensive lending to Estonia.[54]

After the crisis, the EU has pursued greater centralisation in order to mitigate the risk of international financial instability and minimise home-host conflicts. The EU single passport framework was built upon with the introduction of the 'single rulebook'. In addition, the 'maximum harmonisation' of the single market rule has prevailed over national laws and regulations.[55] Moreover, the EU has centralised the enforcement powers at the supranational level, through the functioning of, for example, the European Central Bank (ECB), the Single Supervisory Mechanism (SSM), the Single Resolution Mechanism (SRM) and the Single Resolution Board (SRB).[56]

[51] Stefan Ingves, 'The Crisis in the Baltic—the Riksbank's Measures, Assessments and Lessons Learned', 'Speech' (The Riksdag Committee on Finance, Stockholm, 2 February 2010), 1.

[52] Ringa Raudla et al., 'Policy Learning from Crisis in Financial Regulation and Supervision: Comparative Analysis of Estonia, Latvia and Sweden' (The 12th Conference on Baltic Studies in Europe, Riga, 19–21 June 2017), 7, https://www.researchgate.net/publication/318402640_Policy_Learning_from_Crisis_in_Financial_Regulation_and_Supervision_Comparative_Analysis_of_Estonia_Latvia_and_Sweden, accessed 4 June 2025.

[53] Ibid.

[54] Riksbank, 'The Financial Crisis 2007–2009', https://www.riksbank.se/en-gb/financial-stability/the-riksbanks-financial-stability-tasks/preparedness-to-manage-a-financial-crisis/the-financial-crisis-2007-2009/, accessed 4 June 2025.

[55] Teixeira (n 14) 544–545.

[56] Stefaan De Rynck, 'Changing Banking Supervision in the Eurozone: The ECB as a Policy Entrepreneur', Bruges Political Research Paper No. 34 (December 2014), 4.

1.2.2 International Bank Lending and Systemic Risk

The level of financial integration in ASEAN can also be measured by a quantity-based approach.[57] Quantity-based measures are concerned with the volume of capital flows that actually take place. Quantity-based variables include, for example, international bank lending.[58] In this monograph, the data from the Bank for International Settlements (BIS) will be used in order to demonstrate the degree of ASEAN financial integration and concerns regarding financial stability and systemic risk.[59]

Figure 1.2 shows the percentage of the amounts outstanding of foreign claims of banks headquartered in ASEAN states in the third quarter of 2019. Given the available data, nine creditor countries (i.e., Japan, USA, the UK, France, Taiwan, Switzerland, Australia, Germany and Korea) are selected as the amounts outstanding to them are the largest ones for banks headquartered in most of ASEAN states. The data have revealed a pattern that banks in ASEAN-5 countries have the largest exposure to the UK, USA and Japan. Meanwhile, banks from Laos, Myanmar and Vietnam have a large exposure to Japan and Taiwan. With regards to Brunei, it has the largest exposure to the UK, France and USA. As for Cambodia, Taiwan and France are the main creditor countries.

According to the BIS data on international bank lending, ASEAN risks financial instability and systemic risk for several reasons. First, the level of financial integration in ASEAN could increase the speed of the propagation of shocks from outside the region, in the case that banks in an ASEAN state are affected by it. For example, Singapore and Malaysia, which are the financial hubs in this region, could transmit shocks they received from a country outside ASEAN to the sub-region. According to the BIS consolidated banking statistics (CBS), the UK has had the

[57] Other measures are regulatory-based and price-based approaches.

[58] Chaipat Poonpatpibul et al., 'The Role of Financial Integration in East Asia in Promoting Regional Growth and Stability', BOT Symposium 2006 (August 2006), 6, https://www.researchgate.net/publication/254395988_The_Role_of_Financial_Integration_in_East_Asian_Promoting_Regional_Growth_and_Stability, accessed 4 June 2025.

[59] There is no single definition of systemic risk which is accepted by the financial community, despite the fact that there are some attempts by academics to define it. For example, Acharya et al. have defined systemic risk as 'the failure of a significant part of the financial sector leading to a reduction in credit availability that has the potential to adversely affect the real economy'. Acharya et al., 'How to calculate systemic risk surcharge', in Joseph G. Haubrich, and Andrew W. Lo (eds), *Quantifying Systemic Risk* (University of Chicago Press 2013).

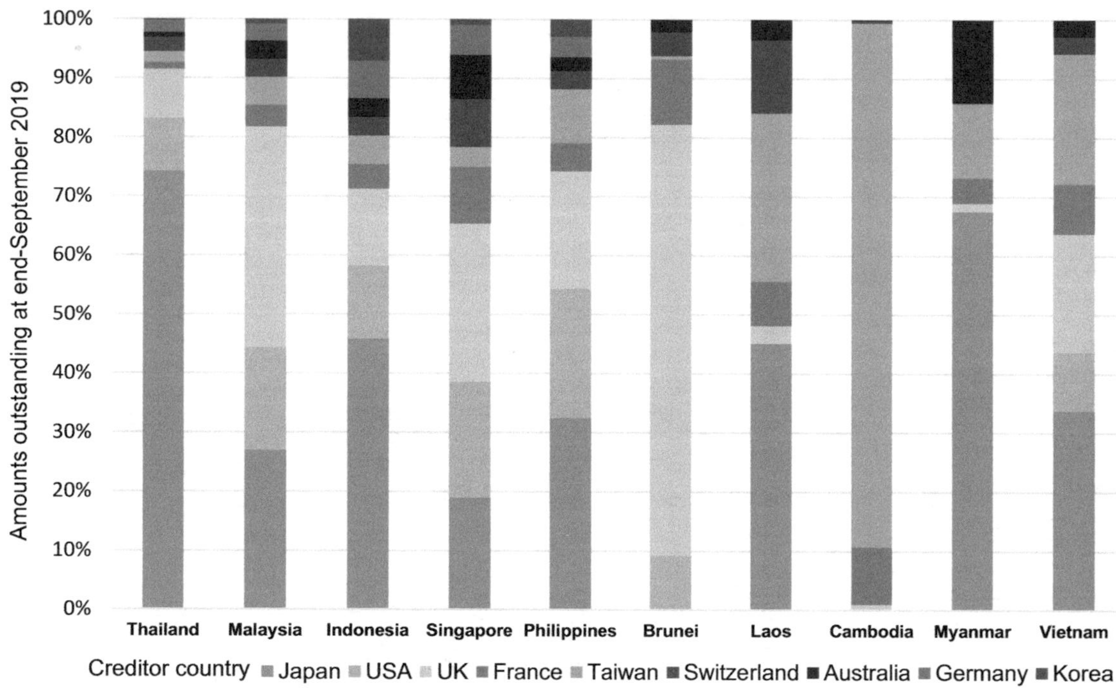

Fig. 1.2 Amounts outstanding of foreign claims of banks headquartered in ASEAN (Q3 2019) – selected creditor countries (share in %) (*Source* BIS consolidated banking statistics)

highest amount of claims, on an immediate counterparty basis, from both Singapore and Malaysia, when compared with other counterparty countries between 2001–2019.[60] In addition, both Singapore and Malaysia have had a large exposure to claims from Japan and the US. In the event that the counterparties in the UK, Japan or the US are in distress, Singapore and Malaysia would be heavily affected by it. These shocks could, then, propagate to the Philippines, which has a large exposure to Singapore.[61] Indonesia which has a large exposure to the Philippines would, in turn, be heavily affected by them.[62]

Secondly, financial integration could increase the magnitude and speed of spillover effect via a common lender channel. According to Remolona and Shim, the common lender can create systemic risk in two main ways: (i) transmit shocks from its home country to many host countries simultaneously; and (ii) cut exposures in other countries as a result of losses it incurs in a host country.[63] Concerning the first scenario, Pontines and Siregar have constructed 'macro-and micro-panel data on international bank lending' to ASEAN-5 countries and Korea.[64] The results suggest that international banks respond to shocks in their own economies by

[60] The BIS consolidated banking statistics is a more useful measure of total risk exposure of the banking system when compared with the BIS locational banking statistics. The former provides the information on an 'aggregate foreign claims of banks headquartered in a particular location on a worldwide consolidated basis'. Meanwhile, the latter is based on the residence principle. The BIS consolidated statistics on an immediate borrower basis have some limitations in measuring aggregate exposures of the banking system to a given country. For example, they are not adjusted for net risk transfers. As a result, the statistics might not be able to provide the information regarding where the ultimate risk resides. Stefan Avdjiev, 'Measuring Banking Systems' Exposures to Particular Countries' (June 2010) BIS Quarterly Review, https://www.bis.org/publ/qtrpdf/r_qt1006y.htm, accessed 4 June 2025.

[61] BIS locational banking statistics, https://www.bis.org/statistics/bankstats.htm, accessed 4 June 2025.

[62] Ibid.

[63] Eli Remolona and Ilhyock Shim, 'The Rise of Regional Banking in Asia and the Pacific' (September 2015) BIS Quarterly Review.

[64] According to Pontines and Siregar, the significance of international bank lending can be considered from the size of loans. They find that Japan, USA and UK are the most important lenders for the 6 Asian countries. Victor Pontines and Reza Siregar, 'How Should We Bank with Foreigners? An Empirical Assessment of Lending Behaviour of International Banks to Six East Asian Countries' (2012) CAMA Working Paper Series 4/2012, 2.

cutting their lending to the six Asian countries.[65] In addition, the study finds the common lender effect, in that adjustments regarding lending by international banks to one state create spillover effect to other countries that share the same creditors.[66]

The results of this study could be used in order to analyse the potential transmission of shocks by banks which operate across borders to the ASEAN sub-region. According to the BIS CBS, Japan was the most important creditor in the third quarter of 2019 for Thailand, Indonesia, the Philippines, Vietnam, Laos and Myanmar. Meanwhile, the United Kingdom was the largest creditor for Singapore, Malaysia and Brunei.[67] Hence, the transmission of shocks by creditors from the UK and Japan could create spillover effects to ASEAN member states which share the same creditors. This could result in a massive impact upon financial stability in this sub-region through the common lender channel.

As for the second scenario, global banks have to rebalance their lending towards safer borrowers under the condition of uncertainty. Rebalancing only occurs towards advanced economies, rather than towards emerging market economies.[68] The Asian financial crisis (AFC) and the GFC situation could be considered as an example: after the AFC broke out, Japan had cut back its lending to ASEAN countries, as it exposed a large amount of loss in the countries at the epicentre of the crisis. Similarly, since the GFC, European banks have reduced their lending in Asia because they faced large losses as a result of their US exposures.[69]

[65] Ibid., 24.

[66] Ibid., 21. Moreover, the study results suggest that foreign subsidiaries rather than foreign branches of international banks help mitigate the impact of a crisis in the 6 East Asian economies. This is the case when the shock stems from the advanced economies. Ibid., 26.

[67] In addition, Taiwan has the largest claims on an immediate counterparty basis against Cambodia. Despite the fact that the US is not the largest creditor of any ASEAN countries, Singapore and the Philippines have a large exposure to the US claims. BIS consolidated banking statistics, https://www.bis.org/statistics/consstats.htm, accessed 4 June 2025.

[68] Sangyup Choi and Davide Furceri, 'Uncertainty and Cross-border Banking Flows' (January 2018) IMF Working Paper, https://www.imf.org/en/Publications/WP/Issues/2018/01/05/Uncertainty-and-Cross-Border-Banking-Flows-45539, accessed 4 June 2025. The authors use quarterly stock market volatility as a proxy for uncertainty.

[69] Catherine Koch and Eli Renolona, 'Common Lenders in Emerging Asia: Their Changing Roles in Three Crises' (March 2018) BIS Quarterly Review, https://www.bis.org/publ/qtrpdf/r_qt1803b.htm, accessed 4 June 2025.

1.3 Part II: The Role of Law in the Financial Trilemma

According to Schoenmaker, if the intensity of international banking has exceeded some basic level, then coordination failure will become a real concern. National authorities would act in a way which is 'individually rational' and protect their national interests. As a result, the common good of financial stability will be jeopardised. In order to minimise the financial trilemma, Schoenmaker has developed model-based solutions: he argues that a legal basis for cooperation is key to an effective cooperation during a crisis. Soft law and voluntary cooperation would not create adequate incentives for national authorities to follow them.[70]

Underlying Schoenmaker's proposal is the utilisation of law as a solution to the problem. In the realm of international financial regulation, there are various actors involving in this enterprise: the IFIs, governance networks, national authorities and in the case of ASEAN, its institutions. These actors employ varied legal conceptions and tools in order to achieve their objectives. For example, some of them have expressly used the rhetoric of the rule of law in pursuing their goals which contribute to the financial trilemma (e.g., financial integration and financial stability). Meanwhile, others' agendas are highly related to the rule of law.

I argue that the conceptions of the rule of law they use, either expressly or impliedly, might be different and conflicting with each other. The meanings of the rule of law depend upon a person who uses it or the context in which the rule of law is situated. I will illustrate the different conceptions of the rule of law as well as relevant legal tools adopted by the IFIs, governance networks and national authorities of ASEAN states in the following sections.

[70] According to D'Hulster, the only instance in which both home and host authorities have strong incentives to openly share accurate and timely information is when the host operations have a materiality to the operations of the group in the home country and the operations of the foreign financial institution is systemic to the host country. When there are problems in either the parent bank or the subsidiary bank, there are no instances in which both home and host supervisors have strong incentive to do so. In addition, due to weak secrecy protection, some supervisors might be deterred from sharing sensitive information to the authorities in other jurisdictions. Katia D'Hulster, 'Cross-border Banking Supervision: Incentive Conflicts in Supervisory Information Sharing between Home and Host Supervisors' (2011) Journal of Banking Regulation 13 (4), 305–309.

1.3.1 The Role of Law and Financial Integration

With regards to the goal of financial integration in the financial trilemma, the increase of financial integration and financial openness in ASEAN has raised questions regarding the role of law in this context. Currently, the International Monetary Fund (IMF) has presented the rule of law as an important tool in furthering the degree of financial integration. The underlying philosophy of the IFIs' rule-of-law enterprise is that of the Post-Washington Consensus (PWC) and the World Bank. The PWC originated from critics of the Washington Consensus, such as Joseph Stigliz. The Washington Consensus supported the free-market economic policies (e.g., privatisation). The PWC differs from the Washington Consensus, in that the former has added to the latter issues of governance and the rule of law.[71]

Under the PWC, the World Bank considers the rule of law as a necessary component of sustainable economic growth policy. The philosophical underpinnings of the World Bank on the issues of law and justice are the 'Shihata doctrine'. This is a specific economic theory of law. It is a Weberian theory of legal, formal rationality in the world of capitalism. It has been developed by Chicago School of law and economics and the New Institutional Economics (NIE).[72] When creating this economic theory of law, the NIE intended to underline the importance of the rule of law, from the perspectives of both means and ends.[73]

The ideological influence of the NIE upon the World Bank could be considered from the World Bank's policies. For example, according to the World Bank's 'World Development Report', the rule of law prevails where (i) 'the government itself is bound by the law'; (ii) 'all in society are treated equally under the law'; (iii) 'the government authorities, including the judiciary, protect the human dignity of its citizens'; and (iv) 'justice

[71] Per Bergling, *Rule of Law on the International Agenda* (Intersentia 2006).

[72] Ibid. The NIE is a 'grand theory of socio-economic development'. John Toye, 'The New Institutional Economics and Its Implication for Development Theory' in John Hariss et al. (eds), *The New Institutional Economics and Third World Development* (Routledge 1997), 64. Douglas North, a leading NIE scholar, argues that a 'long-run economic growth entails development of the rule of law and the protection of civil and political freedoms'. Douglas North, 'The New Institutional Economics and Third World Development' in John Hariss et al. (eds) (n 72), 25.

[73] Rachel Kleinfeld Belton, 'Competing Definitions of the Rule of Law: Implications for Practitioners' (January 2005) Carnegie Papers No. 55, 17.

is accessible for its citizens'. In a society where the rule of law has taken a firm root, there would be 'transparent legislation, fair laws, predictable enforcement, and accountable governments to maintain order, promote private sector growth, fight poverty, and have legitimacy'.[74]

As for the IMF, promoting good governance includes 'ensuring the rule of law, improving the efficiency and accountability of the public sector, and tackling corruption, as an essential element of a framework within which economies can prosper'.[75] In the area of economic law, good governance will include, for example, 'supporting the development and maintenance of a transparent and stable economic and regulatory environment conductive to efficient private sector activities (e.g., price systems, exchange and trade regimes, and banking systems and their related regulations)'.[76]

However, when practitioners turn the ideas regarding the rule of law into practice, the means become conflated with the ends. Eventually, the conceptions of the rule of law used in practice highlight institutional attributes, rather than the rule-of-law ends. For example, some commentators from the IMF have argued that in order to reap the benefits of financial integration, ASEAN needs sound institutional framework (e.g., the rule of law).

According to Yiqun Wu et al., institutional quality matters for regional financial integration. In other words, good institutional quality (e.g., good governance and business-friendly environment) is linked to greater financial integration.[77] In addition, Ananchotikul et al. have found that the lack of regulatory harmonisation has more negative effect on intra-Asia investment.[78] Moreover, 'restrictions on cross-border capital flows,

[74] World Bank, 'World Development Report 2002: Building Institutions for Markets' (Oxford University Press 2002), 3.

[75] IMF, 'Good Governance: The IMF's Role' (August 1997), https://www.imf.org/external/pubs/ft/exrp/govern/govindex.htm, accessed 4 June 2025.

[76] Ibid., 3.

[77] Yiqun Wu et al., 'The Future of ASEAN-5 Financial Integration' in Ana Corbacho and Shanaka J. Peiris (eds), *The ASEAN Way: Sustaining Growth and Stability* (International Monetary Fund 2018).

[78] Nasha Ananchotikul et al., 'Drivers of Financial Integration—Implications for Asia' (2015) IMF Working Paper WP/15/160, https://www.imf.org/external/pubs/ft/wp/2015/wp15160.pdf, accessed 4 June 2025.

informational asymmetries, barriers to foreign bank entry, and differences in regulatory and institutional quality create obstacles to financial integration' in Asia.[79]

Nevertheless, the analysis regarding the importance of the rule of law in supporting financial integration by the IFIs is subject to some qualifications. First, the causal connection between the means of financial integration and the end goal of economic growth, which the rule of law is required to support, is not conclusive. For example, according to Nicolas Coeurdacier et al., the benefits of financial integration are 'quantitatively small, even for riskier and capital scarce emerging economies'.[80] In addition, Jose De Gregorio has found that financial integration does not generate a direct effect on economic growth. He is of the view that the gains from financial integration that benefit economic growth come mainly via the channel of the development of domestic financial system.[81]

Secondly, the validity of the analysis regarding the role of the rule of law depends upon whether or not the conception of the rule of law used represents the current rule-of-law situation in the assessed countries. The reliance upon a conception of the rule of law which emphasises institutional attributes might leave out many important dimensions of the rule of law. This is due to the fact that the rule of law is not merely a technical and legal institution—it has cultural, historical and political dimensions.[82]

For example, there are various conceptions of the rule of law among the ASEAN member states. In Vietnam, the law was primarily utilised to preserve Confucian hierarchies and social order.[83] Legal rules were not

[79] Ibid., 5.

[80] Nicolas Coeurdacier et al., 'Financial Integration and Growth in a Risky World' (2019) NBER Working Paper No. 21817, https://www.nber.org/papers/w21817.pdf, accessed 4 June 2025. Their paper concludes that 'financial integration may bring sizable gains but their magnitude is sensitive to the cross-country correlation of long-run (or disaster) risk'. Financial integration has very heterogeneous effects depending upon other factors (e.g., the stochastic structure of shocks, the size of countries and their initial degree of capital scarcity).

[81] Joes De Gregorio, 'Financial Integration, Financial Development and Economic Growth' (1999) Estudios de Economia 26 (2), 159.

[82] Kleinfeld Belton (n 73).

[83] Confucians have a higher respect for morality and virtuous leaders than law. In a Confucian system, law is considered as a tool serve the interests of the state. Randy Peerenboom, 'Competing Conceptions of Rule of Law in China' in Randall Peerenboom

immutable divine principles.[84] As for the rule of law in Malaysia, there are competing conceptions. Hoong Phun Lee has argued that it is unlikely that in Malaysia 'a thick rule of law as obtained in a liberal democracy will operate in the foreseeable future'.[85] The rule of law in Malaysia must be partly sacrificed for the sake of economic and social advancement.[86]

In the case of Thailand, after the revolution in 1932, Thai rule of law has moved towards Western notions of the rule of law.[87] The People's Constitution of 1997 was part of this trend. The term 'the rule of law' has been stipulated for the first time in some sections of the Constitution of 2007.[88] Meanwhile, some academics have proposed that the rule of law in Thailand should embrace some concepts in Buddhism—unsurprising, as over 90 per cent of Thai people are Buddhist. For instance, Thanin Kraiwichian, a Thai former judge and law professor, has argued that the meaning of Thai rule of law should have a substantive meaning of justice. This substantive meaning could be enriched by incorporating a Buddhist concept of *Awirothana* (i.e., conformity to the law and non-deviance from righteousness).

Besides this, the role of the rule of law in ASEAN is different from those of some regional integration projects (e.g., the EU). In the EU, the rule of law has been central to the achievement of the European integration since its inception. It has increased the legitimacy and integrity of the EU. In contrast, the initial purpose of the establishment of ASEAN

(ed), *Asian Discourses of Rule of Law: Theories and Implementation of Rule of Law in Twelve Asian Countries, France and the U.S.* (Routledge 2004), 114–115.

84 John Gillespie., 'Concepts of Law in Vietnam: Transforming Statist Socialism' in Peerenboom (ed), Ibid., 149.

85 Hoong Phun Lee, 'Competing Conceptions of Rule of Law in Malaysia', in Peerenboom, Ibid., 246.

86 Ibid., 244.

87 The term 'the rule of law' was translated and used for the first time by Prof. Wikrom Maolanont. He translated the Act of Athens 1955 into Thai language. Then, the term 'the rule of law' has gained attention in the Thai society especially among lawyers. Thanin Kraiwichian, *The Rule of Law* (Chuanpim Ltd 2010) (in Thai), 1. The meaning of the rule of law, according to Thai dictionary (1999), is the basic principle of law.

88 For example, Section 3(2) of the 2007 Constitution states that 'the performance of duties of the National Assembly, the Council of Ministers, the Courts, the Constitutional organisations and State agencies shall be in accordance with the rule of law'. According to Prof. Kraiwichian, the term 'the rule of law' was debated and selected by the drafters over the term 'legal state' or 'Rechtsstaat'.

was to create a platform to develop a collective voice of the member states regarding security matters of the region. From its inception, the sovereignty and state autonomy were to be preserved, and not to be tamed. In addition, the rule of law has remained the prerogative of each member state government.

Unsurprisingly, the original architecture of ASEAN was not designed to support regional enforcement and ensure regulatory compliance. There is no legal enforcement organisation which could perform functions similar to those of the European Commission; the closest ASEAN institution to the European Commission is the ASEAN Secretariat. It takes charge of monitoring the implementation of community decisions and rulings of the member governments. However, the ASEAN Charter does not equip the Secretariat with a legal power to resolve disputes among ASEAN states.

In the case of a conflict between ASEAN countries, the diplomatic norms known as the 'ASEAN Way' might take precedence over the rule of law. The 'ASEAN Way' emphasises non-interference in the internal affairs of other member states. Hence, within ASEAN, operations and decision-making are characterised by 'non-binding decision-making, consensus-building, and soft institutions'.[89]

Thirdly, in analysing the importance of the rule of law to financial integration, the aforementioned papers rely upon the rule-of-law index of the World Bank's Worldwide Governance Indicators (WGI). The definition of the WGI indicator for Rule of Law is that it is the 'perceptions of the extent to which agents have confidence in and abide by the rules of society, and in particular the quality of contract enforcement, property rights, the police, and the courts, as well as the likelihood of crime and violence'.[90] However, as MA Thomas has argued, 'there is a substantial difference between measuring a thing and measuring perceptions of it'.[91] In other words, the perception of the rule of law might not be a good representation of the rule of law itself.

[89] Jorn Dorsh, 'Regional Answers to the Global Crisis? Asia–Pacific Multilateral Organisations and the Economic Downturn' in Jorn Dosch and Christopher Dent (eds), *The Asia–Pacific, Regionalism and the Global System* (Cheltenham: Edward Elgar 2012), 134.

[90] World Bank, 'Worldwide Governance Indicators', https://info.worldbank.org/governance/wgi/Home/FAQ, accessed 4 June 2025.

[91] M.A. Thomas, 'What Do the Worldwide Governance Indicators Measure?' (2010) European Journal of Development Research 22 (1), 36.

1.3.2 *The Role of Law in Maintaining International Financial Stability*

The second main policy goal in the financial trilemma is financial stability. Schoenmaker has proposed that a supranational approach to resolution would be the first-best solution to maintain financial stability.[92] A resolution regime would help ensure that financial institutions, especially global and regional banks, would fail in an orderly way, in order to minimise losses to society at large. According to Schoenmaker, deposit insurance and resolution are intertwined. In addition, a fiscal backstop, which provides incentive for cooperation, is a tool to be utilised at the last stage in governance framework. In the case that the fiscal backstop is fully national, international cooperation will remain fragile.[93]

The current governance regime regarding cross-border bank resolution mainly utilises 'soft law'. Hard law has only been promulgated in some states (e.g., the EU has the Bank Recovery and Resolution Directive (BRRD) since 2014).[94] The use of soft law could raise a concern regarding its normative status, as soft law has no legally binding force. Concerning this issue, legal scholars have different views upon whether or not soft law *is*, in fact, law. For example, according to the conventional legal positivist conception of law, a binary binding/non-binding divide is used to distinguish soft law from hard law. Scholars who follow this approach would consider soft law as non-law.[95] Meanwhile, some authors adopt an alternative definition, which considers law as a continuum.

[92] Schoenmaker (n 5).

[93] Ibid.

[94] European Parliament and Council Directive 2014/59/EU of 15 May 2014 establishing a framework for the recovery and resolution of credit institutions and investment firms and amending Council Directive 82/891/EEC, and Directives 2001/24/EC, 2002/47/EC, 2004/25/EC, 2005/56/EC, 2007/36/EC, 2011/35/EU, 2012/30/EU and 2013/36/EU, and Regulations (EU) No 1093/2010 and (EU) No 648/2012, of the European Parliament and of the Council [2014] OJ L173/19.

[95] Oana Stefan et al., 'EU Soft Law in the EU Legal Order: A Literature Review' (2019) King's College London Law School Research Paper, 30, https://papers.ssrn.com/sol3/papers.cfm?abstract_id=3346629, accessed 4 June 2025.

According to this assumption, soft law occupies a space in between legal norms and non-legal positions.[96]

Regardless of one's preferred classification of hard and soft legal provisions, the normative effects of the former might not be significantly different from those of the latter. One of the reasons is the fact that the effects of both hard and soft legal instruments still depend largely on the interpretation and implementation they receive from the 'interpretive community' (e.g., the regulatee, the courts and the states).[97] For example, utilising hard law does not guarantee legal compliance, as the regulator may 'go by the book'.[98] Besides, the regulatee may conduct regulatory arbitrage.

In addition, soft law may possess a disciplining power, as well as produce similar effects to hard law. For instance, soft law can generate a reasonable expectation to which parties will conform—otherwise, a social or reputational sanction might be applied. Moreover, according to Brummer, regulators can be viewed as second-class citizens within their own larger regulatory body. They can face a social opprobrium from their counterparts in the relatively close-knit regulatory community for failing to deliver on the group's regulatory programme.[99] Furthermore, institutions can create new market costs, by implying or arguing that non-cooperative jurisdictions suffer from poor domestic oversight and market supervision. Hence, they are risky places to do business. Any firm operating in such jurisdiction can potentially incur higher costs of capital. As a result, those countries may find it more difficult to attract firms to enter their borders.[100]

In the realm of international financial regulation, these arguments could be considered from the practice of international standard setters

[96] Fabien Terpan, 'Soft Law in the European Union: The Changing Nature of EU Law' (2013) Sciences Po Grenoble Working Paper No. 7, 2, https://halshs.archives-ouvertes.fr/halshs-00911460/document, accessed 4 June 2025.

[97] Julia M. Black, *Rules and Regulators* (Clarendon Press 1997).

[98] Eugene Bardach and Robert A. Kagan, *Going by the book: The Problem of Regulatory Unreasonableness* (Temple University Press 1982). The authors state that regulators sometimes complained of being compelled to 'go by the book' as a result of regulatory unreasonableness. They argue for regulation which is more responsive and reasonable with inspectors having discretion to fulfill the spirit rather than the letter of the law.

[99] Chris Brummer, 'Why Soft Law Dominates International Finance-and not Trade' (2010) 13 (3) Journal of International Economic Law 623.

[100] Ibid.

and governance networks. These institutions have been a major force in creating international 'soft law' in this area. For instance, since April 2009, the Financial Stability Board (FSB), an institutional continuation of the Financial Stability Forum (FSF), has played a leading role in tackling the issue of systemic risk. The FSB has brought together participants from ministries of finance, central banks, financial regulators, major standard-setting bodies (e.g., the Basel Committee, International Organisation of Securities Commission (IOSCO) and International Association of Insurance Supervisors (IAIS) and the IFIs (e.g., the IMF and the World Bank).[101]

Despite the fact that the FSB has no legal personality and its principles are not legally binding, many countries followed its principles.[102] Hence, some commentators have argued that the FSB has emerged as an informal international lawmaking (IN-LAW) body. According to J Pauwelyn, IN-LAW generates normative effects despite the fact that it is not governed by international law.[103] The demarcation line between the FSB's 'soft law' and international hard law is blurred by the fact that the principles created by the FSB have a very strong political commitment among states, as FSB members are willing to participate in the standard-making process.[104]

[101] Nathan Sheets, 'Race to the Top: The Case for the Financial Stability Board' (April 2017) PIIE Paterson Institute for International Economics, Policy Brief, 2.

[102] Ariticle 23 of the FSB Charter states that 'this Charter is not intended to create any legal rights or obligations'. Ibid., 8.

[103] According to J. Pauwelyn, IN-LAW is characterised by 'Cross-border cooperation between public authorities, with or without the participation of private actors and/or international organisations, in a forum other than a traditional international organisation (process informality), and/ or as between actors other than traditional diplomatic actors (such as regulators/agencies) (actor informality) and/ or which does not result in a formal treaty or traditional source of international law (output informality)'. Joost Pauwelyn, 'Informal International Lawmaking: Framing the Concept and Research Questions' in Joost Pauwelyn et al. (eds), *Informal International Lawmaking* (Oxford University Press 2012), 22.

Douglas Arner and Michael Taylor, 'The Global Financial Crisis and the Financial Stability Board: Hardening the Soft Law of International Financial Regulation?' (2009) University of New South Wales Law Journal 32, 6.

[104] Shawn Donnelly, 'Informal International lawmaking: Global Financial Market Regulation' in Ayelet Berman et al. (eds), *Informal International Lawmaking: Case Studies* (Torkel Opsahl Academic EPublisher 2012), 213. Nevertheless, the creation of these international financial standards is not transparent. The agenda of the FSB is still set by powerful member states. In the case that those states disagree with a particular topic, this issue will not come up on the table. As Arner and Taylor have stated, 'no criteria have

In addition, FSB members are encouraged to converge their regulatory regimes to meet international standards through legislative changes. For example, in the case of cross-border resolution, the FSB has created the Key Attributes of Effective Resolution Regimes for Financial Institutions in 2014 (the Key Attributes). The Key Attributes have provided resolution tools and powers which the members should incorporate into their jurisdictions by means of national legislation.[105]

Moreover, non-member states may want to participate in the FSB's standard-making process through consultation; therefore, they may be more inclined to follow the FSB's principles. Furthermore, some states may be obliged by their obligations under the mandates of the IMF (the Financial Sector Assessment Programmes (FSAPs), the World Bank (the Reports on Observance of Standards and Codes (ROSCs)) or MOUs to observe the FSB's standards.[106]

1.3.3 The Home-Host Conflicts and the Role of Law

The last main policy goal according to the financial trilemma is national financial policies. National states are likely to pursue their national interest at the expense of the public good of international financial stability. In this scenario, there might be conflicts between the home and host authority. Schoenmaker's idea is influenced by the work of Richard J. Herring. According to Herring, the home-host conflicts in financial regulation and supervision could potentially occur for three main reasons: (i) asymmetry of resources; (ii) asymmetry of accounting, legal and institutional infrastructures; and (iii) asymmetry regarding exposure to financial instability. For example, a bank might be systemically important for the host country, while it might not be so for the home state.[107]

The Key Attributes have created guidelines in order to minimise the home-host conflicts in many ways. According to Key Attribute 7.3, the

ever been published for determining priorities in selecting issues on which to develop standards, for designating standard areas and standards as 'key', or for selecting appropriate standard-setting organisations'. Arner and Taylor, ibid., 6.

[105] Financial Stability Board, 'Key Attributes of Effective Resolution Regimes for Financial Institutions' (15 October 2014), 4, https://www.fsb.org/wp-content/uploads/r_141015.pdf, accessed 4 June 2025.

[106] Donnelly (n 104).

[107] Herring (n 1).

host authority should have the powers to support the resolution decision of the home authority. However, in exceptional circumstances in which the home authority does not take any action or takes into account insufficient concerns regarding financial stability of the host country, the latter could take its own resolution initiative.

In addition, Key Attribute 7.5 states that jurisdictions should give effects to foreign resolution measures. This could be pursued by way of two countries mutually recognising each other's resolution processes. Alternatively, the host authority could take measures under their domestic regime which support the measures taken by a foreign home authority. Moreover, Key Attributes 7.6 and 7.7 require FSB members to provide legal capacity and protection for the resolution authority regarding information sharing with foreign authorities.

However, most of the ASEAN states are not FSB members. Given the limited participation in the FSB by ASEAN member states, the Key Attributes might have negligible persuasive authority for non-member ASEAN states.[108] Currently, cross-border cooperation in ASEAN will be conducted via home-host supervisory relationships, the establishment of a supervisory college, and MOUs.[109]

In addition, unlike the EU Banking Union, in which a banking group is supervised by a single supervisor, ASEAN has not created a harmonised regulatory and supervisory regime for its QAB scheme.[110] As Lupo-Pasini has stated, it is unclear whether the QAB system operates as a

[108] As of 16 February 2020, Singapore and Indonesia are the only ASEAN member states which are members of the FSB.

[109] Vivien Chen et al., 'Cross-border Cooperation in Bank Resolution: A Framework for Asia' (2016) Singapore Journal of Legal Studies 1–28.

[110] In the EU, subsidiaries of banks are still subject to remaining national powers and individual requirements of supervisors of each subsidiary. J. Deslandes et al., 'Banking Union: Defusing the 'Home/Host' Debate' (July 2019) IPOL Economic Governance Support Unit, Briefing, 1, https://www.europarl.europa.eu/RegData/etudes/BRIE/2019/634373/IPOL_BRI(2019)634373_EN.pdf, accessed 4 June 2025. In addition, the BRRD covers only the insolvency of branches of credit institutions. It does not include subsidiaries of the banking groups in other Member States. Rosa M. Lastra, 'Northern Rock and Banking Law Reform in the UK', in Franco Bruni and David T. Llewellyn (eds), *The Failure of Northern Rock: A Multi-dimensional Case Study* (January 2009), https://www.suerf.org/docx/s_5d6646aad9bcc0be55b2c82f69750387_2141_suerf.pdf, accessed 4 June 2025.

home country model led by the home supervisor, or a host country-model in which banks will be supervised by the host authority.[111] Hence, there is a possibility that QABs might be treated differently depending upon the national financial policies of the country in which it is established. For instance, the Philippines has taken the view that QABs in their country will be regulated under the BSP regulations. The Republic Act (RA) No. 10641 will provide the legal framework for the QABs in the Philippines.[112]

The lack of harmonised cross-border banking regulation and supervision in ASEAN could increase the likelihood of home-host conflicts during a financial crisis. Apart from the home-host conflicts in bank supervision, the home-host dilemma could also occur in resolution, deposit insurance and crisis-management. For instance, the lack of a recognition of foreign resolution measures in the majority of the member states could cause a problem of conflict of laws. This could, in turn, increase legal uncertainty during and after a financial crisis.

1.4 Towards an ASEAN Bank Crisis Management Framework: A Chapter Summary

The remainder of this monograph develops the argument that the financial trilemma poses a significant challenge to cross-border bank crisis management in ASEAN. In addition, it explores how legal and institutional frameworks—particularly soft law mechanisms—might be leveraged to address this problem effectively. Moreover, it draws comparative insights, particularly from the European Union, to inform ASEAN's approach.

Chapter 2 elaborates the use of soft laws and government networks in the area of bank supervision. With regard to government networks, they could be considered into horizontal and vertical networks. The former comprises a group of national agencies from different countries which produce a horizontal non-binding agreement. Meanwhile, in the latter case, governing authority is delegated to a supranational organisation. While ASEAN currently engages with the horizontal network of the

[111] Lupo-Pasini (n 16) 140.

[112] Ben O. de Vera, 'PH, Indonesia Start Talks for Entry of Qualified ASEAN Banks' *Philippine Daily Inquirer* (Manila, 6 June 2017), https://business.inquirer.net/230857/ph-indonesia-start-talks-entry-qualified-asean-banks, accessed 4 June 2025.

Basel Committee on Banking Supervision (BCBS), the chapter critiques this model for its technical and contextual limitations, particularly for emerging markets. Drawing lessons from the European Union's Single Supervisory Mechanism (SSM), the chapter suggests that ASEAN may benefit from transitioning towards a vertical model. However, it should be borne in mind that although the SSM is advanced, it manifests some weaknesses due to the persistent discretion retained by national competent authorities (NCAs) and the enforcement constraints faced by the European Central Bank (ECB).

Chapter 3 turns to cross-border bank resolution, a field that remains underdeveloped in ASEAN. Some ASEAN states still use national (bank) insolvency proceedings in dealing with bank failures, as they have not created a bank resolution regime. In addition, ASEAN countries utilise supervisory college and home-host supervision in facilitating cross-border bank resolution. The differences of rules which are applicable in different states could raise an issue of unequal treatment in cross-border cases. This chapter analyses the EU's Bank Recovery and Resolution Directive (BRRD) and the Single Resolution Mechanism (SRM) as a potential model, while also identifying shortcomings such as legal uncertainty, the risk of contagion through the bail-in tool, and inequality of treatment in cross-border cases. These observations offer critical insights for ASEAN in considering its own framework.

Chapter 4 illustrates the significant impact that soft law can have in shaping financial governance by examining deposit insurance systems. The Core Principles developed by the International Association of Deposit Insurers (IADI) and the BCBS demonstrate how non-binding norms may exert strong influence, particularly when tied to the conditions of international financial assistance. In contrast, the EU Deposit Guarantee Schemes Directive (DGSD) regime, which utilises a hard-law approach, has manifested weaknesses due to the incompatibility of the DGSD regime with other financial safety-net systems, as well as the incompleteness of the EU vertical network. The EU has not created a European deposit guarantee system. As a result, most of the tasks of the Deposit Guarantee Schemes (DGSs) are performed at the national level. This chapter argues that there must be a well-functioning rule of law in the background for an ASEAN Deposit Insurance System to perform its tasks effectively.

Chapter 5 addresses the role of state support measures and fiscal backstops in managing a banking crisis. Those measures are categorised into lender of last resort (LOLR), guarantees, recapitalisation and troubled asset relief or asset management corporation (AMC). This chapter demonstrates that the use of those state supports during the Asian financial crisis resulted in the financial trilemma as the Member States were willing to protect only their local banks. It argues that the horizontal network of the Chiang Mai Initiative Multilateralisation (CMIM) created by ASEAN + 3 countries (i.e. China, Japan and Korea) as well as its surveillance unit, ASEAN + 3 Macroeconomic Research Office (AMRO), could help minimise the financial trilemma. Nevertheless, both the CMIM and AMRO need to be equipped with more power, resources and capacity.

Chapter 6 concludes the monograph by reaffirming the central thesis that the financial trilemma model is strongly applicable in the context of bank crisis management in ASEAN. It proposes the use of soft laws, MOUs and government networks as a solution to the financial trilemma rather than that of the hard-law approach proposed by Schoenmaker. The chapter ends with seven policy recommendations designed to guide ASEAN in crafting a framework that is both legally coherent and operationally effective in mitigating systemic risk and minimising the financial trilemma in this sub-region.

References

Acharya et al., 'How to calculate systemic risk surcharge', in Joseph G. Haubrich, and Andrew W. Lo (eds), *Quantifying Systemic Risk* (University of Chicago Press 2013)

Aizenman J. and Sengupta R., 'The Financial Trilemma in China and a Comparative Analysis with India' (2013) 18(2) Pacific Economic Review 123–146

Ananchotikul N et al, 'Drivers of Financial Integration – Implications for Asia' (2015) IMF Working Paper WP/15/160

'ASEAN Economic Community Blueprint'

Asian Development Bank, 'ASEAN Banking Integration Framework (ABIF)'

Arner D and Taylor M, 'The Global Financial Crisis and the Financial Stability Board: Hardening the Soft Law of International Financial Regulation?' (2009) University of New South Wales Law Journal 32

Avdjiev S, 'Measuring Banking Systems' Exposures to Particular Countries' (June 2010) BIS Quarterly Review

Bangko Sentral ng Pilipinas, Working Committee on ASEAN Banking Integration Framework (WC-ABIF)

Bangkok Bank, 'Bangkok Bank to Strengthen Regional Position through Acquisition of Permata in Indonesia from Standard Chartered Bank and Astra International' (*Press Release*, 12 December 2019)

'Bangkok Bank Buys Standard Chartered's Indonesian Bank for $3.65 Billion' *The Straits Times* (Singapore, 13 December 2019)

Bardach E and Kagan R, Going by the book: The Problem of Regulatory Unreasonableness (Temple University Press 1982)

Bergling P, Rule of Law on the International Agenda (Intersentia 2006)

BIS, 'ASEAN Banking Integration and Lessons from Europe' (13 September 2015) BIS Quarterly Review

Black J, Rules and Regulators (Clarendon Press 1997)

Brana S and Lahet D, 'The Push-Pull Determinants of Cross-border Bank Claims on Emerging Countries: The Role of Parent Banks and their Subsidiaries' (2015)

Brummer C., 'Why Soft Law Dominates International Finance-and not Trade' (2010) 13 (3) Journal of International Economic Law 623

Chan A et al, 'Depositor Preference and Deposit Insurance Schemes – Challenges for Regulatory Convergence and Regulatory Coordination in Asia' in Douglas W Arner et al. (eds), Research Handbook on Asian Financial Law (Edward Elgar Publishing 2020)

Choi S and Furceri D, 'Uncertainty and Cross-border Banking Flows' (January 2018) IMF Working Paper

Chen V. et al., 'Cross-border Cooperation in Bank Resolution: A Framework for Asia' (2016) Singapore Journal of Legal Studies 1–28

Coeurdacier N et al., 'Financial Integration and Growth in a Risky World' (2019) NBER Working Paper No. 21817

De Gregorio J, 'Financial Integration, Financial Development and Economic Growth' (1999) 26 (2) Estudios de Economia

Demirguc-Kunt A et al., The Global Findex Database 2017: Measuring Financial Inclusion and the Fintech Revolution (The World Bank 2018)

De Rynck S, 'Changing Banking Supervision in the Eurozone: The ECB as a Policy Entrepreneur', Bruges Political Research Paper No. 34 (December 2014)

Deslandes J et al, 'Banking Union: Defusing the 'Home/Host' Debate' (July 2019) IPOL Economic Governance Support Unit, Briefing

De Vera B., 'PH, Indonesia Start Talks for Entry of Qualified ASEAN Banks' *Philippine Daily Inquirer* (Manila, 6 June 2017)

Donnelly S, 'Informal International lawmaking: Global Financial Market Regulation' in Ayelet Berman et al (eds), Informal International Lawmaking: Case Studies (Torkel Opsahl Academic EPublisher 2012)

Dorsh J, 'Regional Answers to the Global Crisis? Asia-Pacific Multilateral Organisations and the Economic Downturn' in Jorn Dosch and Christopher Dent

(eds), The Asia-Pacific, Regionalism and the Global System (Cheltenham: Edward Elgar 2012)
D'Hulster K, 'Cross-border Banking Supervision: Incentive Conflicts in Supervisory Information Sharing between Home and Host Supervisors' (2011) Journal of Banking Regulation 13 (4)
Eukeik .ee, 'What Would Happen in the Retail Business When UOB Acquire Citigroup?' (*Marketeer*, 14 January 2022) (in Thai)
Fernandez-Arias E, 'The New Wave of Private Capital Inflows: Push or Pull?' (1994) World Bank Policy Research Working Paper 1312
Fiechter J. et al., 'Subsidiaries or Branches: Does One Size Fit All?' (7 March 2011) IMF Staff Discussion Note
Financial Stability Board, 'Key Attributes of Effective Resolution Regimes for Financial Institutions' (15 October 2014)
Gillespie J., 'Concepts of Law in Vietnam: Transforming Statist Socialism' in Peerenboom R. (ed), Asian Discourses of Rule of Law: Theories and Implementation of Rule of Law in Twelve Asian Countries, France and the U.S. (Routledge 2004)
Government of Timor-Leste, 'Timor-Leste Welcomes ASEAN Decision to Admit Timor-Leste as 11th Member' (28 May 2025)
Herring R., 'Conflicts between Home and Host Country Prudential Supervisors' in Douglas Evanoff et al (eds), International Financial Stability: Global Banking and National Regulation (World Scientific 2007)
IMF, 'Good Governance: The IMF's Role' (August 1997)
Ingves S., 'The Crisis in the Baltic – the Riksbank's Measures, Assessments and Lessons Learned', 'Speech' (The Riksdag Committee on Finance, Stockholm, 2 February 2010)
Kleinfeld Belton R, 'Competing Definitions of the Rule of Law: Implications for Practitioners' (January 2005) Carnegie Papers No. 55
Koch C. and Remolona E., 'Common Lenders in Emerging Asia: Their Changing Roles in Three Crises' (March 2018) BIS Quarterly Review
Kraiwichian T., The Rule of Law (Chuanpim Ltd 2010) (in Thai)
Lastra R, 'Northern Rock and Banking Law Reform in the UK', in Franco Bruni and David T. Llewellyn (eds), The Failure of Northern Rock: A Multi-dimensional Case Study (January 2009)
Lee H.P., 'Competing Conceptions of Rule of Law in Malaysia', in Peerenboom R. (ed), Asian Discourses of Rule of Law: Theories and Implementation of Rule of Law in Twelve Asian Countries, France and the U.S. (Routledge 2004
Lupo-Pasini F., 'Banking Integration in ASEAN and the Challenges of Regulatory Cooperation', in Pasha L. Hsieh and Bryan Mercurio (eds), ASEAN Law in the New Regional Economic Order: Global Trends and Shifting Paradigm (Cambridge University Press 2019)

Mathis J., 'Corrigendum to "The Financial Trilemma" [Economic Letters 111 (2011) 57–59]' (2023) 224 Economics Letters

Murphy P., 'Systemic Risks and Financial Stability Frameworks' in Corbacho A. and Peiris S. (eds), The ASEAN Way: Sustaining Growth and Stability (International Monetary Fund 2018)

Nardo M et al., 'Financial Integration in the EU28 Equity Markets: Measures and Drivers' (2022) 57 Journal of Financial Markets

Njoroge L., 'The Financial Trilemma and Macroeconomic Instability: Empirical Evidence from Kenya' (2015) 2(2) American Journal of Trade and Policy

North D., 'The New Institutional Economics and Third World Development' in John Hariss et al (eds), The New Institutional Economics and Third World Development (Routledge 1997)

Pauwelyn J., 'Informal International Lawmaking: Framing the Concept and Research Questions' in Pauwelyn J. et al. (eds), Informal International Lawmaking (Oxford University Press 2012)

Peerenboom P., 'Competing Conceptions of Rule of Law in China', in Peerenboom R. (ed), Asian Discourses of Rule of Law: Theories and Implementation of Rule of Law in Twelve Asian Countries, France and the U.S. (Routledge 2004)

Pontines V. and Siregar R., 'How Should We Bank with Foreigners? An Empirical Assessment of Lending Behaviour of International Banks to Six East Asian Countries' (2012) CAMA Working Paper Series 4/2012

Poonpatpibul C et al, 'The Role of Financial Integration in East Asia in Promoting Regional Growth and Stability', BOT Symposium 2006 (August 2006)

Raudla R. et al, 'Policy Learning from Crisis in Financial Regulation and Supervision: Comparative Analysis of Estonia, Latvia and Sweden' (The 12th Conference on Baltic Studies in Europe, Riga, 19–21 June 2017)

Remolona E and Shim I, 'The Rise of Regional Banking in Asia and the Pacific' (September 2015) BIS Quarterly Review

Riksbank, 'The Financial Crisis 2007–2009'

Rillo A., 'ASEAN Financial Integration: Opportunities, Risks, and Challenges' (2018) 14 (5) Public Policy Review

Schinasi G, *Safeguarding Financial Stability: Theory and Practice* (International Monetary Fund 2005)

Schoenmaker D., 'The Financial Trilemma' (2011) 111(1) Economics Letters 57

Schoenmaker D, *Governance of International Banking: The Financial Trilemma* (Oxford Scholarship Online 2013)

Sheets N., 'Race to the Top: The Case for the Financial Stability Board' (April 2017) PIIE Paterson Institute for International Economics, Policy Brief

Shimizu S., 'ASEAN Financial and Capital Markets – Policies and Prospects of Regional Integration' (2014) RIM Pacific Business and Industries Vol. XIV, No. 54

Stefan O. et al., 'EU Soft Law in the EU Legal Order: A Literature Review' (2019) King's College London Law School Research Paper

Supattha, 'Examining Five Issues Leading to the Permata Bank Deal of BBL' *(Marketeer,* 13 December 2019) (in Thai)

Teixeira P., 'The Legal History of the Banking Union' (2017) Eur Bus Org Law Rev 18

Terpan F., 'Soft Law in the European Union: The Changing Nature of EU Law' (2013) Sciences Po Grenoble Working Paper No. 7

Thomas M.A., 'What Do the Worldwide Governance Indicators Measure?' (2010) European Journal of Development Research 22 (1)

Toye J., 'The New Institutional Economics and Its Implication for Development Theory' in John Hariss et al (eds), The New Institutional Economics and Third World Development (Routledge 1997)

Vinokurov E., 'Regional Financial Integration in ASEAN in the Comparative Perspective' (4 December 2017) MPRA Paper No. 83022

Wihardja M, 'Financial Integration Challenges in ASEAN beyond 2015' (November 2013) ERIA Discussion Paper Series

Wijaya H. et al., 'ASEAN Banking Integration and Its Impact on the Banking Industry in Indonesia' (3rd International Conference on Globalization of Law and Local Wisdom, Surakarta, 7–8 July 2019)

World Bank, 'World Development Report 2002: Building Institutions for Markets' (Oxford University Press 2002)

Wu Y. et al., 'The Future of ASEAN-5 Financial Integration' in Corbacho A. and Peiris S. (eds), *The ASEAN Way: Sustaining Growth and Stability* (International Monetary Fund 2018)

Case

Vishipco Line v. Chase Manhattan Bank 660 F 2d 854 (1981)

CHAPTER 2

Cross-border Banking Supervision in ASEAN

2.1 Introduction

In her famous book, *A New World Order*, Anne-Marie Slaughter has argued that states are disaggregated rather than unitary. This is because their institutions (e.g., regulators, judges and legislators) operate not only within their national borders, but also in the international realm, in the form of transnational organisations.[1] In addition, as governments find that their ability to utilise hard power is increasingly restricted, they have to resort to soft powers in order to achieve their objectives (e.g., persuasion and exchange of information).[2] This is especially so for cross-border businesses, for which operations transcend state territories. Governments' functions are increasingly carried out by 'government networks', which are devoid of a formal status in the eyes of international law.

The 'government networks' bring together state institutions, in order to exchange information as well as create best practice. Their networks could produce horizontal non-binding agreements whereby agencies from different countries cooperate with each other (e.g., the Basel Committee on Banking Supervision (BCBS)). Alternatively, the government networks could manifest themselves in the form of vertical systems, whereby

[1] Anne-Marie Slaughter, *A New World Order* (Princeton University Press 2009), 33.

[2] Ibid., 6.

© The Author(s), under exclusive license to Springer Nature Singapore Pte Ltd. 2025

W. Kun-amornpong, *The Financial Trilemma and Cross-border Bank Crisis Management in ASEAN*,
https://doi.org/10.1007/978-981-95-0512-8_2

governing authority is delegated to a supranational organisation (e.g., the EU). According to Slaughter, both horizontal and vertical government networks help create 'a new world order'.[3]

In my view, this evolving 'new world order' has a potential to minimise the financial trilemma for ASEAN, which has occurred as a result of increasing financial integration in this sub-region. For example, the ASEAN Banking Integration Framework (ABIF) has accelerated banking integration by guaranteeing equal treatment to qualified banks in ASEAN under the scheme of QABs.[4] One of the issues of the financial trilemma is the fact that countries face a paradox of requiring government on the global and regional scale, in order to solve the global problem of financial instability; however, they also need to keep centralisation of decision-making power and coercive authority as close as possible to those governed. A centralisation of power would affect their national sovereignty.[5] The 'government networks' could help resolve this paradox, by distributing information, enforcing regulation, providing training and technical assistance, building capacity or harmonising national laws.

This chapter will explore the way in which 'government networks' could minimise the financial trilemma in ASEAN, with a focus upon cross-border banking supervision. In addition, it will discuss possible and existing obstacles to the success of 'government networks' in so doing. The chapter will proceed as follows: part I will consider the roles as well as weaknesses of horizontal networks in ASEAN. In part II, the arguments for creating a vertical network for banking supervision in this sub-region will be elaborated. Part II will also use the experience of the EU in analysing the effectiveness of vertical networks in minimising the financial trilemma. The chapter will conclude by providing recommendations regarding cross-border banking supervision in ASEAN.

[3] Ibid.

[4] As for the securities market, the ASEAN Trade Link was established in 2012 in order to resemble the Markets in Financial Instruments Directive (MiFID) in the EU. However, due to its lack of a centralised clearing and settlement system, it was undesirable for day-trading investors. Hence, this initiative was ended in 2017. Oliver Ward, 'The Missed Opportunity of the ASEAN Trade Link' (*ASEAN Today,* 21 October 2017), https://www.aseantoday.com/2017/10/the-missed-opportunity-of-the-asean-trade-link/, accessed 4 June 2025.

[5] Slaughter (n 113) 8.

2.2 Part I: Horizontal Networks and the Minimisation of Financial Trilemma

There are some existing horizontal networks in ASEAN; the BCBS is a prominent example among them. After the AFC, the Basel principles have taken a firm root in some ASEAN nations. For instance, in 1999, following the advice of the World Bank, Thailand began to use a risk-based approach for its financial supervision.[6] In addition, the country incorporated Basel II and the Basel Core Principles (BCPs) into its supervisory system as the 'best practice'.[7]

Moreover, a review of FSAP reports has shown that ASEAN states have increasingly implemented the BCPs. This is despite the fact that Indonesia and Singapore are the only Basel committee members in this sub-region.[8] With regards to the comprehensiveness and credibility of information in the reports, it could be argued that FSAP reports are a 'negotiated space'. In other words, states could object to some contents, which might potentially harm their reputation, being published in the reports. If this is the case, the IMF and the World Bank normally produce a confidential report which is not publicly available for a state in question. However, the IFIs would not distort the information in any FSAP report.

Table 2.1 provides the information about ASEAN states' compliance with the BCPs on some important aspects of cross-border banking supervision. These measures are a framework to support cross-border cooperation and information sharing; a requirement for prior consent from home supervisor to license in a host state; a practice to obtain consent or inform host supervisor for ongoing supervision; a recognition of foreign resolution actions; confidentiality requirements for sharing information; and a legal protection to supervisors, employees and agents.

All of the aforementioned measures which implement the BCPs are in place in Singapore, Malaysia and Thailand. With regards to the Philippines, there has been an improvement in information sharing with foreign supervisors. However, the legal protection to supervisors, employees and agents is still insufficient. For instance, according to an FSAP report, 'the

[6] Nawaporn Ruengsakul, *The Report on the Study of the Command of Permanent Closure of 56 Financial Institutions* (2005) (in Thai), 41. The idea of risk-based approach was introduced in the US after the S&L crisis in the 1980s and 1990s while it was used in the UK since the Labour government.

[7] The BIS ratio was first used in Thailand in 1992.

[8] Malaysia is an observer.

Table 2.1 Compliance of the basel core principles for effective banking supervision in ASEAN states

Topic	*Singapore*	*Malaysia*	*Thailand*	*Philippines*	*Indonesia*	*Vietnam*	*Laos*	*Cambodia*	*Myanmar*	*Brunei*
Information sharing & cooperation	✔	✔	✔	✔	N/A	✔	N/A	N/A	N/A	N/A
Prior consent from home supervisor for licensing	✔	✔	✔	N/A	N/A	N/A	N/A	N/A	N/A	N/A
Consent/ informing host supervisor for ongoing supervision	✔	✔	✔	N/A	N/A	✔	N/A	N/A	N/A	N/A
Recovery & resolution plan has statutory footing	✔	✔	✔	N/A	N/A	N/A	N/A	N/A	N/A	N/A
Confidentiality requirements set out in law	✔	✔	✔	N/A	N/A	N/A	N/A	N/A	N/A	N/A
Legal protection to supervisors, employees & agents	✔	✔	✔	Inadequate	Inadequate	N/A	Inadequate	N/A	N/A	N/A

Source Financial Sector Assessment Programme reports and central banks' websites

Table 2.2 The Basel Capital Compliance of ASEAN Member States

Country	*Basel II*	*Basel III*						
	Capital adequacy requirement (%)	*Liquidity ratio (%)*		*CET 1 (%)*	*Leverage ratio (%)*	*Capital buffers*		
		LCR	*NSFR*			*Counter cyclical buffer (%)*	*Capital conservation buffer (%)*	*Systemically important banks buffer (%)*
Brunei	10							
Cambodia	7.5					0–2.5	2.5	
Indonesia		85[+]	85[+]	4.5	3	0–2.5	2.5	1–2.5
Lao PDR	8							
Malaysia		100	100	4.5	3	0–2.5	2.5	*
Myanmar	8							
Philippines		70[#]	70[#]	6	5	0–2.5	2.5	1–2.5
Singapore		100	100	6.5	3	0–2.5	2.5	2
Thailand		100	100	4.5	3	0–2.5	2.5	1
Vietnam	8							

Source Central Banks' websites
[+] This ratio was effective until March 2021. It had previously been required at 100%.
[#] The ratio has been reduced to 70% due to the Covid-19 pandemic. It was previously set at 100%.
*The government requires Higher Loss Absorbency (HLA) of 0.5% for Public Bank and 1% for Maybank and CIMB. This requirement has been effective since 31 January 2021

legal text that considers supervisors not civilly liable only if they can prove that they applied 'extraordinary diligence' is still in force'.[9] Similarly, legal protections in Indonesia and Laos are inadequate. For example, the IMF FSAP report in 2018 states that the lack of immunity from prosecution in the lawful performance of supervisory duties has led to supervisory forbearance in Laos.[10]

[9] IMF and the World Bank, 'Technical Note: FSAP Update, Philippines, Focused Update of the Basel Core Principles for Effective Banking Supervision' (April 2010), 3–4, http://documents1.worldbank.org/curated/en/992381468144566289/pdf/792320WP0Phili0Box0377370B00Public0.pdf, accessed 4 June 2025.

[10] IMF, 'Technical Assistance Report, Lao People's Democratic Republic, The Development of Risk-based Supervision' (May 2018), 13, https://www.imf.org/en/Publications/CR/Issues/2018/05/31/Lao-Peoples-Democratic-Republic-Technical-Assistance-Report-The-Development-of-Risk-Based-45919, accessed 4 June 2025.

With regards to the Basel Accords, central banks in ASEAN states have imposed requirements on banks in compliance with the standards. Table 2 shows numerical figures of capital adequacy requirements and other ratios in ASEAN countries. ASEAN states could be considered in two groups: states which have implemented Basel II, and those which have followed Basel III recommendations. The former group comprises Brunei, Cambodia, Lao PDR, Myanmar and Vietnam. Cambodia has incorporated Basel II standards into its regulatory framework with an aim to move towards Basel III. Hence, some Basel III measures have already been implemented in the country (i.e., the requirements of counter cyclical buffer and capital conservation buffer).[11] Similarly, Vietnam set the deadline in 2020 in order to comply with the Basel II standards.[12] In addition, Basel III requirements such as liquidity coverage ratio and net stable funding ratio have already been incorporated into the regulations of the State Bank of Vietnam (SBV), although there is no public commitment to Basel III.[13] As for Lao PDR, its central bank is revising

[11] National Bank of Cambodia, 'Prakas on Capital Buffer in Banking and Financial Institutions' (22 February 2018), https://www.nbc.org.kh/download_files/legislation/prakas_eng/3.Prakas_on_Capital_Buffer_in_BFIs_ENG.pdf, accessed 4 June 2025.

[12] IMF, 'Vietnam: 2018 Article IV Consultation—Press Release and Staff Report' (July 2018), 15–16, https://www.imf.org/en/Publications/CR/Issues/2018/07/10/Vietnam-2018-Article-IV-Consultation-Press-Release-and-Staff-Report-46064, accessed 4 June 2025.

[13] Que-Giang Tran-Thi and Tu-Anh Vu Thanh, 'Vietnam: The Dilemma of Bringing Global Financial Standards to a Socialist Market Economy' in Emily Jones (ed), *The Political Economy of Bank Regulation in Developing Countries: Risk and Reputation* (Oxford Publishing Press USA—OSO 2020), 306. According to Article 15(3)(c) of Circular 36/2014, 30-day liquidity coverage ratio (LCR) for commercial banks and branches of foreign banks is 50% for Vietnamese dong. As for foreign currencies, 30-day LCR for commercial banks is 10% for commercial banks and 5% for branches of foreign banks (Article 15(3)(d) of Circular 36/2014). Meanwhile, net stable funding ratio (NSFR) for commercial banks and branches of foreign banks is 10% (Article 15(2)(d) of Circular 36/2014). State Bank of Vietnam, Circular No. 36/2014/TT-NHNN Stipulating Minimum Safety Limits and Ratios for Transactions Performed by Credit Institutions and Branches of Foreign Banks (20 November 2014), https://vanbanphapluat.co/circular-no-36-2014-tt-nhnn-minimum-safety-limits-ratios-for-credit-institutions-branches-foreign-banks, accessed 4 June 2025.

the central bank law and banking law and regulations relating to risk-based regulation in order to support the implementation of the Basel II capital framework.[14]

The final group is composed of ASEAN-5 states: Indonesia, Malaysia, the Philippines, Singapore and Thailand. For example, the Bank of Thailand (BOT) has switched its capital framework from Basel II to Basel III since 2013.[15] Currently, the BOT demands five domestic systemically important banks (D-SIBs)[16] in Thailand to satisfy the Basel III standards regarding the Common Equity Tier 1 (CET1) requirement and the capital adequacy ratio.[17]

2.2.1 *Soft Law and its Effectiveness in Minimising the Financial Trilemma*

Many commentators have questioned the effectiveness of the BCPs and the Basel Accords in helping supervisors maintain financial stability and harmonise law in action.[18] For example, a research result by Demirguc-Kunt and Detragiache finds that better compliance with the BCPs has

[14] IMF, 'Lao People's Democratic Republic: Technical Assistance Report—Implementation of Risk-based Supervision' (November 2018), 16, https://www.imf.org/en/Publications/CR/Issues/2018/11/14/Lao-Peoples-Democratic-Republic-Technical-Assistance-Report-Implementation-of-Risk-Based-46364, accessed 4 June 2025.

[15] Bank of Thailand, 'Re: Regulation on Capital Supervision of Financial Business Groups' Bank of Thailand Notification No. FPG. 9/2561, 2, https://www.bot.or.th/Thai/FIPCS/Documents/FPG/2561/EngPDF/25610131.pdf, accessed 4 June 2025.

[16] They are Bangkok Bank, Krungthai Bank, Bank of Ayudhya, Kasikornbank and Siam Commercial Bank.

[17] Pawee Sirimai and Somreudi Banchongduang, 'BoT Embraces Basel III Rule' *Bangkok Post* (Thailand, 27 September 2017), https://www.bangkokpost.com/business/1331879/bot-embraces-basel-iii-rule, accessed 4 June 2025.

[18] Allen and Saunders (2002) argue that the Basel capital requirements do not focus upon systemic risk sufficiently. For example, the use of 'institution-level value-at-risk (VaR) which is designed to address the risk of an individual institution have persisted in regulation-assessing risks of the financial system as a whole'. Viral Acharya et. al., 'Measuring Systemic Risk' (2017) 30 (1) *The Review of Financial Studies 2*, 3. In addition, Hall Scott questions whether measures in the Basel Accord (e.g., capital requirements, liquidity requirements, and loss-imposing resolution procedures) can adequately address the problem of contagious runs that can quickly spread through the financial system. Hall Scott, 'Interconnectedness and Contagion', Committee on Capital Market Regulation (20 Novermber 2012), 7, https://www.capmktsreg.org/wp-content/uploads/2014/11/2012.11.20_Interconnectedness_and_Contagion.pdf, accessed 4 June 2025.

'no robust statistical relationship' with 'bank soundness' and systemic stability.[19] Nonetheless, their findings must be treated with caution, as the research result was limited by the availability and quality of data. For instance, Demirguc-Kunt and Detragiache state that their findings may be attributable to low quality of the assessments of BCP compliance, especially in low-income countries. In those countries, law and regulations on the books may not reflect how they are implemented in practice.[20]

With regard to legal concerns, one of the main issues is the fact that the Basel standard is soft law, and not legally binding. As a result, it lacks legal enforcement and sanctions which help secure compliance. According to Brummer, when there are significant distributional trade-offs and the risk-adjusted cost of defection is lowered, the likelihood of non-compliance will be heightened.[21] For example, there are weak monitoring mechanisms which have rendered the BCPs ineffectual.[22]

In addition, soft law allows large discretion on the part of national regulators and supervisors. Hence, when applying soft law, a national authority could prioritise national interest over the common good of financial stability. For instance, the Chairman of Indonesian Financial Services Authority's (Otoritas Jasa Keuangan (OJK)) Board of Commissioners, Wimboh Santoso, stated that the OJK would 'implement the Basel III framework with emphasis on national interests in mind'.[23] Besides, the OJK will use zero per cent risk-weighted assets (RWA) for government bonds which constitute sovereign exposures to banks' assets.[24]

[19] Ash Demirguc-Kunt and Enrica Detragiache, 'Basel Core Principles and Bank Soundness: Does Compliance Matter?' (2009) World Bank Policy Research Working Paper 5129, 13, https://elibrary.worldbank.org/doi/abs/10.1596/1813-9450-5129, accessed 4 June 2025.

[20] Ibid., 4–5.

[21] Chris Brummer, 'How International Financial Law Works (And How It Doesn't) (2011) Georgetown Law and Economics Research Paper No. 11–15, 264.

[22] Ibid., 303.

[23] Otoritas Jasa Keuangan, 'Basel III Implementation to be Adapted to National Interests' Press Release (8 December 2017), https://www.ojk.go.id/en/berita-dan-kegiatan/siaran-pers/Pages/Press-Release-Basel-III-Implementation-to-be-Adapted-to-National-Interests.aspx, accessed 4 June 2025.

[24] Ibid.

However, it could be argued that the effects of soft law and hard law might not be significantly different—soft law could be as coercive as hard law in many ways. The former could generate reputational costs, since regulators might face institutional sanctions and shaming.[25] As Giovanoli has argued in the context of the Basel Accords, these standards reflect mutual commitments resulting from intense negotiations. Therefore, their incentives for compliance and sanctions for non-compliance are serious.[26]

Apart from instrumental motivations (e.g., incentives and sanctions), soft law could produce social motivations (e.g., legitimacy of authorities) which are more influential to people's rule behaviour than instrumental drives. According to Tom Tyler, social motivations are the main factors which form 'cooperation, especially voluntary cooperation'.[27] In addition, social motivation leads to both 'compliance' and 'voluntary deference to rules'. Moreover, Murphy, Taylor and Curtis (2009) find that there is a strong causal connection between an acceptance of rules and procedural justice. The latter is important in providing legitimacy to the law.[28]

In the case of the Basel standards, the rule-making process of the BCPs, Basel II and Basel III were transparent, inclusive and participatory. This process has increased accountability and legitimacy of these soft instruments from the perspective of non-member nations.[29] For instance, central bankers and supervisors from non-G-10 and developing countries were invited to participate in the creation of these soft laws.[30] In addition, the BCBS has conducted a notice and comment process, whereby its proposed soft laws are published and open to comments by the public, in creating and revising these tools. Moreover, the Basel Standards have

[25] Brummer (n 133) 263.

[26] Mario Giovanoli, 'The Reform of the International Architecture after the Global Crisis' (2009) 42 (81) International Law and Politics, https://nyujilp.org/wp-content/uploads/2013/02/42.1-Giovanoli.pdf, accessed 4 June 2025.

[27] Tom Tyler, Why People Cooperate: The Role of Social Motivations (Princeton University Press 2011).

[28] Ibid.

[29] Michael S. Barr and Geoffrey P. Miller, 'Global Administrative Law: The View from Basel' (2006) 17 (1) The European Journal of International Law, 40.

[30] Ibid., 27–28.

been embraced into 'domestic notice and comment rule-making process' by national supervisors and central banks.[31]

Nevertheless, in my view, there are still some weaknesses which render the Basel standards ineffective in maintaining financial stability and increasing supervisory cooperation. These shortcomings are not attributable mainly to their soft law nature, but their design. Their design is flawed for three main reasons. First, the Basel Accords relies upon complex risk model of which benefits in maintaining financial stability is doubtful. Secondly, there is no widely accepted rationale and measurement of the Basel liquidity requirements. Lastly, the design of these standards is inept for developing countries and emerging markets. This has, in turn, discouraged those states from complying with the soft laws. The next sections will provide details of these issues.

2.2.1.1 Complex Risk Model[32]

The simple risk model of the 1988 Basel Accord (Basel I) was replaced by Basel II in 2004. The designers of Basel II believed that more sophisticated models would be able to help reduce regulatory arbitrage and risk-shifting incentives which were created by simpler regulation of Basel I. In the context of banking regulation, M Hiterschweiger et al. (2018) state that risk-shifting had effects on the riskiness of banks' portfolios. Shareholders of the banks were incentivised to invest in risky assets or projects as they might generate higher portfolio returns while the banks did not need to keep a higher level of capital.[33]

One of the most sophisticated mechanisms of Basel II was the utilisation of risk-weighted assets in calculating the denominator of the regulatory capital ratios. For each type of risk, various approaches which increased risk-sensitivity and sophistication were used.[34] Nonetheless,

[31] Ibid., 17.

[32] Some parts of this section (i.e., (i) complex risk model) have been published in Financial Regulation International. *See* Sharon Kun-amornpong, 'The Role of the Basel Accords in Mitigating Systemic Risk' (2019) Financial Regulation International.

[33] Marc Hinterschweiger et al., 'Risk Sensitivity and Risk Shifting in Banking Regulation' (2018) Financial Stability Paper No 44, 20, https://www.bankofengland.co.uk/-/media/boe/files/financial-stability-paper/2018/risk-sensitivity-and-risk-shifting-in-banking-regulation.pdf?la=en&hash=1C68C5AC14E0A518950547193679B5BCDEFEA8EA, accessed 4 June 2025.

[34] Andrew Taylor, 'What Is Basel II and Why Has It Got 3 Pillars?' (2004) 19 Butterworths Journal of International Banking & Financial Law, 123.

the success of Basel II in reducing the incentive to risk-shift has been supported by very few empirical studies. One of those studies is research by M Hinterschweiger et al (2018) which concludes that overly simple approaches may lead to risk shifting. The study supports the view that Basel II may have mitigated risk-shifting incentives better than Basel I.

Concerning the issue of regulatory arbitrage, Basel II was expected to help reduce this problem by aligning economic and regulatory capital, as well as creating incentives for banks to develop their own risk management systems. However, financial institutions in the GFC, especially systemically important financial institutions (SIFIs), conducted 'regulatory capital arbitrage' by, for example, utilising special purpose vehicles (SPVs) to perform off-balance sheet financing. Those financial institutions could exploit 'the difference between capital as measured for regulatory purposes and the banks' true economic capital'.[35] The result was that financial institutions which were badly affected in the GFC were highly leveraged. Their managers took excessive risks.

The Basel Committee responded to the shortcomings in Basel II by introducing Basel III. Basel III requires banks to maintain capital against a wider range of risks including liquidity risk and sets out formulae for those capital cushions.[36] Basel III also enhances capital standard for global systemically important banks (G-SIBs). In addition, there are additional buffers in order to increase financial stability (e.g., countercyclical capital buffers, capital conservation buffers and systemic risk buffers). However, many commentators have questioned the effectiveness of Basel III in helping the regulator to achieve regulatory objectives. For example, Ismail Erturk argues that Basel III would not be able to solve the problem of regulatory arbitrage as it does not change the business model of firms. According to Erturk, the root cause is the shareholder value-driven business models, which give incentives for managers to make risky investments in order to raise return on equity (ROE).[37]

[35] Bunea-Bontas et al. discuss this issue in the context of 'cosmetic changes' where an increase in capital ratio of banks was manipulated so as not to raise probability of failure of those banks. Cristina Bunea-Bontas et al., 'Capital Adequacy and Risk Management—Premises for Strengthening Financial System Stability' (2009) MPRA Paper No. 18132.

[36] Erik Gerding, 'The Dialectics of Bank Capital' (2016) 55 Washburn Law Journal, 367.

[37] Isamil Erturk, 'Financialization, Bank Business Models and the Limits of Post-Crisis Bank Regulation' (2016) 17 Journal of Banking Regulation 60, 62.

In addition, the accuracy of a risk model in portraying risk in an individual financial institution and aggregate risk of the financial market would depend largely upon the quality of the underlying assumptions of the model itself. If the underlying assumptions are incomplete or incorrect, the risk model would inevitably be error-prone. For example, a factor model is widely used among financial institutions; however, it underestimates the importance of changing correlations. This is despite the fact that the 'large swings in correlations' are important factors in a financial crisis. Hence, during the GFC, the predictive power of this model decreased significantly. Besides this, the risk of errors increases when the modelling process becomes more complicated.[38]

Moreover, Basel III has not eliminated the complexity of regulation by models. It has merely introduced some simpler risk identifiers (e.g., leverage ratio and liquidity risk) to be used in addition to the more complex ones (i.e., risk-weighted ratio). In my view, solving the complexity of the financial market by using a complex tool might neither reduce the arbitrage incentives nor produce the best regulatory outcome, for the following reasons. First, the state and its regulator do not have sufficient capacity to check the truthfulness of the information produced by a complex risk model, as risk weights are based on private information held by banks.[39] According to H Benink et al., supervisors have already faced great difficulties in checking the truthfulness of estimates of probabilities of default (PD). Hence, it is possible that financial institutions could conduct a regulatory risk arbitrage when they use sophisticated internal risk-based models.

Secondly, the superiority of a more complex tool (i.e., risk-weighted ratio) in identifying risk when compared with a simpler one is doubtful. There are some studies, undertaken after the GFC, which support the view that greater complexity of Basel II rules does not always lead to a better risk identification. In addition, a complex model is subject to greater variance, which yields more inaccurate predictions of risk. Moreover, in an environment where larger banks faced complex risks with

[38] Jon Danielsson, 'Blame the Models' (2008) 4 Journal of Financial Stability, 324–325.

[39] Harald Benink et al., 'On the Role of Regulatory Banking Capital' (2008) 17 (1) Financial Markets, Institutions and Instruments 85, https://notendur.hi.is/ajonsson/kennsla2006/Basel_grein.pdf, accessed 4 June 2025.

limited data, a simpler leverage ratio produces a more accurate prediction of bank failures than a risk-weighted approach.[40]

Lastly, complex rules have higher administrative costs than simple ones. According to R Epstein, administrative costs include compliance costs, the public cost of enforcing legal norms, costs of inspection, monitoring and supervising and error costs[41] in operating the legal system. As R Epstein states, 'the more complicated the legal rules, the greater the likelihood that these administrative costs, including error costs, will be high'.[42] Financial institutions have already spent a large amount of money and manpower in order to ensure compliance with the Basel requirements. The cost of compliance to the complex rules under Basel III has become increasingly prohibitive. Besides, the complexity of the model could consume a vast amount of resource which, in turn, could potentially undermine the Pillar II Supervisory Review process. The resources of the private and public sectors are sacrificed for unclear effects in improving the financial stability and reducing systemic risk in the financial system.

2.2.1.2 The Lack of a Wide Agreement Regarding the Rationale and Measurement of Liquidity Regulation

The BCBS has introduced LCR and NSFR as part of the Basel III reforms to deal with liquidity risk of banks.[43] Liquidity risk can arise due to factors such as maturity mismatch, bank run and recessionary economic conditions.[44] The LCR is intended to ensure that banks have an ongoing ability to meet short-term obligation. It is calculated by dividing the sum of High Quality Liquid Asset (HQLA) by the total amount of net

[40] Andrew Haldane and Vasileios Madouros, 'The Dog and the Frisbee', 'Speech' (The Federal Reserve Bank of Kansas City's 366th Economic Policy Symposium, Wyoming, 31 August 2012), https://www.bis.org/review/r120905a.pdf, accessed 4 June 2025.

[41] The error costs could occur where legal determinations are uncertain and unreliable. Richard Epstein, *Simple Rules for a Complex World* (Harvard University Press 1995), 31.

[42] Ibid.

[43] BIS, 'Net Stable Funding Ratio (NSFR)—Executive Summary (28 June 2018), https://www.bis.org/fsi/fsisummaries/nsfr.htm, accessed 4 June 2025.

[44] Ahmed Arif and Ahmed Nauman Anees, 'Liquidity Risk and Performance of Banking System' (2012) 20 (2) Journal of Financial Regulation and Compliance, 182–195.

cash outflows, arising from both actual and contingent exposures, over a 30-day stress scenario.[45]

Meanwhile, the NSFR concerns maturity transformation.[46] One of the objectives of creating the NSFR is to reduce systemic risk arising as a result of funding shocks. The NSFR is expected to incentivise banks to maintain resilience over a longer time horizon. In order to comply with the NSFR requirement, banks have to fund their activities with more stable sources of funding.[47] The NSFR is measured by the ratio of banks' available stable funding (ASF) to the banks' required stable funding (RSF). This ratio must be at or above 100 per cent. ASF is its capital and the liabilities that will be reliable sources of funds for more than one year. With regards to RSF, the amount of stable funding required to hold is determined by taking into accounts the 'liquidity characteristics and residual maturities of its assets and the contingent liquidity risk arising from its off-balance sheet exposures'.[48]

Some commentators have supported the use of liquidity regulation as it could yield some benefits to the financial system. For example, the LCR and NSFR could act as a second-best solution to the lender of last resort (LOLR) of central banks in preventing a liquidity crisis.[49] In other words, liquidity regulation would reduce the likelihood of the need for the LOLR intervention. This would minimise associated costs of the LOLR.[50] These associated costs partly reflect Type I and Type II errors in a decision-making process. In the case of Type I error, the LOLR might fail to provide liquidity to an illiquid but solvent bank. As for Type II error, the LOLR could back deposits of an insolvent banks and, effectively, bail out

[45] Deutsche Bank, 'Liquidity Coverage Ratio' Annual Report 2017, https://annualreport.deutsche-bank.com/2017/ar/risk-report/risk-and-capital-management/liquidity-risk-management/liquidity-coverage-ratio.html, accessed 4 June 2025.

[46] Stephen Cecchetti and Anil Kashyap, 'What Binds? Interactions between Bank Capital and LiquidityRregulations' in Hartmann P. (ed), *The Changing Fortunes of Central Banking* (Cambridge University Press 2018), 194.

[47] BIS (n 155).

[48] Ibid.

[49] Mari.e.,Hoerova et al., 'Benefits and Costs of Liquidity Regulation' ECB Working Paper Series (July 2018), 3, https://www.ecb.europa.eu/pub/pdf/scpwps/ecb.wp2169.en.pdf, accessed 4 June 2025.

[50] Ibid., 14.

those banks.[51] These errors derive in part from asymmetric information about bank assets' value that renders obtaining a true quality of illiquid bank balance sheets very challenging.

In addition, the use of LCR and NSFR as a second-best solution to the LOLR intervention might prevent central banks from breaching the 'Fundamental Constraint'. According to Sir Paul Tucker, the Fundamental Constraint is a 'principle that central banks should not lend to firms that they know to be fundamentally bust or broken'.[52] This principle has its roots in the constitutional democracies, in which the rule of law and the constitutional doctrine of separation of power prevent an arbitrary use of power. Tucker has argued that in a constitutional democracy, taxation powers should be separated from monetary policy.[53] In other words, tax policy should be decided by an elected lawmakers rather than an independent central bank. Consequently, liquidity assistance in the form of LOLR operation that would amount to a fiscal measure should be avoided. This form of the LOLR could occur in two main circumstances. The first situation is where the LOLR intervention results in a prioritisation of repayment to short-term unsecured creditors over long-term creditors of the same hierarchy of claims. Meanwhile, in the second scenario, all creditors receive repayment due to the fact that the LOLR provides funds to a bank. However, the repayment is made at the expense of taxpayers as losses are effectively transferred to them.[54]

Moreover, there is some empirical research regarding the relationship between liquidity requirement and banks' profitability, which demonstrates that the former increases the level of the latter. For instance, Rasidah Mohd Said finds that the NSFR is an important factor which affects his sample Malaysian commercial banks' profitability. There is a

[51] Ibid., 13.

[52] Sir Paul Tucker, 'Solvency as a Fundamental Constraint on LOLR Policy for Independent Central Banks: Principles, History, Law' (2020) 2 (2) Journal of Financial Crises, 2.

[53] Ibid., 3–4.

[54] Ibid., 9.

positive relationship between the NSFR and indicators of profit performance (i.e., return on assets (ROA),[55] ROE (i.e., return on equity)[56] and net interest margin (NIM)[57]).[58]

However, requiring banks to meet liquidity standards does not rule out the need for the LOLR intervention. For example, the historical experience of the US has provided a lesson that reserve requirements may lead to additional pressure on the banks during a crisis. That is because non-regulated institutions may reduce their reserves and rely more on banks as a source of liquidity. In addition, the liquidity of assets could change during a crisis.[59] Moreover, a complete removal of the LOLR function would result in the need for liquidity requirements to be set at a much higher level.[60] This policy would be undesirable as it would significantly reduce banks' capacity to make loans.[61]

Apart from the LOLR concerns, the empirical evidence regarding the effects of liquidity upon banks' profitability is inconsistent.[62] Some scholars have suggested that liquidity holdings have a negative impact upon financial development.[63] For example, the findings of Nguyen et al. suggest that banks which hold more liquid asset lacks market power while dominant banks hold less liquid asset.[64] In addition, there is a lack of a wide agreement regarding theories and measurement of

[55] ROA is an indicator of the efficiency of a company in utilising its assets. It measures net income against total assets of a company.

[56] ROE is calculated by dividing a company's net income by shareholders' equity. ROE is considered a return on net assets.

[57] NIM compares net interest income of a financial firm with outgoing interest payment.

[58] Rasidah Mohd Said, 'Net Stable Funding Ratio and Commercial Banks Profitability' (2014) 76 (7) IPEDR, 34.

[59] Mark Carlson, 'Lessons from the Historical Use of Reserve Requirements in the United States to Promote Bank Liquidity' (2015) 11 (1) International Journal of Central Banking, 193.

[60] Hoerova et al. (n 161) 35.

[61] Carlson (n 171).

[62] Olga Golubeva et al., 'The Impact of Liquidity Risk on Bank Profitability: Some Empirical Evidence from the European Banks Following the Introduction of Basel III Regulations' (2019) 18 (4) Accounting and Management Information Systems 455, 461.

[63] Ibid., 457.

[64] My Nguyen et al., 'Bank Market Power, Asset Liquidity and Funding Liquidity: International Evidence' (2017) 54 International Review of Financial Analysis, 23.

liquidity ratios. As Allen and Gale have stated, 'with capital regulation there is a huge literature but little agreement on the optimal level of requirements. With liquidity regulation, we do not even know what to argue about'.[65] For instance, there is no conclusive answer 'whether liquidity should correspond to short-term real assets or to monetary instruments'.[66] Furthermore, the requirement of the LCR could exacerbate the problem of systemic risk as it could increase banks' exposure to similar and correlated assets.[67]

2.2.1.3 *Unsuitability for Conditions in Developing Countries and Emerging Markets*

The Basel standards are not originally designed to suit conditions in developing countries and emerging markets. This is despite the fact that there were representatives from some less-developed countries participating in developing the BCPs (e.g., Thailand, Indonesia and Malaysia) and the Basel Accords.[68] The unsuitable design stems, in part, from the fact the Basel Committee has made a decision on a consensus basis. Consequently, smaller states were unwilling to take a minority position by objecting to proposals of economically powerful countries (e.g., USA and the UK).[69]

Nevertheless, less-developed countries still adopt these international standards. According to Jones, the decisions of peripheral countries to do so have been driven by political considerations rather than 'technocratic concerns' regarding the most effective or suitable regulation for banks in their countries.[70] For example, there is a concern that international standards allow large domestic banks to gain access to foreign markets by

[65] Franklin Allen and Douglas Gale, 'How should bank liquidity be regulated?' (2017) SSRN, 25, https://papers.ssrn.com/sol3/papers.cfm?abstract_id=2956304, accessed 4 June 2025.

[66] Ibid., 24.

[67] Daniel Roberts et al., 'Bank Liquidity Creation, Systemic Risk and Basel Liquidity Regulations' Federal Reserve Bank of New York Staff Reports No. 852 (June 2018), 1, https://www.newyorkfed.org/medialibrary/media/research/staff_reports/sr852.pdf, accessed 4 June 2025.

[68] BCBS, 'Core Principles for Effective Banking Supervision' (September 1997), 1–2, https://www.bis.org/publ/bcbs30a.pdf, accessed 4 June 2025.

[69] Kern Alexander, 'Global Financial Standard-Setting, the G10 Committees, and International Economic Law' (2009) 34 (3) Brook.J.Int'L L., https://www.ius.uzh.ch/dam/jcr:00000000-39e6-3af1-0000-00000f966d59/KAGFSS.pdf, accessed 4 June 2025.

[70] Jones (ed.) (n 125) 4.

showing potential host supervisors that they are regulated in accordance with international best practice in their home country.[71]

The incompatibility of design of these standards with economic and institutional contexts in peripheral countries could reduce their effectiveness in minimising the financial trilemma for various reasons. First, the goals of these standards do not include financial policies which are important to low-income countries like some of ASEAN states (e.g., financial inclusion (i.e., 'greater access to financial services for low-income households and small firms, as part of their overall strategies for economic and financial development')[72] and financial development[73]). For example, financial stability is the only criterion in evaluating supervisors or regulation according to the BCPs.[74] Hence, when these policies are in conflict with each other, a state might choose to prioritise policies which are its immediate concerns over financial stability and compliance with international standards.

However, it could be argued that financial stability goes hand in hand with other financial policies, especially financial inclusion. Therefore, a conflict between those policies is unlikely to occur. For instance, Maria Jose Roa Garcia has reviewed studies regarding the relationship between financial inclusion and financial stability. The majority of the reviewed studies suggest that greater financial inclusion reduces financial instability. That is because financial inclusion results in 'a more diversified and stable retail deposit base', a 'more efficient intermediation of resources', and an 'enhanced household capacity to manage vulnerabilities and shocks'.[75] In addition, Morgan and Pontines find that increasing financial inclusion by lending to small and medium-sized enterprises (SMEs) contributes to financial stability. This is due to the fact that doing so helps decrease

[71] Ibid.

[72] Peter J. Morgan and Victor Pontines, 'Financial Stability and Financial Inclusion' ADBI Working Paper Series No. 488 (July 2014), 3.

[73] Financial development is considered in terms of 'depth, access, and efficiency'. Ratna Sahay et al., 'Rethinking Financial Deepening: Stability and Growth in Emerging Markets' IMF Staff Discussion Notes No. 15/8 (2015), 6.

[74] Jones (ed) (n 125) 39.

[75] Maria Jose Roa Garcia, 'Can Financial Inclusion and Financial Stability Go Hand in Hand?' (2016) 21 (2) Economic Issues, 94.

probability of default and non-performing loans (NPLs) of financial institutions.[76]

Nevertheless, some scholars suggest that the relationship between financial inclusion and financial stability is not conclusive. For example, Ardic et al. (2013) find that financial inclusion in terms of deposit account penetration leads to 'neither positive nor negative correlations' with the World Bank's Global Financial Development database (GFDD).[77,78] Moreover, when there is no appropriate regulation and supervision in place, overly-aggressive policies of financial inclusion and excessive credit growth could generate highly negative effects upon financial stability.[79] Furthermore, the requirements of higher capital requirements in Basel III, while potentially help maintain financial stability, could deprive people from access to finance as well as aggravate the problem of financial exclusion in emerging economies.[80] For example, Li Ma et al. find that the imposition of higher capital requirements disadvantaged small businesses in China by discriminating them.[81]

Apart from the abovementioned financial policies, in some developing countries, the governments have pursued national polices of 'policy-directed credit' (e.g., East Asian tiger economies). According to this developmental state model, states play an important role in allocating credits. Hence, it would be impossible for the regulator to be completely free from any political interference. However, the assumption underlying the Basel standards is that banks should be supervised under a market-based allocation of credit. In other words, governments should take a steering role and intervene in the market only when there is a

[76] Morgan and Pontines (n 184) 3.

[77] 'Examples of data on financial stability in the GFDD include bank Z-scores (an indicator of the probability of default of the country's banking system), the ratio of NPLs, the ratio of bank credit to bank deposits, the ratio of bank regulatory capital to risk-weighted assets, and the ratio of bank liquid assets to deposits and short-term funding'. Ibid.

[78] Garcia (n 187) 90.

[79] Ibid., 82.

[80] Aurelio Gurrea-Martinez and Nydia Remolina, 'The Dark Side of Implementing Basel Capital Requirements: Theory, Evidence, and Policy' Working Paper Series 2/2017, 35–36.

[81] Li Ma et al., 'Capital Requirements of Commercial Banks and Lending Discrimination against Small Businesses: Theory and Empirical Evidence from China' (2013) 14–2(A) Annals of Economic and Finance.

market failure.[82] For example, Principle 2 of the BCPs assesses supervisory compliance against the criteria that 'there is no government or industry interference which compromises the operational independence of the supervisor'. The supervisors should also have 'full discretion' in conducting their supervision or taking a decision on banks and banking groups.[83]

Encountering conflicting demands between the requirement of the Basel standards and their national policies, some regulators have exercised regulatory forbearance and left regulations unenforced. This practice is termed 'cosmetic or mock compliance'.[84] For example this could be considered from the Vietnamese experience. In Vietnam, economic integration and the adoption of international best practices are still 'valued only as long as it does not interfere with the party-state's legitimacy and its control of the economy'.[85] Hence, the SBV has practised 'mock compliance' with regard to the Basel Accords. The SBV has allowed the utilisation of 'compromised and falsified data by banks'.[86] During the banking crisis between 2008 and 2012, the SBV 'largely overlooked' the capital adequacy requirement of banks.[87]

Secondly, the sophistication and complexity of the Basel tools require infrastructure, resources, capacity and expertise in order to implement them properly. Developing countries might find these requirements challenging. For instance, in Vietnam, the shortage of competent technocrats in the SBV and domestic commercial banks is part of the reason for a high level of forbearance in implementing the Basel standards.[88] In addition, the countercyclical buffer of Basel III needs macroeconomic knowledge on the part of the regulators. The regulators must be able to anticipate credit bubbles accurately. However, regulators in some developing

[82] Jones (n125) 16.

[83] BCBS, 'Core Principles for Effective Banking Supervision' Consultative Document (December 2011), 22–23, https://www.bis.org/publ/bcbs213.pdf, accessed 4 June 2025.

[84] Jones (n 125) 14.

[85] Ibid., 319.

[86] Ibid., 312.

[87] Ibid.

[88] Ibid., 229.

countries might not have capacity to do so, as large swings in economic performance are common.[89]

Moreover, Pillar 2 assessments of Basel III need to be forward-looking and generate a comprehensive view of banks' risks and capital adequacy.[90] Supervisors have to collect both quantitative and qualitative assessments in so doing. This requires massive regulatory resources, that developing countries might not be able to afford.[91] Besides this, some of the assessments (e.g., standardised approach of the capital adequacy requirement) still have to rely on credit rating agencies. Nonetheless, there are wide segments of emerging markets and developing countries which are not covered by credit ratings.[92] Furthermore, there are limited high-quality liquid assets which are necessary to meet Basel III liquidity requirements in developing countries.[93]

89 Emily Jones and Peter Knaack, 'Global Financial Regulation: Shortcomings and Reform Options' (2019) 10 (2) Global Policy, 196.

90 Caio Ferreira et al., 'From Basel I to Basel III: Sequencing Implementation in Developing Economies' IMF Working Paper WP/19/127 (June 2019), 25, https://www.imf.org/en/Publications/WP/Issues/2019/06/14/From-Basel-I-to-Basel-III-Sequencing-Implementation-in-Developing-Economies-46895, accessed 4 June 2025.

91 For example, the banking sector in Vietnam has 'faced a shortage of people who have experience in working with Basel II. Banks need to invest time to build and develop adequate human resources to operate risk management under Basel II. There are problems in gathering sufficient data to measure and run analysis as banks need exact and copious amounts of historical data. It can take up to three years to collect enough data to build a model with low error rate'. 'Basel II: The Precursor of an Integrated Risk Management Framework for Vietnamese Banks' *The Asian Banker* (Vietnam, 18 October 2016), https://www.theasianbanker.com/updates-and-articles/basel-ii-the-precursor-of-an-integrated-risk-management-framework-for-vietnamese-banks, accessed 4 June 2025.

92 Jones and Knaack (n 201) 196.

93 BCBS, 'Impact and Implementation Challenges of the Basel Framework for Emerging Market, Developing and Small Economies' Working Paper No. 27 (November 2014), 1, https://www.bis.org/bcbs/publ/wp27.pdf, accessed 4 June 2025.

2.3 Part II: Vertical Network and the Financial Trilemma

2.3.1 The ASEAN and the Need to Create a Vertical Network for Banking Supervision

Cross-border externalities from bank failure in ASEAN have become increasingly large. As ASEAN has moved towards expanding financial integration, the possibility that banks would face stress would simultaneously increase.[94] In addition, externalities are potentially higher in ASEAN, because businesses would be subject to fewer barriers to entry across the sub-region.[95] As discussed in the previous section, the horizontal network of the BCBS has some weaknesses which could reduce its effectiveness in minimising the financial trilemma. This would, in turn, raise a concern regarding whether or not ASEAN should create its own supranational authority for banking supervision. Currently, ASEAN has not indicated that it is forming a single supervisory mechanism. Instead, the member states have pursued regulatory harmonisation.[96]

I argue that ASEAN would need a supranational authority for banking supervision for some reasons. First, a supranational authority would help ensure that supervisory practice in the member states is harmonised. This is crucially important, as a mere regulatory harmonisation might not yield the expected result, if the supervisory practice within the member states is not sound and consistent. As the European Commission has commented, 'regulation, no matter good, cannot overcome poor supervision'.[97] In

[94] Thorsten Beck and Wolf Wagner, 'Supranational Supervision: How Much and for Whom?' (2016) 12 (2) International Journal of Central Banking, 228–229, https://www.ijcb.org/journal/ijcb16q2a5.pdf, accessed 4 June 2025.

[95] Ibid.

[96] Ratna Sahay et al. (eds), *The Future of Asian Finance* (International Monetary Fund 2015), 230, https://www.elibrary.imf.org/doc/IMF071/22239-9781498317191/22239-9781498317191/Other_formats/Source_PDF/22239-9781513555591.pdf?redirect=true, accessed 4 June 2025.

[97] European Commission, 'Capital Requirement—CRD IV/CRR—Frequently Asked Questions' EU Commission Memo (16 July 2013), 25, https://ec.europa.eu/commission/presscorner/detail/en/MEMO_13_690, accessed 4 June 2025.

addition, uneven supervisory quality in host markets could hide vulnerabilities in the financial system.[98] Moreover, an ASEAN supervisor would be the most suitable authority to oversee systemic ASEAN banks. The centralisation of authority would help ensure that nationality dominance is avoided when dealing with these banks.[99]

Furthermore, a diverse supervisory practice could increase the costs of doing business to international and regional banks. According to a study by the Organisation for Economic Co-operation and Development (OECD) in 2015, regulatory divergence costs financial institutions 5–10 per cent of their annual turnover. These costs consume scarce resources that could otherwise be utilised in order to identify emerging risks in the financial system. The study also concludes that these costs, which are more than US$780 billion annually, are a barrier to international growth.[100] A supranational banking supervision in ASEAN could reduce fragmentation in the supervisory framework by providing consistent guidelines and practice of banking supervision. This would, in turn, help reduce the compliance costs to international and regional banks.

Secondly, an ASEAN banking supervision is a necessary step for coordination in other regulatory aspects (e.g., risk-sharing). In my view, coordination in the regulatory framework should be pursued holistically, as a piecemeal approach could generate detrimental effects. As Acharya has warned, 'a less than full step toward complete coordination can be more harmful than no step at all'.[101] For example, coordinating capital adequacy ratios across countries is not sufficient if it is not combined with coordination in other regulatory dimensions (e.g., resolution policies).[102]

Thirdly, a vertical network could help strengthen the existing horizontal network of the BCBS. For example, there is no mandatory mediating process for resolving disagreement among supervisors in a college of supervisors under the Basel principles. During the GFC, the

[98] Geert Almekinders et al., 'ASEAN Financial Integration' IMF Working Paper (February 2015), 24.

[99] Ibid., 18.

[100] International Federation of Accountants and Business at OECD, 'Regulatory Divergence: Costs, Risks, Impacts' (February 2018), 4, http://biac.org/wp-content/uploads/2018/04/IFAC-OECD_Regulatory-Divergence_V9_singles.pdf, accessed 4 June 2025.

[101] Viral V. Acharya, 'Is the International Convergence of Capital Adequacy Regulation Desirable?' (2003) 58 (6) The Journal of Finance, 2747.

[102] Ibid.

lack of mediation led EU national supervisors to avoid coordination and act unilaterally to the detriment of the interest of other countries. For example, in the case of Fortis, the Dutch government decided to nationalise the Dutch operations of the bank.[103] Consequently, the Belgium government was forced to broker the deal for BNP Paribas to take over Fortis operations in Belgium and Luxembourg.[104]

In addition, supranational supervisors can coordinate more efficiently in resolving problems than national supervisors.[105] This argument could be considered from the work of Joint Supervisory Teams (JSTs) of the ECB. The JSTs benefits from their clear decision-making processes and chain of command. These mechanisms allow them to deliver better work than their preceding supervisory colleges.[106] For instance, the problem of information sharing previously resulted in the host authority took a suboptimal caution from a consolidated prudential perspective.[107] The JSTs have improved this situation by creating connected databases with a common data format for the ECB and the national competent authorities (NCAs). Besides, there is a legislative framework which guarantees that the pooling of supervisory information would be sufficient.[108]

In creating a vertical network for ASEAN, the European model could be helpful. ASEAN could learn lessons from Europe's experience in order to find an appropriate approach for this sub-region. The following section will provide an overview of the European vertical network in banking supervision. It will also argue that the European model has some weaknesses which reduce its effectiveness in banking supervision.

103 Duncan Alford, 'Supervisory College: The Global Financial Crisis and Improving International Supervisory Coordination' (2010) 24 Emory Int'l L. Rev. 57, 28.

104 Gwen Robinson, 'BNP Takes Control of Fortis in €14.5bn Deal' *Financial Times* (6 October 2008), https://www.ft.com/content/a979d518-9390-11dd-9a63-0000779fd18c, accessed 4 June 2025.

105 Giacomo Calzolari et al., 'Multinational Banks and Supranational Supervision' (2018) 32 (8) The Review of Financial Studies.

106 Dirk Schoenmaker and Nicolas Veron (eds), 'European Banking Supervision: The First 18 Months' Blueprint Series 25 (June 2016), 22, https://www.researchgate.net/publication/304497260_European_Banking_Supervision_The_first_18_months, accessed 4 June 2025.

107 Ibid.

108 Ibid.

2.3.2 *The European Model of Banking Supervision*

One promising model for a vertical network of ASEAN banking supervision is that of the EU. The EU needs greater centralisation, uniformity and harmonisation in order to achieve its goal of advancing integration. However, the pursuance of a greater degree of centralisation would pose a threat to the sovereignty of its member states, which is politically inconceivable.[109] This tension has led to a political compromise as vindicated in the EU governance framework. On the one hand, the EU approach is based on the principles of 'home country control and mutual recognition'.[110] On the other hand, the EU has moved towards regulatory harmonisation.[111] The EU governance framework is made possible by the fact that there is a 'vertical network' of national officials. This network ensures that those officials and actors who are responsible for implementing EU policies behave consistently in performing their tasks.[112]

The Banking Union is part of this vertical network. The member states transfer their responsibility for banking policy to the EU supranational organisations. The SSM is one of the two pillars of the Banking Union,[113] comprising the ECB and the NCAs of the participating member states. The objectives of the SSM are to 'ensure the safety and soundness of the European banking system', 'increase financial integration and stability', as well as 'ensure consistent supervision'.[114] Under the SSM regime, the

109 Slaughter (n 113) 8.

110 The principles of home control and mutual recognition were incorporated for the first time in the 1989 Second Banking Directive. Jean Dermine, 'Home Country Control and Mutual Recognition' (SUERF Conference on the Financial Institutions in Europe under New Competitive Conditions, Nice, October 1989), 6. Second Council Directive 89/646/EEC of 15 December 1989 on the coordination of laws, regulations and administrative provisions relating to the taking up and pursuit of the business of credit institutions and amending Directive 77/780/EEC [1989] OJ L386/1.

111 The 1977 First Banking Directive 'is a fist steps towards the harmonisation of regulation'. Ibid., 5.

112 Slaughter (n 113) 8.

113 Another pillar is the SRM. There is a plan to set up the third pillar which is the Common Deposit Guarantee.

114 European Central Bank, 'Single Supervisory Mechanism', https://www.bankingsupervision.europa.eu/about/thessm/html/index.en.html, accessed 4 June 2025.

ECB acts as the main supervisor of the eurozone banks. It has a supervisory authority over credit institutions whose assets exceed 30 billion euros, or ratio of total assets to gross domestic product (GDP) of the home member state exceeding 20 per cent. Alternatively, the NCAs could define an institution as significant. In addition, according to Article 6(4) SSMR,[115] the ECB could utilise the power to take a direct supervision on any bank on its own initiative.[116] Meanwhile, less significant credit institutions are under the supervision of the NCAs.

Coordination and cooperation are key to the success of this vertical network. In order to maintain a consistent supervision throughout the Union, the ECB works in close cooperation with the NCAs as well as other Union institutions (e.g., the European Banking Authority (EBA)). Nevertheless, there are some weaknesses in the network which ASEAN should take into account when considering the EU approach for its banking supervision. The next section will elaborate these weaknesses by considering them into two main issues: (a) the cooperation between the ECB and the NCAs and (b) the role of the EBA.

[115] The Council Regulation (EU) 1024/2013 of 15 October 2013 on conferring specific tasks on the European Central Bank concerning policies relating to the prudential supervision of credit institutions [2013] OJ L 287/63 (2013). 'The legal basis of the SSM Regulation is Article 127, para 6 TFEU (repeated in Article 25.2 of the Statute of the European System of Central Banks and of the European Central Bank), which contains an enabling clause (known as the 'sleeping beauty clause')'. Christos V. Gortsos, 'The Role of the European Banking Authority (EBA) after the Establishment of the Single Supervisory Mechanism (SSM)' in M. Andenas, G. Deipenbrock (eds), *Regulating and Supervising European Financial Markets* (Springer International Publishing Switzerland 2016), 282.

[116] Guido Ferrarini, 'Single Supervision and the Governance of Banking Markets: Will the SSM Deliver the Expected Benefits?' (2015) 16 European Business Organization Law Review 513–537, 521. According to the EU General Court (EGC) in the L-Bank case, the ECB's exclusive competence to supervise credit institutions under the SSM regulation is an important factor in determining the legitimacy of the ECB's decision regarding whether or not a bank is a 'significant entity'. Kern Alexander, 'The ECB's Macroprudential Tasks and Home-Host Supervision in the SSM: Tasks, Powers and Supervisory Gaps' in Gianni Lo Schiavo (ed), *The European Banking Union and the Rule of Law* (Edward Elgar Publishing Limited 2019), 164. Case T-122/15 *Landeskreditbank Baden-Wurttemberg-Forderbank v European Central Bank* [2017] OJ C 213/26. The case was appealed to the Court of Justice of the European Union (CJEU) under Article 56 of the Statute of the Court of Justice of the European Union. In Case C-450/17 P *Landeskreditbank Baden-Wurttemberg*, the CJEU dismissed the Bank's appeal to annul Decision ECB/SSM/15/1 of the ECB.

2.3.2.1 Cooperation Between the ECB and the NCAs

The EU Treaties provide limited competence to EU regulatory agencies.[117] This is, in part, due to political compromise and difficulties in designing the internal governance of the regime. According to Dehousse, the EU has pioneered 'regulation by networks' in that regulatory agencies are 'expected to act as network coordinators, rather than as central regulators'.[118] As for the SSM, Ferrarini has argued that when taking into account the EBA's position against the ECB, European bank supervision in the eurozone area is based on a 'model of semi-strong centralisation'. However, the SSM does not depart substantially from the models of the EU general framework. The supervision of non-eurozone countries is still based on the EU model of enhanced cooperation and leads supervision.[119]

The ECB has worked closely with the NCAs as each significant credit institution is supervised under the JST. The JST comprises staff members from both the ECB and the NCAs.[120] In addition, the ECB utilises the Single Rulebook and the Supervisory Manual in order to help harmonise rules and supervisory practice under the SSM. The former 'aims at bringing about a unified regulatory framework'.[121] Meanwhile, the purpose of the latter is to 'set out the approach to be followed by the SSM in carrying out its supervisory tasks'.[122] Both of them form,

[117] According to Dehousse, 'most have been confined to regulation by information and the few agencies granted the power to prepare or take decisions are operating under Commission control'. Renaud Dehousse, 'Regulation by Networks in the European Community: The Role of European Agencies' (1997) 4 (2) Journal of European Public Policy, 258.

[118] Ibid., 246.

[119] Guido Ferrarini, 'Cross-border Banking and the SSM' in Giorgio Barba Navaretti et al. (eds) *Single Supervision and Cross-border Banking* (Europeye Srl 2015), 62, https://european-economy.eu/wp-content/uploads/2016/03/EE_2015_3.pdf, accessed 4 June 2025.

[120] Laura Wissink, 'Challenges to an Efficient European Centralised Banking Supervision (SSM): Single Rulebook, Joint Supervisory Teams and Split Supervisory Tasks' (2017) 18 European Business Organization Law Review 431–456.

[121] Jerome Deslandes et al., 'Banking Union: Completing the Single Rule Book' Briefing (July 2019), 1, https://www.europarl.europa.eu/RegData/etudes/BRIE/2019/634375/IPOL_BRI(2019)634375_EN.pdf, accessed 4 June 2025.

[122] European Central Bank, 'SSM Supervisory Manual—European Banking Supervision: Functioning of the SSM and Supervisory Approach' (March 2018), 3, https://www.bankingsupervision.europa.eu/ecb/pub/pdf/ssm.supervisorymanual201803.en.pdf, accessed 4 June 2025.

in the words of the CJEU, 'rules of practice from which the administration may not depart in an individual case without giving reasons that are compatible with the principle of equal treatment'.[123]

Despite the aforementioned efforts, there are some weaknesses which could undermine the effectiveness of this vertical network. First, the Single Rulebook does not fully harmonise regulation under the SSM. National laws still have a role to play in many areas, especially when they are utilised to implement a Directive. According to Article 4 (3) SSMR, the ECB has to apply national legislation which transposes a Directive. In addition, the ECB will have to utilise national legislation exercising options in the case that Regulations grant those options for the member states. These tasks of the ECB could raise a concern regarding its competence. As Wissink has argued, it would be challenging for the ECB to have a comprehensive knowledge regarding national laws of every member state.[124]

Moreover, the Single Rulebook leaves a large amount of discretion to the NCAs in many areas. As a result, there might be inconsistencies between the ECB and the NCAs in supervising and interpreting national laws, which implement a Directive. For instance, there are many national options and discretion within the CRD IV[125] and CRR.[126] According to Enria (2015), these options and discretions are often used by national

[123] Paragraph 209 of the judgement of the CJEU in Joined Cases C-189/02, C-202/02, C-205/02 to C-208/02 and C-213/02 *Dansk Rørindustri and Others v Commission of the European Communities* [2005] ECR I-5425.

[124] Wissink (n 232) 440.

[125] CRD IV is European Parliament and Council Directive 2013/36/EU of 26 June 2013 on access to the activity of credit institutions and the prudential supervision of credit institutions and investment firms, amending Directive 2002/87/EC and repealing Directives 2006/48/EC and 2006/49/EC [2006] OJ L176/338. CRD V is European Parliament and Council Directive 2019/878 of 20 May 2019 amending Directive 2013/36/EU as regards exempted entities, financial holding companies, mixed financial holding companies, remuneration, supervisory measures and powers and capital conservation measures [2019] OJ L150/253. CRD V has come into force since December 2020. The national transposition for most provisions in CRD V was 28 December 2020.

[126] European Parliament and Council Regulation (EU) 575/2013 of 26 June 2013 on prudential requirements for credit institutions and investment firms and amending Regulation (EU) No 648/2012. The majority of CRR II provisions have come into force on 28 June 2021. European Parliament and Council Regulation (EU) 2019/876 of 20 May 2019 amending Regulation (EU) No 575/2013 as regards the leverage ratio, the net stable funding ratio, requirements for own funds and eligible liabilities, counterparty

authority for the purpose of protecting national interests as well as supervisory forbearance. Besides, the experience of ECB's senior officials has shown that the way in which national supervisors conduct supervision in accordance with transposing law is diverse than what they expected (Lautenschlager, 2015).[127]

Furthermore, the Supervisory Review and Evaluation Process (SREP), which is a holistic assessment of business model, governance as well as capital and liquidity risks, may not be able to help narrow different supervisory practices among the member states. This is because the functionality of SREP depends on the underlying Rulebook, and consequently, the SREP may perpetuate the home country domination that has existed in the current supervisory regime. In addition, there has been very little information provided by the ECB as to how proportionality and uniformity of the SREP is to be achieved at the EU-wide level of the SSM.[128]

Secondly, the limited capacity of the ECB could result in 'enforcement arbitrage'.[129] The ECB has to rely upon NCAs in imposing penalties in some instances. For example, the ECB can only impose administrative pecuniary penalties upon a legal person. This power could be used when there is a breach of requirement under directly applicable acts of Union law in accordance with Article 18 (1) SSMR.[130] In addition, according

credit risk, market risk, exposures to central counterparties, exposures to collective investment undertakings, large exposures, reporting and disclosure requirements, and Regulation (EU) No 648/2012.

[127] Elisabetta Montanaro, 'The Process towards the Centralization of the European Financial Supervisory Architecture: The Case of the Banking Union' (2016) FESSUD Working paper, 17.

[128] Michael Meissner, 'The Supervisory Review and Evaluation Process (SREP): Ultimate Test for the Banking Union?' (2016) 31(6) J.I.B.L.R., 6.

[129] Dalvinder Singh, 'The Centralisation of European Financial Regulation and Supervision: Is There a Need for a Single Enforcement Handbook?' (2015) 16 Eur Bus Org law Rev, 461.

[130] 'Intentionally or negligently, breach a requirement under relevant directly applicable acts of Union law in relation to which administrative pecuniary penalties shall be made available to competent authorities under the relevant Union law, the ECB may impose administrative pecuniary penalties of up to twice the amount of the profits gained or losses avoided because of the breach where those can be determined, or up to 10 % of the total annual turnover, as defined in relevant Union law, of a legal person in the preceding business year or such other pecuniary penalties as may be provided for in relevant Union law'.

to Article 18 (5) SSMR, in the case that there is a breach of national law implementing a Directive, the ECB may require NCAs to open proceedings in order to impose appropriate penalties.[131] Consequently, the ECB has to effectively comply with the interpretation of NCAs regarding the relevant transposing law.[132]

Thirdly, an agency problem between the ECB and the NCAs could arise in attaining the information which is necessary for conducting supervisory tasks. For instance, a large amount of sensitive information about credit institutions which the ECB needs for its supervision is collected by the NCAs.[133] This is, in part, due to the fact that the ECB might not be able to build the same level of trust with credit institutions as what the NCAs can. Besides, the agency problem could be acute when there is an incentive on the part of NCAs to protect their national interests and/or banks. In such circumstances, there is a risk that the NCAs might delay information transferring, adversely select or withhold some information, or present biased information to the ECB.

Furthermore, in the case of consolidated supervision, the ECB will be a consolidated supervisor for a eurozone bank. Hence, a host state would be under an obligation to supply information and data to the EBC. However, the home state authority is not under a reciprocal obligation to

[131] Wissink (n 232) 442. 'In the cases not covered by paragraph 1 of this Article, where necessary for the purpose of carrying out the tasks conferred on it by this Regulation, the ECB may require national competent authorities to open proceedings with a view to taking action in order to ensure that appropriate penalties are imposed in accordance with the acts referred to in the first subparagraph of Article 4(3) and any relevant national legislation which confers specific powers which are currently not required by Union law. The penalties applied by national competent authorities shall be effective, proportionate and dissuasive'.

[132] Singh (n 241).

[133] The scope of the power of the ECB includes, for example, the investigation of credit institutions and on-site inspections at business premises. Ferrarini (n 228) 522. 'While the NCAs are first in line for the collection of supervisory data and quality control, the ECB has established further quality controls to ensure consistent data quality standards across all supervised banks, and is gradually building up integrated information systems. The supervisory banking data system (SUBA in ECB lingo) allows for communication and data-sharing between the ECB and NCAs'. Schoenmaker and Veron (n 218) 11.

transfer the information to the host state. Hence, during a crisis, the host state might be in a weak position to obtain the information.[134]

2.3.2.2 The Role of the EBA

The SSM has to interact with the European System of Financial Supervision (ESFS). The latter 'aims to ensure consistent and coherent financial supervision in the EU'.[135] The ESFS consists of the European Systemic Risk Board (ESRB), the three European supervisory authorities (ESAs), the Joint Committee of the ESAs and NCAs. The ESAs comprise the European Banking Authority (EBA), the European Securities and Markets Authority (ESMA) and the European Insurance and Occupational Pensions Authority (EIOPA).[136] The ECB has to interact with these EU bodies, especially the EBA.

The EBA has undertaken a leading role in formulating regulatory policy and technical standards which become the foundation of the Single Rulebook.[137] It also safeguards consistent application of the Single Rulebook by utilising tools such as guidelines and recommendations.[138] In performing its tasks, the EBA plays a facilitative role rather than exercising its intervention powers.[139] For example, it will act as a dispute mediator in resolving a disagreement between home and host supervisors in a supervisory college.[140]

However, the EBA might not be able to perform a perfect role for some reasons. First, the scope of the EBA's power is limited by design.

[134] Dalvinder Singh, 'Should Non-Participating Member States Join the Banking Union? A legal Perspective' in Stefan Grundmann and Hans-W Micklitz (eds), *The European Banking Union and Constitution: Beacon for Advanced Integration or Death-Knell for Democracy?* (Hart Publishing 2019), 306.

[135] Radostina Parenti, 'European System of Financial Supervision' Factsheets on the European Union (2022), 1, https://www.europarl.europa.eu/factsheets/en/sheet/84/european-system-of-financial-supervision-esfs, accessed 4 June 2025.

[136] Ibid.

[137] Vitor Constancio, 'Implication of the SSM on the ESFS', 'Speech' (Public Hearing on Financial Supervision in the EU, Brussels, 24 May 2013), https://www.ecb.europa.eu/press/key/date/2013/html/sp130524.en.html, accessed 4 June 2025.

[138] Valia Babis, 'The Single Rulebook and the European Banking Authority' University of Cambridge Faculty of Law Research Paper No. 45/2018 (2018), 18.

[139] Ellis Ferran, 'The Existential Search of the European Banking Authority' (2016) 17 Eur Bus Org Law Rev, 285.

[140] Montanaro (n 239) 15.

The EBA can only issue draft technical standards if it is delegated powers by Level 1 instruments.[141] According to *Meroni* decision, 'EU institutions may only delegate defined executive powers which do not entail a wide margin of discretion'.[142] Secondly, there is risk of politicisation of the EBA due to the fact that its Board of Supervisors comprises representatives of national authorities. It is possible that national authorities might put a priority on their national interest when performing their tasks on the Board. Another possible risk is that the EBA could draft technical standards which are general in order to accommodate the diverging views of the member states.[143]

2.4 Conclusion

As argued in Part I, the horizontal network of the BCBS that exists in ASEAN might not be adequate in minimising the financial trilemma, especially during a crisis. Hence, ASEAN should consider creating a vertical network in order to increase supervisory coordination as well as mitigate systemic risk in this sub-region. However, ASEAN should bear in mind that not all member states will benefit from the creation of a supranational authority equally. In addition, the model of the EU has to be examined carefully in order to identify its aspects which would be applicable to the ASEAN context. As Ayadi et al. have stated, 'regulatory structures that will succeed in some countries may not constitute best practice in other countries that have different institutional settings'.[144] Moreover, according to Barth et al (2013), there is no broad cross-country evidence regarding which regulations or supervisory practices are best to promote financial stability.[145] Therefore, a solution to the issue of cross-border banking supervision in ASEAN could be different from that of the EU.

In creating a vertical network for ASEAN banking supervision, I argue that there are three main steps that ASEAN should pursue, in order to

[141] Babis (n 250) 22.

[142] Ibid., 21.

[143] Ibid., 23.

[144] Rym Ayadi et al., 'Does Basel Compliance Matter for Bank Performance?' (2015) IMF Working Paper WP/15/100, 4.

[145] James Barth et al., 'Do Bank Regulation, Supervision and Monitoring Enhance or Impede Bank Efficiency?' (2013) 37(81) Journal of Banking & Finance 2879–92.

ensure that the member states are ready for an ASEAN banking supervisory system. First, ASEAN needs to strengthen its capacity-building and training programmes which would help enable Brunei, Cambodia, Lao PDR, Myanmar and Vietnam (BCLMV) to catch up with current financial development in ASEAN-5 countries. In addition, these programmes should focus on building up the ability of BCLMV states to develop regulatory frameworks which are in line with international standards.[146] By narrowing the gaps between the development of financial system and regulation in ASEAN-5 and that of BCLMV countries, the latter group of states would be more willing and ready to transfer their national authority regarding banking supervision to an ASEAN organ.

Secondly, ASEAN has to empower existing ASEAN institutions to cope with the issue of the financial trilemma while a supranational authority for banking supervision has not been created. As mentioned in Chapter 1, the rule of law has not taken a firm root in ASEAN. There is no equivalent ASEAN institution to the EU Commission. In addition, the power of the ASEAN Secretariat is limited by the Charter. The Secretariat has no legal power in resolving disputes among the member states. Its main responsibility, according to Article 27(1) of ASEAN Charter, is monitoring the 'compliance with the findings, recommendations or decisions resulting from an ASEAN dispute settlement mechanism'. Moreover, the member states have been reluctant to use the Enhanced Dispute Settlement Mechanism, which is an independent dispute mechanism in ASEAN. Instead, they prefer pursuing their case in other international fora.

In order to build confidence among the member states in ASEAN institutions, a rule-based norm in this sub-region has to be strengthened. For example, the ASEAN Secretariat should be given a stronger role in facilitating financial integration and regulatory harmonisation. Its role should include not only monitoring a process for financial integration but also ensuring that community decisions and rulings of the member governments are strictly implemented.[147] In addition, ASEAN could increase the legitimacy of and support for its organs by securing participation from stakeholders or a wide-ranging group of people who are affected by its policies. For example, in formulating rules or policies regarding

146 Danupon Ariyasajjakorn et al., 'Evolution of ASEAN Financial Integration in the Comparative Perspective' (2020) ADBI Working Paper Series No. 1123, 27.

147 Ibid.

cross-border banking supervision, ASEAN institutions should utilise a process of a notice and comment in obtaining inputs from those on the receiving end. This process would also help provide ASEAN organs with local knowledge regarding the issue with which they are dealing.

Lastly, ASEAN should consider taking a bold initiative in creating a supranational authority for banking supervision. Financial instability and systemic risk could occur in increasingly interconnected financial market in ASEAN. Nevertheless, ASEAN should accept the fact that BCLMV countries might not be moving at the same pace as ASEAN-5 countries, and hence, it might utilise a dual-track approach by setting up an ASEAN banking supervisory system while simultaneously providing capacity-building and training programmes to BCLMV countries. In my view, it is possible to do so as ASEAN has previously used 'ASEAN minus X' approaches for dealing with other issues (e.g. intra-ASEAN trade).[148] An ASEAN-minus-X formula allows those countries that are ready to join and benefit from a scheme, while the rest of the member states could participate when they are ready. This would reduce objection from the member states which are less developed than other countries.

References

Acharya V, 'Is the International Convergence of Capital Adequacy Regulation Desirable?' (2003) 58 (6) The Journal of Finance

Acharya V et al, 'Measuring Systemic Risk' (2017) 30 (1) The Review of Financial Studies 2

Alexander K., 'Global Financial Standard-Setting, the G10 Committees, and International Economic Law' (2009) 34 (3) Brook.J.Int'L L

Alexander K., 'The ECB's Macroprudential Tasks and Home-Host Supervision in the SSM: Tasks, Powers and Supervisory Gaps' in Gianni Lo Schiavo (ed), *The European Banking Union and the Rule of Law* (Edward Elgar Publishing Limited 2019)

Alford D., 'Supervisory College: The Global Financial Crisis and Improving International Supervisory Coordination' (2010) 24 Emory Int'l L. Rev. 57

Almekinders G. et al., 'ASEAN Financial Integration' IMF Working Paper (February 2015)

[148] ASEAN Information Center, 'Jump Starting 'ASEAN Minus X' (11 February 2016), http://www.aseanthai.net/english/ewt_news.php?nid=918&filename=index#:~:text=This%20process%20is%20known%20as,%2Fculture%E2%80%94is%20very%20urgent, accessed 4 June 2025.

Allen F and Gale D, 'How should bank liquidity be regulated?' (2017) SSRN

Arif A. and Anees A., 'Liquidity Risk and Performance of Banking System' (2012) 20 (2) Journal of Financial Regulation and Compliance

Ariyasajjakorn D. et al., 'Evolution of ASEAN Financial Integration in the Comparative Perspective' (2020) ADBI Working Paper Series No. 1123

ASEAN Information Center, 'Jump Starting 'ASEAN Minus X' (11 February 2016)

Ayadi R. et al., 'Does Basel Compliance Matter for Bank Performance?' (2015) IMF Working Paper WP/15/100

Babis V., 'The Single Rulebook and the European Banking Authority' University of Cambridge Faculty of Law Research Paper No. 45/2018 (2018)

Bank of Thailand, 'Re: Regulation on Capital Supervision of Financial Business Groups' Bank of Thailand Notification No. FPG. 9/2561

Barr M. and Miller G., 'Global Administrative Law: The View from Basel' (2006) 17 (1) The European Journal of International Law

Barth J. et al., 'Do Bank Regulation, Supervision and Monitoring Enhance or Impede Bank Efficiency?' (2013) 37(81) Journal of Banking & Finance 2879–92

'Basel II: The Precursor of an Integrated Risk Management Framework for Vietnamese Banks' *The Asian Banker* (Vietnam, 18 October 2016)

BCBS, 'Core Principles for Effective Banking Supervision' Consultative Document (December 2011)

BCBS, 'Core Principles for Effective Banking Supervision' (September 1997)

BCBS, 'Impact and Implementation Challenges of the Basel Framework for Emerging Market, Developing and Small Economies' Working Paper No. 27 (November 2014)

Beck T. and Wagner W., 'Supranational Supervision: How Much and for Whom?' (2016) 12 (2) International Journal of Central Banking

Benink H. et al., 'On the Role of Regulatory Banking Capital' (2008) 17 (1) Financial Markets, Institutions and Instruments 85

BIS, 'Net Stable Funding Ratio (NSFR) – Executive Summary (28 June 2018)

Brummer C., 'How International Financial Law Works (And How It Doesn't) (2011) Georgetown Law and Economics Research Paper No. 11–15

Bunea-Bontas C. et al, 'Capital Adequacy and Risk Management – Premises for Strengthening Financial System Stability' (2009) MPRA Paper No. 18132

Calzolari G. et al., 'Multinational Banks and Supranational Supervision' (2018) 32 (8) The Review of Financial Studies

Carlson M., 'Lessons from the Historical Use of Reserve Requirements in the United States to Promote Bank Liquidity' (2015) 11 (1) International Journal of Central Banking

Cecchetti S. and Kashyap A., 'What Binds? Interactions between Bank Capital and Liquidity Regulations' in Hartmann P. (ed), The Changing Fortunes of Central Banking (Cambridge University Press 2018)
Constancio V., 'Implication of the SSM on the ESFS', 'Speech' (Public Hearing on Financial Supervision in the EU, Brussels, 24 May 2013)
Danielsson J., 'Blame the Models' (2008) 4 Journal of Financial Stability
Dehousse R., 'Regulation by Networks in the European Community: The Role of European Agencies' (1997) 4 (2) Journal of European Public Policy
Demirguc-Kunt A. and Detragiache E., 'Basel Core Principles and Bank Soundness: Does Compliance Matter?' (2009) World Bank Policy Research Working Paper 5129
Dermine J., 'Home Country Control and Mutual Recognition' (SUERF Conference on the Financial Institutions in Europe under New Competitive Conditions, Nice, October 1989)
Deslandes J. et al., 'Banking Union: Completing the Single Rule Book' Briefing (July 2019)
Deutsche Bank, 'Liquidity Coverage Ratio' Annual Report 2017
Epstein R., *Simple Rules for a Complex World* (Harvard University Press 1995)
Erturk I., 'Financialization, Bank Business Models and the Limits of Post-Crisis Bank Regulation' (2016) 17 Journal of Banking Regulation 60
European Central Bank, 'Single Supervisory Mechanism'
European Central Bank, 'SSM Supervisory Manual -- European Banking Supervision: Functioning of the SSM and Supervisory Approach' (March 2018)
European Commission, 'Capital Requirement – CRD IV/CRR – Frequently Asked Questions' EU Commission Memo (16 July 2013)
Ferran E., 'The Existential Search of the European Banking Authority' (2016) 17 Eur Bus Org Law Rev
Ferrarini G., 'Cross-border Banking and the SSM' in Giorgio Barba Navaretti et al (eds) Single Supervision and Cross-border Banking (Europeye Srl 2015)
Ferrarini G., 'Single Supervision and the Governance of Banking Markets: Will the SSM Deliver the Expected Benefits?' (2015) 16 European Business Organization Law Review 513–537
Ferreira C. et al, 'From Basel I to Basel III: Sequencing Implementation in Developing Economies' IMF Working Paper WP/19/127 (June 2019)
Garcia M., 'Can Financial Inclusion and Financial Stability Go Hand in Hand?' (2016) 21 (2) Economic Issues
Gerding E., 'The Dialectics of Bank Capital' (2016) 55 Washburn Law Journal
Giovanoli M., 'The Reform of the International Architecture after the Global Crisis' (2009) 42 (81) International Law and Politics

Golubeva O. et al, 'The Impact of Liquidity Risk on Bank Profitability: Some Empirical Evidence from the European Banks Following the Introduction of Basel III Regulations' (2019) 18 (4) Accounting and Management Information Systems 455

Gortsos C., 'The Role of the European Banking Authority (EBA) after the Establishment of the Single Supervisory Mechanism (SSM)' in M. Andenas and G. Deipenbrock (eds), Regulating and Supervising European Financial Markets (Springer International Publishing Switzerland 2016)

Gurrea-Martinez A. and Remolina N., 'The Dark Side of Implementing Basel Capital Requirements: Theory, Evidence, and Policy' Working Paper Series 2/2017

Haldane A. and Madouros V., 'The Dog and the Frisbee', 'Speech' (The Federal Reserve Bank of Kansas City's 366th Economic Policy Symposium, Wyoming, 31 August 2012)

Hinterschweiger M. et al, 'Risk Sensitivity and Risk Shifting in Banking Regulation' (2018) Financial Stability Paper No 44

Hoerova M. et al, 'Benefits and Costs of Liquidity Regulation' ECB Working Paper Series (July 2018)

IMF, 'Lao People's Democratic Republic: Technical Assistance Report – Implementation of Risk-based Supervision' (November 2018)

IMF, 'Technical Assistance Report, Lao People's Democratic Republic, The Development of Risk-based Supervision' (May 2018)

IMF, 'Vietnam: 2018 Article IV Consultation – Press Release and Staff Report' (July 2018)

IMF and the World Bank, 'Technical Note: FSAP Update, Philippines, Focused Update of the Basel Core Principles for Effective Banking Supervision' (April 2010)

International Federation of Accountants and Business at OECD, 'Regulatory Divergence: Costs, Risks, Impacts' (February 2018)

Jones E and Knaack P, 'Global Financial Regulation: Shortcomings and Reform Options' (2019) 10 (2) Global Policy

Keuangan O, 'Basel III Implementation to be Adapted to National Interests' Press Release (8 December 2017)

Kun-amornpong S, 'The Role of the Basel Accords in Mitigating Systemic Risk' (2019) Financial Regulation International

Ma L. et al., 'Capital Requirements of Commercial Banks and Lending Discrimination against Small Businesses: Theory and Empirical Evidence from China' (2013) 14–2(A) Annals of Economic and Finance

Meissner M., 'The Supervisory Review and Evaluation Process (SREP): Ultimate Test for the Banking Union?' (2016) 31(6) J.I.B.L.R.

Montanaro E., 'The Process towards the Centralization of the European Financial Supervisory Architecture: The Case of the Banking Union' (2016) FESSUD Working paper

Morgan P. and Pontines V., 'Financial Stability and Financial Inclusion' ADBI Working Paper Series No. 488 (July 2014)

National Bank of Cambodia, 'Prakas on Capital Buffer in Banking and Financial Institutions' (22 February 2018)

Nguyen M et al, 'Bank Market Power, Asset Liquidity and Funding Liquidity: International Evidence' (2017) 54 International Review of Financial Analysis

Parenti R, 'European System of Financial Supervision' Factsheets on the European Union (2022)

Roberts D. et al, 'Bank Liquidity Creation, Systemic Risk and Basel Liquidity Regulations' Federal Reserve Bank of New York Staff Reports No. 852 (June 2018)

Robinson G, 'BNP Takes Control of Fortis in €14.5bn Deal' *Financial Times* (6 October 2008)

Ruengsakul N., The Report on the Study of the Command of Permanent Closure of 56 Financial Institutions (2005) (in Thai)

Sahay R. et al., 'Rethinking Financial Deepening: Stability and Growth in Emerging Markets' IMF Staff Discussion Notes No. 15/8 (2015)

Sahay R. et al. (eds), *The Future of Asian Finance* (International Monetary Fund 2015)

Said R., 'Net Stable Funding Ratio and Commercial Banks Profitability' (2014) 76 (7) IPEDR

Schoenmaker D. and Veron N. (eds), 'European Banking Supervision: The First 18 Months' Blueprint Series 25 (June 2016)

Scott H., 'Interconnectedness and Contagion', Committee on Capital Market Regulation (20 Novermber 2012)

Singh D, 'Should Non-Participating Member States Join the Banking Union? A legal Perspective' in Stefan Grundmann and Hans-W Micklitz (eds), *The European Banking Union and Constitution: Beacon for Advanced Integration or Death-Knell for Democracy*? (Hart Publishing 2019)

Singh D., 'The Centralisation of European Financial Regulation and Supervision: Is There a Need for a Single Enforcement Handbook?' (2015) 16 Eur Bus Org law Rev

Sirimai P. and Banchongduang S., 'BoT Embraces Basel III Rule' *Bangkok Post* (Thailand, 27 September 2017)

Slaughter A., *A New World Order* (Princeton University Press 2009)

State Bank of Vietnam, Circular No. 36/2014/TT-NHNN Stipulating Minimum Safety Limits and Ratios for Transactions Performed by Credit Institutions and Branches of Foreign Banks (20 November 2014)

Taylor A., 'What Is Basel II and Why Has It Got 3 Pillars?' (2004) 19 Butterworths Journal of International Banking & Financial Law

Tran-Thi Q. and Thanh T., 'Vietnam: The Dilemma of Bringing Global Financial Standards to a Socialist Market Economy' in Emily Jones (ed), The Political Economy of Bank Regulation in Developing Countries: Risk and Reputation (Oxford Publishing Press USA – OSO 2020)

Tucker P, 'Solvency as a Fundamental Constraint on LOLR Policy for Independent Central Banks: Principles, History, Law' (2020) 2 (2) Journal of Financial Crises

Tyler T, Why People Cooperate: The Role of Social Motivations (Princeton University Press 2011)

Ward O, 'The Missed Opportunity of the ASEAN Trade Link' (*ASEAN Today*, 21 October 2017)

Wissink L., 'Challenges to an Efficient European Centralised Banking Supervision (SSM): Single Rulebook, Joint Supervisory Teams and Split Supervisory Tasks' (2017) 18 European Business Organization Law Review 431–456

Cases

Case C-450/17 P Landeskreditbank Baden-Wurttemberg [2019]

Case T-122/15 Landeskreditbank Baden-Wurttemberg-Forderbank v European Central Bank [2017] OJ C 213/26

Joined Cases C-189/02, C-202/02, C-205/02 to C-208/02 and C-213/02 Dansk Rørindustri and Others v Commission of the European Communities [2005] ECR I-5425

CHAPTER 3

The Future of ASEAN Bank Resolution—Lessons from the European Experience

3.1 Introduction

Cross-border banking benefits the performance of the economy by allocating productive capital to the most efficient firms.[1] Nevertheless, it can also produce risks, if an existing regulatory structure is insufficient, or regulation and supervision is ineffective. In addition, failures of global or regional banks could create financial instability and systemic risk in countries in which they operate, or in which their counterparties conduct business. The magnitude of risk could be large—as can be considered from the failures of banks during the GFC in 2008, when bank resolution measures did not exist in Europe.

It might not be possible to eliminate the risk of bank failure. Therefore, it is crucially important to have an appropriate resolution regime, in order to ensure that financial institutions, especially global and regional banks, would fail in an orderly way, in order to minimise losses to society at large. According to the US Federal Deposit Insurance Corporation (FDIC), the bankruptcy proceedings in the case of Lehman Brothers led to losses of 79 cents on the dollar, which is significantly higher than losses of merely

[1] Remolona and Shim (n 63) 1–2.

© The Author(s), under exclusive license to Springer Nature Singapore Pte Ltd. 2025

W. Kun-amornpong, *The Financial Trilemma and Cross-border Bank Crisis Management in ASEAN*,
https://doi.org/10.1007/978-981-95-0512-8_3

three cents on the dollar that an Orderly Liquidation Authority (OLA) resolution would have produced.[2]

In addition, a resolution regime has an overarching objective of ensuring financial stability. This is pursued by, for example, providing mechanisms in order to resolve a failing bank swiftly.[3] Moreover, resolution aims at safeguarding the continuity of financial institutions' critical functions.[4] These objectives of resolution differ markedly from those of the normal corporate insolvency. The objectives of the latter are, for example, to maximise the returns to the creditors as a whole and to distribute them in a fair and equitable way.[5]

In this chapter, bank resolution measures of the European Union (EU) and those of ASEAN states will be discussed, considering lessons that ASEAN can take from Europe's experience, should it decide to create an ASEAN bank resolution regime. While there are many structural and institutional differences between the two regimes, there are some similarities which warrant a close consideration of these two regimes. For example, most of the ASEAN states have bank-dominated financial sectors.[6] As a result, systemic risk in this region is most likely to arise in the banking sector. Meanwhile, mitigating systemic risks is a priority concern that the EU considered when creating its bank resolution regime in the aftermath of the European debt crisis.

[2] Jeffrey N. Gordon and Wolf-Georg Ringe, 'Bank Resolution in the European Banking Union: A Transatlantic Perspective on What It Would Take' (2015) 115 Columbia Law Review, 1297–1369.

[3] Single Resolution Board, 'Resolution Q & A', https://srb.europa.eu/en/content/resolution-qa, accessed 4 June 2025.

[4] According to Recital 5 of the Bank Recovery and Resolution Directive, new powers should enable the authorities to 'maintain uninterrupted access to deposits and payment transactions, sell viable portions of the institution where appropriate, and apportion losses in a manner that is fair and predictable'.

[5] The rationales for corporate insolvency are varied. For example, in Thailand, the main objectives of corporate insolvency law are to distribute the proceeds of asset realisations fairly and equitably among creditors in accordance with the *pari passu* principle, to investigate and ascertain the causes of the debtor's insolvency, and to preserve viable businesses by giving them a fresh start. Wicha Mahakhun, *A Commentary on Insolvency and Business Rehabilitation Law* (Nitibannakarn Publishing 2016), 17–24.

[6] A. Michael Andrews, 'Effective Resolution Regimes for Financial Institutions in ASEAN + 3', in Iwan J. Azis and Hyun S. Shim (eds), *Global Shock, Risks and Asian Financial Reform* (Edward Elgar 2014), 488.

Part I will elaborate on the bank resolution regime within the EU, analysing the weaknesses of the regime from the perspectives of legal risk and uncertainty, effects upon the macroeconomy and structure of the regime. In Part II, the development of bank resolution and bank insolvency in each ASEAN states will be explored. Moreover, I will discuss whether or not ASEAN needs a cross-border bank resolution regime. This issue will be tackled by, first, approaching this question from a national perspective. Then, I will argue that the home-host conflicts warrant a consideration for creating a supranational solution in dealing with this issue.

3.2 Part I: The European Union and its Bank Resolution Regime

There have been attempts to harmonise insolvency laws at international and supranational levels—for example, the United Nations Commission of International Trade Law (UNCITRAL) has created the Model Law on Cross-Border Insolvency (hereafter, the Model Law).[7] However, the Model Law is not applicable to financial firms.[8] With regard to the harmonisation of law at supra-national level, the EU has principles of unity and universality of bankruptcy in order to deal with this issue. As for cross-border bank insolvency, the EU has created its bank resolution regime by promulgating the Bank Recovery and Resolution Directive (BRRD I)[9] in 2014. The BRRD I has later been amended by the BRRD

[7] The objectives of the Model Law are to promote cooperation between the courts and authorities of states which are involved in cross-border insolvency cases, provide greater legal certainty, produce fair and efficient administration of cross-border insolvencies, protect and maximise value of debtor's assets, and facilitate the rescue of businesses in trouble. United Nations, *UNCITRAL Model Law on Cross-Border Insolvency with Guide to Enactment and Interpretation* (New York 2014), 3. Currently, the Model Law has been implemented in 44 states (46 jurisdictions). Singapore and the Philippines are the only ASEAN states which have adopted the Model.

[8] Financial Stability Board, 'Cross-border Recognition of Resolution Action' Consultative Document (29 September 2004), http://www.fsb.org/wp-content/uploads/c_140929.pdf, accessed 4 June 2025.

[9] Directive 2014/59/EU (n 94).

II in 2019.[10] The Directive covers only the insolvency of branches of credit institutions. It does not include subsidiaries of the banking groups in other Member States.[11]

In addition, the EU lawmakers has passed the Single Resolution Mechanism Regulation (SRMR I),[12] as amended by the SRMR II.[13] According to Recital 10 SRMR I, the SRMR is intended to increase centralisation of decision-making in resolution as the BRRD has merely provided a minimum harmonisation of rule. In other words, national authorities have been given a large discretion by the BRRD in applying resolution tools and using national financing arrangements. The centralisation of power by the SRM is expected to reduce different approaches that the national authorities could take in utilising a resolution power.

Concerning the authorities which deal with the issues of financial stability, systemic risk and bank resolution, there are four major authorities within the Banking Union[14]: The ECB, the EBA, the SRB and the national resolution authorities (NRAs). The ECB operates under the SSM. It exercises power regarding, for example, the determination of the systemic significance of financial institutions and the conduct of stress test. Meanwhile, the EBA, SRB and NRAs deal with the resolution of financial institutions. There are four resolution tools to be used by the resolution authorities: bail-in (i.e., 'unsecured creditors of an institution bear appropriate losses'),[15] bridge institution (i.e., a 'transfer of the business

[10] European Parliament and Council Directive 2019/879 of 20 May 2019 amending Directive 2014/59/EU as regards the loss-absorbing and recapitalisation capacity of credit institutions and investment firms and Directive 98/26/EC [2019] OJ L150/296.

[11] Lastra (n 110).

[12] European Parliament and Council Regulation (EU) 806/2014 of 15 July 2014 establishing uniform rules and a uniform procedure for the resolution of credit institutions and certain investment firms in the framework of a Single Resolution Mechanism and a Single Resolution Fund and amending Regulation (EU) No 1093/2010 [2014] OJ L255/1.

[13] European Parliament and Council Regulation (EU) 2019/877 of 20 May 2019 amending Regulation (EU) No 806/2014 as regards the loss-absorbing and recapitalization capacity of credit institutions and investment firms [2019] OJ L150/226.

[14] The Banking Union applies to states in the euro area. However, non-euro area countries can also join the Banking Union.

[15] Martina Miskova and Lucia Orszaghova, 'MREL: Gone Concern Loss Absorbing Capacity' (2015) Banking Regulation, 18.

to an entity owed by the authorities'),[16] asset separation (i.e., 'a transfer of 'bad' assets to a 'bad bank''),[17] and sale of business (i.e., a total or partial disposal of the business of the entity).[18,19]

3.2.1 *Lessons from the EU Experience*

Despite the fact that the EU resolution regime is one of the most advanced of its kind, there are some issues that ASEAN states should consider carefully, should it decide to follow the EU's path. In this section, I will consider these issues from the perspectives of legal risk and uncertainty, effects upon the macroeconomy and structure of the regime.

3.2.1.1 Legal Risk and Uncertainty

In a cross-border context, bank resolution actions might not be able to perfectly provide a sufficient level of legal certainty and predictability, which are necessary for maintaining financial stability and mitigating systemic risk. The FSB members which include the European Commission and the ECB have recognised these weaknesses and agreed to utilise contractual measures in order to help solve the problems in two main areas. First, the contractual measures will be used for write-down, cancellation or conversion of debt instruments in resolution where instruments are governed by laws of jurisdiction other than that of the resolution entity. Secondly, the effectiveness of temporary stays on early termination rights will be ensured by contractual measures under the International Swaps and Derivative Association, Inc. (ISDA) Protocols.[20]

Write-down, Cancellation or Conversion of Debt Instruments

The BRRD uses the terminology of 'bail-in' for the resolution tool regarding write-down, cancellation or conversion of debt. A bail-in tool

[16] Ibid.

[17] Ibid.

[18] Single Resolution Board's website, https://srb.europa.eu/en/content/resolution-qa, accessed 4 June 2025.

[19] Single Resolution Board's website, https://srb.europa.eu/en/content/resolution-qa, accessed 4 June 2025.

[20] Financial Stability Board (n 268).

is considered an innovative measure which is used to recapitalise a financial institution in resolution, for the institution to continue performing its authorised activity. It could also be used with other resolution tools (i.e., bridge institution, sale of business and asset separation) in order to convert equity or reduce the principal amount of claim or debt instrument.[21] Nevertheless, there are some potential problems in applying the bail-in tool.

First, divergence of substantive laws in different countries regarding the ranking of claims could cause confusion and legal uncertainty for creditors. In a cross-border case, which involves transactions in more than one country, creditors need to secure legal advice from experts in various jurisdictions. With regard to EU Member States, there are different hierarchies of claims in insolvency in different jurisdictions. Article 108 BRRD I, as amended by the Bank Creditor Hierarchy Directive in 2017, has harmonised national orders of creditors in liquidation to some extent.[22] For example, according to Article 108(1)(a), eligible deposits are put in priority to ordinary unsecured claims. In addition, covered deposits and deposit guarantee schemes rank ahead of eligible deposits (Article 108(2)(b)). Moreover, Article 108(3) has created a new class of debt: non-preferred senior debt. These liabilities rank below senior debts; however, they are paid before claims resulting from instruments which could be subject to the bail-in tool under article 48 BRRD I.

Nonetheless, Article 108 does not resolve all problems resulting from different national hierarchies of claims. This issue could be considered from the bank insolvency regime in Spain which has aligned its hierarchies of claims with that of the BRRD. There are still differences between the Spanish hierarchies of creditors in insolvency proceedings and in resolution. For instance, Additional Tier 1 and Tier 2 capitals, which are subordinated debts, are prioritised before claims of other subordinated creditors (e.g., intra-group loans and related persons).[23]

[21] Single Resolution Board's website, https://srb.europa.eu/en/content/tasks-tools, accessed 4 June 2025.

[22] European Parliament and Council Directive 2017/2399 of 12 December 2017 amending Directive 2014/59/EU as regards the ranking of unsecured debt instruments in insolvency hierarchy [2017] OJ L345/96.

[23] Sophie Buckingham et al., 'Study on the Differences between Bank Insolvency Laws and on Their Potential Harmonization: Final Report', Country Report: Spain (2019),

Meanwhile, German law on the adaptation of resolution mechanism to the SRM (*Abwicklungsmechanismusgesetz*) provides for an amendment of the seniority of debt instruments, and the creation of a new subordinated sub-class of ordinary creditors.[24] This new subordinated sub-class ranks lower than other liabilities (e.g., interbank deposits, corporate deposits, money market instruments, certain claims under derivative transactions and structured notes with derivative-linked features) in insolvency proceedings.[25] Concerning Italian law, there has been a new super-priority ranking for eligible deposits above 100,000 euros held by depositors which are not covered by Article 108 BRRD I. The public policy behind this law is the protection of uninsured depositors including corporate clients.[26]

In addition, the issue of the diversity of substantive law becomes more complicated when considering the fact that the prescription of a Minimum Requirement for own funds and Eligible Liabilities (MREL) could be adjusted by a competent authority or resolution authority later. Hence, this would put investors in an uncertain position regarding the risk of their investment as their original assessment of the loss given default (LGD) would have to be changed after the financial problem has occurred.[27]

Secondly, the use of resolution tools raises concerns regarding property rights and unequal treatment of creditors, which could constitute

4, https://ec.europa.eu/info/publications/191106-study-bank-insolvency_en, accessed 4 June 2025.

24 Danielle Myles, 'TLAC's Toll' (2016) 35 Int'l Fin. L. Rev. 24, 29.

25 Anna Gardella, 'Bail-in and the Two Dimensions of Burden-sharing,' in From Monetary Union to Banking Union, on the Way to Captial Markets Union: New Opportunities for European Integration, ECB Legal Conference 2015 (1–2 September2015), https://www.ecb.europa.eu/pub/pdf/other/frommonetaryuniontobankingunion201512.en.pdf, accessed 4 June 2025.

26 Ibid.

27 Tobias H. Troger, 'Why MREL Won't Help Much' (2018) SAFE Working Paper No 180. 'All the resolution authorities should strive to reach a joint decision to set MREL for each subsidiary together. In the absence of a joint decision on the individual MRELs, each resolution authority takes its own decision which is communicated to the college.' Pamela Lintner, De/centralized Decision making Under the European Resolution Framework: Does *Meroni* Hamper the Creation of a European Resolution Authority?, (2017) 18 Eur Bus Org Law Rev (2017) 591, 596.

uncertainty and a legal risk to them. For example, EU law allows resolution authorities a large amount of discretion regarding eligibility for bail-ins—in other words, everything is bail-inable, unless it is explicitly excluded. An exclusion of some liabilities as not eligible for a bail-in could give advantages to creditors of those debts, in comparison to creditors of non-excluded liabilities.[28] This could violate the principle of *pari passu*, that all unsecured creditors must share equally assets or proceeds of assets in insolvent processes in proportion to the debts due to each creditor. It could also disrupt the insolvency law objective of maximisation of recoverable assets.[29]

Nonetheless, it could be argued that the current resolution system has provided sufficient safeguards to protect the interest of creditors. Investors of banks could rely on a protection under the European Convention on Human Rights (ECHR) as well as the 'no creditor worse off' (NCWO) principle. According to article 1 of the First Protocol to the Convention of Human Rights and Fundamental Freedoms (the Protocol) and article 17 of the Charter of Fundamental Rights of the European Union (the Charter), every person is entitled to the peaceful enjoyment of his or her possessions. A deprivation of those possessions must be in the public interest and subject to the conditions provided by law. Besides, a fair compensation must be paid for his or her loss. According to de Seriere and van der Houwen, the EU legislators have utilised the NCWO principle in order to ensure that the interference with property rights would be proportionate in accordance with the Protocol and the Charter.[30]

In a bank resolution, the NCWO principle is used to safeguard the investors' interest in several ways. For example, an independent valuer[31]

[28] Bail-in will be used for largest and most complex firms with balance sheets greater than 15–25 billion pounds. Bank of England, 'The Bank of England's approach to resolution' (October 2017), https://www.bankofengland.co.uk/-/media/boe/files/news/2017/october/the-bank-of-england-approach-to-resolution, accessed 4 June 2025.

[29] Christos Hadjiemmanuil, 'Bank Stakeholders' Mandatory Contribution to Resolution Financing: Principle and Ambiguities of Bail-in' in From Monetary Union to Banking Union, on the way to Captial Markets Union: New Opportunities for European Integration (n 329).

[30] V.P.G. de Seriere and D.M. van der Houwen, "No Creditor Worse Off' in Case of Bank Resolution: Food for Litigation?' (2016) 31(7) Journal of International Banking Law and Regulation, 378.

[31] The valuer has to be independent from both the resolution authority and resolution entity. In addition, there must not be any material common or conflicting interests.

will consider the NCWO principle when conducting an assessment in two main stages: Valuation 2 and Valuation 3. There are three types of resolution valuations: (1) Valuation 1 which is conducted prior to resolution to assess conditions for resolution and the point of non-viability; (2) Valuation 2 which is performed prior to resolution to consider the use of resolution tools; and (3) Valuation 3 which is carried out after resolution to assess the no creditor worse off valuation.

With regards to Valuation 2, it is an assessment conducted prior to resolution which provides information necessary for taking a suitable resolution action. In addition, the outcome of Valuation 2 will indicate the extent of interference with property rights in the assets, rights, liabilities or shares, as well as the value of any consideration to be paid.[32] This process will help ensure that the stakeholders will receive sufficient value in accordance with their fundamental rights and the NCWO principle under Article 73 of the BRRD I.[33]

Moreover, the NCWO principle must be taken into account during Valuation 3. Valuation 3, which is a liquidation valuation, takes place after the execution of resolution. The independent valuer has to conduct a hypothetical gone concern valuation in accordance with applicable insolvency law (Articles 20(16)–(18) of the SRMR I).[34] The NCWO principle attempts to provide a safeguard to the rights of creditors by ensuring that they would not be subject to a larger amount of losses in resolution

See Article 37–41 of Commission Delegated Regulation (EU) 2016/1075, https://eur-lex.europa.eu/legal-content/EN/TXT/PDF/?uri=CELEX:32016R1075, accessed 4 June 2025. Commission Delegated Regulation (EU) 2016/1075 of 23 March 2016 supplementing Directive 2014/59/EU of the European Parliament and of the Council with regard to regulatory technical standards specifying the content of recovery plans, resolution plans and group resolution plans, the minimum criteria that the competent authority is to assess as regards recovery plans and group recovery plans, the conditions for group financial support, the requirements for independent valuers, the contractual recognition of write-down and conversion powers, the procedures and contents of notification requirements and of notice of suspension and the operational functioning of the resolution colleges [2016] OJ L184/1.

[32] European Banking Authority, 'Handbook on Valuation for Purposes of Resolution' (22 February 2019), 12, https://www.eba.europa.eu/sites/default/documents/files/documents/10180/2613666/9f0772ea-a052-49e5-86ce-64c157adff10/Valuation%20Handbook.pdf, accessed 4 June 2025.

[33] Ibid.

[34] Single Resolution Board, 'Framework for Valuation: Q&A' 2, https://srb.europa.eu/sites/default/files/18_02_valuation_qa_002.pdf, accessed 4 June 2025.

than what they would have been in ordinary winding-up.[35] In the case that there is a shortfall, creditors are entitled to compensation from the resolution financing arrangements.[36]

However, it could be counter-argued that there is a large degree of uncertainties in valuations which could dilute the envisaged protection to creditors.[37] For example, in the case of Banco Popular, provisional report (Valuation 2) indicated that the valuation results were 'highly uncertain'.[38] That is, in part, because the independent valuer is likely to have limited time and information for preparing a valuation. In Valuation 2, the valuer is normally notified only shortly before a resolution action is taken.[39] In addition, the valuer needs to determine losses which could arise as a result of mis-selling claims in Valuation 2.[40] It is challenging to accurately estimate those losses at the time of the resolution action.[41] This is especially so in the case of massive or serial mis-selling, where the real total amount of liabilities is very difficult to ascertain.

Moreover, investors may face hurdles in pursuing their claims in order to challenge valuation under the NCWO cause of action. This difficulty could arise due to the fact that there is more than one insolvency regime

[35] Article 34(1)(g) BRRD I.

[36] Article 75 and article 101(1)(e) BRRD I.

[37] Jens-Hinrich Binder, 'Proportionality at the Resolution Stage: Calibration of Resolution Measures and the Public Interest Test' (2020) 21 European Business Organization Law Review, 468, https://papers.ssrn.com/sol3/papers.cfm?abstract_id=2990379, accessed 4 June 2025.

[38] Willem Pieter De Grone, 'Valuation Reports in the Context of Banking Resolution: What Are the Challenges?' (2018), https://www.europarl.europa.eu/RegData/etudes/IDAN/2018/624418/IPOL_IDA(2018)624418_EN.pdf, accessed 4 June 2025.

[39] Ibid., 11.

[40] Recital 16 of the BRRD II has stated that the Directive aims to protect retail investors by ensuring that they do not invest excessively in instruments eligible for the MREL. However, the effectiveness of the BRRD II in preventing mis-selling is questionable. According to Malvagna and Alibrandi, the main flaw of Article 44a of the BRRD II is that it leaves the enforcement of investor protection on an ex-post means. This approach is inadequate to prevent serial or massive mis-selling. By the time that a compensation or restitution is awarded, the bank might already be on the brink of insolvency. Ugo Malvagna and Antoenlla Sciarrone Alibrandi, 'Misselling in Self-Placement and Bank Resolution under BRRD2' (2020) 17(5) European Company and Financial Law Review, 550.

[41] De Grone (n 298) 19.

applicable to a bank's assets, located in various countries.[42] The problem could also be exacerbated by the fact that the resolution authorities have a large degree of discretion. Hence, challenging their decisions would not only lead to a complex case but also long and costly litigation, which those investors might not be able to afford.[43]

Furthermore, the non-uniform application of the NCWO principle across the Banking Union could lead to the problem of inequality before the law, in the case of a bank which operates in different states. Creditors in some jurisdictions might be treated more favourably by the applicable national laws than those in other Member States. Besides, at the supranational level, the CJEU might have to interpret and apply national laws of various Member States. Decisions of the EU officials including the SRB are subject to a judicial review of the CJEU. The judicial review could be brought under, for example, Article 263 of the Treaty on the Functioning of the European Union (TFEU) (i.e., an action for annulment) or Article 267 of the TFEU (i.e., preliminary references).[44] As I have argued in Chapter 2, it may not be assumed that the Court has expertise and competence to interpret and apply local laws.

Apart from the issue of bail-in, a resolution might be challenged in court, as it can take place when a bank is still solvent. This could raise tensions between bail-ins and private rights. The BRRD has not stipulated a clear numerical threshold which would trigger a resolution.[45] Instead, the EU resolution regime utilises a qualitative assessment of recapitalisation levels.[46] In other words, a resolution could be triggered when an institution is 'failing or likely to fail' (FOLTF). The meaning of FOLTF

[42] V.P.G. de Seriere and D.M. van der Houwen (n 290) 380.

[43] Ibid., 384.

[44] Diego Valiante, 'Harmonising Insolvency Laws in the Euro Area: Rationale, Stock-taking and Challenges. What Role for the Eurogroup?' (2016), 19, https://www.europarl.europa.eu/RegData/etudes/STUD/2016/574428/IPOL_STU(2016)574428_EN.pdf, accessed 4 June 2025.

[45] Hadjiemmanuil (n 289).

[46] Anne-Caroline Huser et al., 'The Systemic Implications of Bail-in: A Multi-Layered Network Approach' (2017) European Central Bank Working Paper Series No. 2010/ February 2017, https://www.ecb.europa.eu/pub/pdf/scpwps/ecbwp2010.en.PDF, accessed 4 June 2025.

does not correspond to notions of being insolvent according to corporate insolvency law.[47] In principle, a firm in distress is insolvent when it is either balance-sheet insolvent (i.e., its liabilities exceed assets), or cash-flow insolvent (i.e., inability to pay when debts fall due). However, under the BRRD, there are four resolution triggers when an institution is failing or likely to fail: (1) balance-sheet insolvency; (2) cash-flow insolvency; (3) breach of regulatory requirements sufficiently serious to justify withdrawal of bank's authorisation; (4) the bank's need for 'extraordinary public financial support' (A. 32(4)).

If one of the four triggers is satisfied, there are two further conditions for a resolution to take place: (1) no reasonable prospect that it will be restored with private sector measures or supervisory actions (e.g., early intervention measures/write down/conversion of capital instruments); (2) resolution tools are necessary due to the public interest. According to Article 32(5) of the BRRD I and Article 18(5) of the SRMR I, a resolution action is in the public interest if three conditions are satisfied: (1) it is necessary for the achievement of the resolution objectives;[48] (2) it must be 'proportionate to one or more of the resolution objectives'; and (3) a winding up under insolvency proceedings would not satisfy resolution objectives to the same degree. In the case that the SRB finds that there is no public interest in resolving a bank, national insolvency proceedings (NIPs) will apply to the bank in question.

In the recent crisis management and deposit insurance framework (CMDI) proposed by the Commission, the public interest test has been modified so that its outcome should be negative only in the case that the winding up under normal insolvency proceedings would yield a more effective result than resolution.[49] The Commission's approach, to which

[47] However, there is 'no single legal definition of inability to pay debts'. Vanessa Finch and David Milman, *Corporate Insolvency Law: Perspectives and Principles* (Cambridge University Press 2017), 119. In addition, as Goode has stated, it is almost impossible to pinpoint when a company was first unable to pay debts. Roy Goode, Perpetual Trustee and Flip Clauses in Swap Transactions (2011) 127 Law Quarterly Review 1.

[48] These resolution objectives are: (1) ensuring the continuity of critical functions; (2) maintain financial stability; (3) minimising reliance on public financial support; (4) protecting depositors covered by Directive 2014/49/EU and investors covered by Directive 97/9/EC; and (5) protecting client funds and client assets. Article 31(2) of the BRRD I and Article 14(2) of the SRMR I.

[49] The CMDI reform comprises mainly three legislative proposals amending BRRD I, SRMR I, and the Deposit Guarantee Schemes Directive.

the Parliament has agreed, has been refined by the Council. According to the Council's proposal, there are two stages in conducting the public interest assessment (PIA): (1) assessing whether insolvency would jeopardise the resolution objectives, and (2) analysing whether insolvency would achieve the resolution objectives more effectively than resolution.[50] At the time of writing, the trilogue on the CMDI legislative package between the Commission, the Parliament, and the Council is still ongoing.

A Temporary Stay: Competing Norms

A temporary stay is an important regulatory measure, in order to have an effective resolution regime and prevent systemic risk. Firms normally use the maturity of their trading products for their business and risk management.[51] Harm stemming from an uncertainty regarding the maturity of financial products can be devastating, as in the Lehmann Brothers case. Here, the exercise of early termination rights generated not only disruptive effects upon the contracting parties, but also the macro instability of the financial markets.

Entering into the resolution of a financial institution could constitute an event of default, and consequently, the institution's counterparty would have early termination rights.[52] A temporary stay prevents an exercise of early termination rights by a counterparty of a firm in resolution—currently, resolution authorities in many countries have the power to order a temporary stay. The authorities can use a period of between 24–48 hours during a temporary stay in order to, for example, transfer the assets of a failing bank to a bridge bank. This could be pursued over the resolution weekend.

However, there are some limitations in using a temporary stay in a cross-border case, as a national resolution authority does not have the authority to impose its resolution rules upon the authorities and courts

[50] Proposal for a Directive of the European Parliament and of the Council amending Directive 2014/59/EU as regards early intervention measures, conditions for resolution and financing of resolution action and Directive 2014/24/EU as regards services needed for the preparation, application and exercise of resolution tools and powers.

[51] PWC, 'Successfully Addressing Stay Regulations' (March 2015) RRP Viewpoint, 5, https://www.pwc.ch/en/publications/2017/pwc_online_booklet_rrp_successfully_addressing_stay_regulations_2017_en.pdf, accessed 4 June 2025.

[52] Early termination events could be triggered by many factors (e.g., non-performance on trading liabilities, insolvency, cross-defaults and external rating downgrades). Ibid.

in other jurisdictions. The FSB has provided a guideline in order to solve this problem in the Key Attributes of Effective Resolution Regimes for Financial Institutions (2014).[53] The Key Attributes specify that a resolution authority should have the power to temporarily stay contractual acceleration or early termination rights in the case that they arise only by reason of or in connection with a firm's entry into resolution.[54] Nevertheless, the Key Attributes of the FSB are only soft law. Their authority would still depend on whether or not states are willing to follow them.

Concerning the EU, Article 68(1) BRRD I provides that resolution measures shall not be deemed to be an enforcement event for the purposes of termination clauses or insolvency proceedings under the contract. Moreover, Article 71(1) BRRD I requires the Member States to ensure that their resolution authorities have the power to suspend early termination rights.[55] Nonetheless, a cross-border resolution could involve a party or parties which are not subject to the BRRD. To ensure the effectiveness of a temporary stay, Article 71a BRRD II stipulates that the Member States shall require institutions and relevant entities to include contractual recognition of stay powers clauses in financial contracts governed by non-EU law.

Despite the fact that Article 71a BRRD II mandates such requirement, the effectiveness and enforceability of the temporary stay remain questionable. One reason for this is the difficulty of imposing the required clause in all financial contracts, as evidenced by the experience with Article 55 BRRD I.[56] In addition, BRRD II and the EBA's Regulatory Technical Standards (RTS) do not prescribe a specific form for the required clause. The RTS merely sets out the mandatory components that must

[53] The FSB released a revised version of the Key Attributes in 2024. The 2024 revision incorporates enhanced guidance on the resolution of Financial Market Infrastructures and their participants. However, the twelve Key Attributes from the original 2011 version remain unchanged. Financial Stability Board, *'Key Attributes of Effective Resolution Regimes for Financial Institutions: Revised Version'* (25 April 2024).

[54] Financial Stability Board (n 268), KA. 4.3.

[55] Matthias Lehmann, 'Bail-in and Private International Law: How to Make Bank Resolution Measures Effective Across Borders' (2017) 66 (1) International & Comparative Law Quarterly, 107–142.

[56] Article 55 requires the Member States to ensure that in-scope entities include a contractual clause recognising bail-in powers in non-EU law governed contracts. However, in practice, including such a clause might be illegal for some types of contracts. EBA, *'Final Report: Draft Regulatory Technical Standards on the Contractual Recognition of Stay Powers under Article 71a(5) of Directive 2014/59/EU'* (16 December 2020), 16.

be included in financial contracts. Hence, contracting parties may utilise a variety of forms of the required clause. According to the EBA's RTS document, in-scope institutions indicated a preference for using standard clauses or standard market documentation pursuant to the requirements of Article 71a BRRD II.[57] On the one hand, the use of standard clauses can enhance efficiency and effectiveness for market participants. On the other hand, it may lead to legal uncertainty, as in the case of standard clauses provided by ISDA.

ISDA has taken a leading role in this area by publishing the Resolution Stay Protocol in 2014,[58] the Universal Resolution Stay Protocol (UP) in 2015, the Resolution Stay Jurisdictional Modular Protocol (JMP) in May 2016, and the U.S. Resolution Stay Protocol in 2018. ISDA has suggested that users of its Master Agreement (MA) adhere to these protocols by signing up with them. By adhering to the protocols, an annex will be automatically added to their contracts.[59]

According to ISDA, the UP has been created in order to enable parties to Protocol Covered Agreements[60] to amend the terms of such Protocol Covered Agreement, in order to contractually recognise the cross-border application of special resolution regimes.[61] With regards to the JMP, the purpose of publishing it is to enable contracting parties to Protocol Covered Agreements to 'comply with certain legislative and regulatory requirements applicable to certain financial companies in different jurisdictions that address the exercise of early termination and related rights upon the resolution or insolvency of such financial companies'.[62]

The ISDA's initiative has been welcomed by regulators and financial institutions in many countries. For example, the UK Prudential Regulation Authority (PRA) published rules in November 2015. These rules require new financial contracts subject to foreign laws to contain

[57] Ibid., 25.

[58] The 2014 Protocol has been replaced with the Universal Resolution Stay Protocol in 2015.

[59] Lehmann (n 315).

[60] Protocol Covered Agreements are defined as 'any agreement that is a Covered Agreement for purposes of such Jurisdictional Module. ISDA, 'ISDA Resolution Stay Jurisdictional Modular Protocol' (3 May 2016), 12, http://assets.isda.org/media/f253b540-95/83d17e3d-pdf/, accessed 4 June 2025.

[61] ISDA, 'ISDA 2015 Universal Stay Protocol' (4 November 2015), http://assets.isda.org/media/ac6b533f-3/5a7c32f8-pdf/, accessed 4 June 2025.

[62] ISDA (n 320).

contractual terms with the effect that a counterparty should recognise the application of a stay applied to firms under the UK resolution regime.[63] According to the Bank of England (2017), 23 systemically important banks adhered to the ISDA 2015 Universal Resolution Stay Protocol.[64] In addition, as a consequence of Brexit, the UK became a third country, since 1 January 2021. In response to changes made to the PRA rulebook following Brexit, ISDA has created the ISDA 2020 UK (PRA Rule) Jurisdictional Module (the PRA Module). The effect of incorporating the PRA Module is that its terms will replace the terms of the 2016 UK Module in their entirety.[65]

Moreover, in 2021, ISDA launched the BRRD II Omnibus Jurisdictional Module, a new module to the JMP, in order to help firms comply with Article 71a BRRD II. Adhering Parties will be either (i) 'Regulated Entities' subject to a BRRD II Stay Recognition Requirement under the national law of EU Member State and are listed in the EU Stay Law Annex,[66] or (ii) 'Module Adhering Parties' that adhere in order to help their counterparties satisfy the BRRD II Stay Recognition Requirements.[67] By adhering to the Module, a Module Adhering Party consents to modify the agreements specified in the Module that 'it has entered into with, provided to or received from' any Regulated Entity.[68]

[63] Bank of England (n 288).

[64] Ibid.

[65] Section 4(a) of the PRA Module. ISDA, 'ISDA Resolution Stay Jurisdictional Modular Protocol 2020 UK (PRA Rule) Jurisdictional Module' (22 December 2020), http://assets.isda.org/media/d7328137/0502946e-pdf, accessed 4 June 2025.

[66] ISDA will add Member States to the EU Stay Law Annex after those countries have transposed A. 71a BRRD II into their national laws and market participants have provided adequate support for ISDA to take such action. The Member States currently listed in the EU Stay Law Annex are Austria, Belgium, Bulgaria, Croatia, Cyprus, Czech Republic, Denmark, Estonia, France, Finland, Germany, Gibraltar, Greece, Hungary, Ireland, Italy, Lithuania, Luxembourg, Malta, Netherlands, Romania, Slovakia, Spain, and Sweden. ISDA, 'BRRD II Omnibus Jurisdictional Module—FAQs', 8–9, https://www.isda.org/protocol/brrd-ii-omnibus-jurisdictional-module-to-the-isda-resolution-stay-jurisdictional-modular-protocol/, accessed 4 June 2025.

[67] Ibid., 2.

[68] ISDA, 'ISDA Resolution Stay Jurisdictional Modular Protocol BRRD II Omnibus Jurisdictional Module' (14 September 2021), 1, https://www.isda.org/protocol/brrd-ii-omnibus-jurisdictional-module-to-the-isda-resolution-stay-jurisdictional-modular-protocol/, accessed 4 June 2025.

The ISDA MA and Protocols provide an illustration of how the private sector could help reduce the ineffectiveness and enforcement gap of supranational law in transnational and cross-border contexts. However, in my view, the authority and effectiveness of ISDA MA and Protocols in a cross-border context still depends to a large extent upon the states' supports, especially those of national courts. In the case that national courts do not provide an appropriate legal enforcement in accordance with the spirit of ISDA MA and Protocols, problems of conflict of laws might arise. The application of the ISDA MA and Protocols depends upon national courts in many ways.

First, the ISDA MA and Protocols need national courts to interpret and provide clarifications to the terms in the agreements. In the EU, many contracts made under the ISDA MA are governed by English law.[69] The English courts have provided clarification to the meaning of ISDA MA in some cases. For example, in the case of *Lehman Brothers Special Financing Inc. v. (1) National Power Corp; (2) Power Sector Assets and Liabilities Management Corp*, Knowles J held that the words regarding close-out provisions of the 2002 ISDA MA required objective reasonableness, rather than merely a rationality standard, in order to determine the close-out amount.[70]

In addition, in the case of *Lomas v JFB Firth Rixon*, Longmore LJ held that Section 2(iii)(a) of ISDA MA meant that the suspended payment obligations continued indefinitely if an Event of Default had not been cured.[71] The Court of Appeal decision in *Lomas* was celebrated, as it dispelled legal uncertainty caused by the High Court decision which was not in line with the market expectation. Moreover, since 2015 a special panel called the 'Financial List' has been created as part of the Court of First Instance. Judges in the Financial List are experts in dealing with complex financial cases. The Financial List could help provide clarification to technical terms in the context of international financial market at the level of the Court of First Instance.

[69] After Brexit, governing laws of some contracts might be French or Irish laws.

[70] *Lehman Brothers Special Financing Inc. v. (1) National Power Corp; (2) Power Sector Assets and Liabilities Management Corp* [2018] EWHC 487 (Comm).

[71] *Lomas v JFB Firth Rixon* [2012] EWCA Civ 419.

Secondly, ISDA MA and Protocols are *lex mercatoria* or merchant law. Their authority would depend on the extent which national courts recognise them, especially in the case that they are not backed up by a statute. Moreover, national courts are likely to deliver a decision in accordance with statute mandatory rules rather than the ISDA MA and/or Protocols if there are conflicts between them.[72] According to Hugh Collins, national rules have not yet admitted an exception that ordinary national rules of property law and insolvency law should only be applied in a manner that respects the authorities of the ISDA MA, and its purpose of regulating and supporting international financial transactions.[73] For example, a voluntary waiver of creditors' rights may not be effective and recognised by the national courts, if it derogates fundamental principles of public law, essential elements of domestic property, insolvency and company laws.[74]

Collin's view could be supported by the argument that party autonomy and freedom of contract are crucially important in providing legal certainty. Without a sufficient degree of legal certainty, an economic integration as well as efficiency of international commercial transactions could be jeopardised. Nonetheless, it could be counter-argued that public welfare as well as the interests of all stakeholders, which could be affected by the non-application of mandatory laws of the jurisdiction, are no less important than the concern regarding freedom of contract. In other words, a regulatory state has a duty to ensure that the fundamental rights of third parties as well as its essential interests (e.g., political, economic and social organisation) are protected.[75]

[72] Hugh Collins, 'Flipping Wreck: Lex Mercatoria on Shoals of Ius Cogens', in Stefan Grundmann et al. (eds), *Contract Governance: Dimensions in Law and Interdisciplinary Research* (Oxford University Press 2015). According to Collins, national courts should seek to reconcile financial *lex mercatoria* with state mandatory rules based on public policy and constitutional principles rather than grant automatic priority or hierarchy to the latter. They should try to understand the demands of both normative systems and how they can be reconciled.

[73] ibid. Collins argues that conception of privately created transnational norms with legal effects has yet been incorporated into the court's perspective on its governing rule of recognition for laws regarding the financial markets.

[74] Federico Lupo-Pasini, *The Logic of Financial Nationalism: The Challenges of Corporation and the Role of International Law* (Cambridge University Press 2017), 115.

[75] Jan Kleinheisterkamp, 'Overriding Mandatory Laws in International Arbitration' (2018) I.C.L.Q. 67(4), 905.

3.2.1.2 Effects Upon the Macroeconomy—Effectiveness of Resolution Tools Mitigating Systemic Risk

Mitigating systemic risk is a dominant driver of financial reform efforts. The creation of resolution tools is part of this enterprise. Nevertheless, the effectiveness of resolution tools in mitigating systemic risk is questionable for some reasons. First, in a financial crisis, bail-ins of bail-inable products could potentially contribute to a contagion and chains of insolvency via balance sheet transmission.[76]

Banks are incentivised to hold bail-inable bank bonds, because a lower risk weight would be applied to bank exposures than to corporate exposures.[77] Currently, a large proportion of bail-inable bonds are held within the financial sector, especially the banking sector.[78] The European banking system has been financed with a large amounts of subordinated debt.[79] According to Anne-Caroline Huser et al., there is a case where a counterparty fails after the write-down at the bank under resolution, as a result of the increased exposure of that counterparty via the interbank market channel.[80]

Secondly, bail-ins could create a banking panic and bank runs by depositors and investors.[81] According to G Gordon, a 'banking panic'

[76] Giovanni Dell'Ariccia et al., 'Trade-offs in Bank Resolution' (February 2018) IMF Staff Discussion Note, 7, https://www.imf.org/en/Publications/Staff-Discussion-Notes/Issues/2018/02/09/Trade-offs-in-Bank-Resolution-45127, accessed 4 June 2025.

[77] Dirk Schoenmaker, 'A Macro Approach to International Bank Resolution' (2017) Working Paper Series No. 56/ November 2017, 14.

[78] Ibid., 4. However, this argument could be contrasted with a conclusion in a working paper by Anne-Caroline Huser et al. which studied systemic implications of bail-in. The authors are of the view that there is 'no direct contagion to creditors in sense that no creditor bank defaults due to bail-in at one of its counterparties.' In addition, the paper shows that spill-overs tend to be small because there are low levels of securities cross-holdings in the network of their sample of 26 banks. These 26 banking groups represent 59 per cent of total euro area banking sector assets. The authors conclude that the low interbank cross-holdings of bank bail-inable debt in network appear to prevent direct contagion. Huser et al. (n 306), 2–3.

[79] Schoenmaker (n 337), 4. 'The euro-area banks (i.e., credit institutions) hold the largest share of bail-inable bonds issued by euro-area banks, with holdings close to € 500 billion'.

[80] Huser et al. (n 306), 35.

[81] According to the ECB, a write down could generate information contagion to the wider European banking system. Schoenmaker (n 337), 14–15.

occurs when 'informationally-insensitive' debt becomes 'informationally-sensitive' due to shock.[82] I would argue that in the case of bail-ins, the asymmetry of the information could turn 'informationally-insensitive' debts (i.e., bail-inable bonds) into an 'informationally-sensitive' products. As for a depositors' run as a result of bail-ins, its magnitude could be large, as households hold a high proportion of bail-inable bonds.[83] This could occur because depositors are 'imperfectly informed about the type of shocks hitting banks and about their physical exposure to each other'.[84]

Concerning a run by investors holding bail-inable bonds, investors who experience losses would be forced to 'rebalance their portfolio and sell their claims on the initially non-distressed banks'.[85] This would, in turn, threaten the stability of these other banks, despite the fact that their financial position is originally healthy.[86] This concern could be exacerbated by the fact that resolution authorities have a large discretion regarding eligibility of assets for bail-ins. This would increase uncertainty with respect to bail-ins. As a result, there might be a run on a distressed bank which could, in turn, threaten its liquidity position.[87]

Thirdly, bail-ins may impose negatives externalities upon society which could dampen the financial markets in which the measures are used, as well as those of other countries. According to the IMF, these negative externalities can involve insolvency costs, heightened macro-financial uncertainty and the deterioration of economic outlook.[88] The severity of the negative externalities would depend on economic conditions

[82] Gary Gordon, 'Slapped in the Face by the Invisible Hand: Banking and the Panic of 2007' (2009) SSRN Paper, https://papers.ssrn.com/sol3/papers.cfm?abstract_id=1401882, accessed 4 June 2025.

[83] Schoenmaker (n 337), 4.

[84] ibid. From the households' perspective, these products provide high rates of interest. However, they may not fully understand the inherent risks of these bonds as these products are highly complex. Besides, banks normally do not disclose clearly the risks involved in the products to their customers. Dell'Ariccia et al. (n 336).

[85] According to the IMF, a 'bail-in could create expectations for further bail-ins in other banks.' Dell'Ariccia et al. (n 336).

[86] Ibid., 6.

[87] Clas Wihlborg, 'Bail-ins: Issues of Credibility and Contagion' (January 2017) SUERF Policy Note Issue No. 10, 8.

[88] Dell'Ariccia et al. (n 336) 7.

prevailing at that time. In an extreme distressed period, negative externalities are likely to generate a larger extent of spillover effects. Countries which have larger and more interconnected financial sectors may be affected to a greater extent by the negative externalities.[89]

In addition, bail-ins can lead to an immediate reassessment of bank risk. This, in turn, can undermine banks' market access, as well as have negative repercussions for credit supply and GDP.[90] Moreover, bail-in could lead to claims for compensation (e.g., depositors in Cyprus) and strategic defaults on bank loans.[91] The non-performing loans which are created as a result of strategic defaults could be one of the factors which cause a financial crisis. Furthermore, imposing losses on unsecured creditors might have an effect upon the equity prices for banks in other countries. For example, according to the IMF Staff Discussion Note, in 11 out of 16 cases, equity prices for banks were negatives with significant changes despite the facts that those banks were not in the country in which the bail-in took place.[92]

3.2.1.3 Structural Concerns of the European Union Resolution Regime

After the global financial crisis, the Banking Union has been fragmented with a lesser degree of cross-border financial integration than its pre-crisis level.[93] This is despite of achievements in the Banking Union in terms of 'balance sheets cleaning, regulatory harmonisation, and deepening institutional integration'.[94] This fragmentation stems, in part, from an insufficient confidence of the Member States in the EU regulations which are to manage a crisis in their jurisdictions.[95] I argue that the current

[89] Ibid., 8.

[90] Ibid.

[91] Ibid., 21.

[92] Ibid.

[93] Andrea Enria, 'Fragmentation in Banking Markets: Crisis Legacy and the Challenge of Brexit', 'Speech' (BCBS-FSI High Level Meeting for Europe on Banking Supervision, 17 September 2018), https://eba.europa.eu/documents/10180/2353431/Andrea+Enria+speech+on+Fragmentation+in+banking+at+BCBS-FSI+High+Level+Meeting+170918.pdf, accessed 4 June 2025.

[94] Ibid., 3.

[95] Jean-Mari.e.,Andres et al., 'Optimizing the Banking Union: Proposals for Member States to Benefit from Private Risk Sharing within the Banking

structure of the EU resolution regime might create obstacles in mitigating systemic and cross-border risks. It could also reduce the confidence of the Member States in the Banking Union for various reasons.

First, an unclear scope of power of related authorities could create confusions and enforcement gap to the parties to a resolution agreement.[96] There could be an 'institutional vacuum' when financial institutions fall into the power of neither the SRB nor the EBA.[97] The power of the SRB and the EBA under the regime of the SRM could overlap, as the SRMR does not provide a demarcating line for their jurisdictional boundaries.[98] The SRB possesses an exclusive power for bank resolution under the SRM. Meanwhile, the EBA has an authority regarding the supervision and resolution of EU banks.[99] In the case of incentive misalignments between the European authorities and the NRA, it is unclear whether the EBA can utilise its quasi-enforcement power if the SRB decides not to take an action against the NRA.[100]

Secondly, the possibility of objections by the European Commission and the European Council may lead to a delay, which might not be compatible with time constraints under which restructurings must be carried out.[101] Under the SRMR, the SRB does not have a full decision-making power.[102] Instead, the SRB has to submit its decision to the European Commission.[103] The Commission, then, has to decide whether or not it will endorse the resolution scheme.

Union', 3, https://www.eurofi.net/wp-content/uploads/2018/06/SOFIA_EUROFI_BANKING_UNION.pdf, accessed 4 June 2025.

[96] Under the European supervisory structure, the European authorities coordinate with the national authorities and allow the latter to supervise financial institutions directly.

[97] Andromachi Georgosouli, 'Regulatory Incentive Realignment and the EU Legal Framework of Bank Resolution' (2016) 10 Brook. J. Corp. Fin. & Com. L., 362.

[98] Ibid., 361.

[99] Ibid., 348.

[100] Ibid., 362.

[101] Lehmann (n 315).

[102] The EU legislator does not provide supranational powers to the SRB in making its decisions. This is because, under the Meroni doctrine, powers of the Commission cannot be delegated to any new EU body which is not foreseen in the primary law. Ibid., 16.

[103] Jens-Hinrich Binder, 'Cross-border coordination of bank resolution in the EU: All problems resolved?', in Matthias Haentjens (ed), *Research Handbook on Cross-Border Bank Resolution* (Edgar Elgar 2019).

In addition, the Commission may refer the scheme to the European Council. The Council could obstruct the execution of the proposed scheme for reasons of, for example, public interest (Article 18(1)(c) and (5) of the SRMR).[104] According to Binder, the Member States could use their bargaining power with the Council in order to obstruct the execution of a proposed scheme. This would allow the Member States to bring the case back into a national sphere.[105]

Thirdly, national resolution authorities have some degree of discretion which allows them to depart from an agreed cross-border resolution scheme. This problem would be exacerbated by the fact that national authorities tend to protect their national interest. During a financial crisis, the misalignment of incentives between the European authorities and the NRAs is likely to be high. For example, national regulators might not cooperate in Single-Point-of-Entry (SPOE) resolution (i.e., where the resolution of a banking group is conducted at the level of the ultimate parent company) when *ex-post* cross-jurisdictional transfers are excessively large. They might instead ring-fence assets in their own jurisdictions.[106]

In addition, in Multiple-Point-of-Entry (MPOE) resolution (i.e., where the resolution is performed at different operating subsidiaries by the local authorities in different jurisdictions),[107] incentive compatibility constraints of national resolution authorities might arise in some circumstances. For example, different national authorities might propose inconsistent resolution actions with each other at each point of entry into resolution. Moreover, cross-resolution clauses could entitle a host authority to sell a solvent subsidiary in their jurisdiction when a resolution procedure has been triggered for a company in the same group in

[104] Ibid.

[105] Ibid.

[106] Patrick Bolton and Martin Oehmke, 'Bank Resolution and the Structure of Global Banks' (2018) Paul Wooley Centre Working Paper No. 59, http://www.lse.ac.uk/fmg/assets/documents/papers/discussion-papers/DP778.pdf, accessed 4 June 2025. For example, experience from the Fortis Bank shows that national authorities would protect the national interest. They were concerned with minimising the losses to stakeholders and taxpayers in their jurisdiction. Li Li Chong, 'Legal Issues of Cross-border Bank Resolution in the EU Context: The Desirability and Feasibility of Having an EU Cross-border Bank Resolution Framework' (LLM. Thesis, Ghent University 2012), 10.

[107] Article 1 of the BRRD II has introduced the concepts of 'resolution entity' and 'resolution group' which have increased clarity regarding definitions of institutions which could be affected by the SPOE and MPOE approaches.

another country. This could be done at the detriment of the parent's and other subsidiaries' creditors.[108]

3.3 Part II: ASEAN and a Bank Resolution Regime

3.3.1 ASEAN States Cross-border Banking and Systemic Risk

Financial integration of the ASEAN states is likely to spur cross-border activities in this region. However, the benefits of financial integration could come at a cost of greater likelihood of systemic risk. As Corbacho and Peiris have stated, the 'greater the degree of interconnectivity between banks, the greater the likelihood that financial stress in one bank could trigger spillovers of financial stress to other banks, thereby increasing systemic risks'.[109] Currently, many ASEAN banks have become regional banks (e.g., DBS, OCBC, UOB, MayBank, CIMB, RHB Bank, and Bangkok Bank). This expansion could be considered from the data in Fig. 1.1 (see Chapter 1). For instance, Fig. 1.1 illustrates that banks headquartered in Malaysia have the highest number of overseas branches and subsidiaries in ASEAN states (1,308 branches / subsidiaries). According to the available data from Orbis Bank Focus, the five largest commercial banks by assets headquartered in Malaysia are MayBank, CIMB, Public Bank Berhad, RHB Bank and Hong Leong Bank Berhad. All of these institutions have their overseas branches and/or subsidiaries in at least four ASEAN Member States. For example, Maybank has a total number of 116 overseas branches and subsidiaries in every ASEAN country except Thailand. The majority of those overseas branches and subsidiaries are located in the Philippines (74 branches/subsidiaries).

In addition, ASEAN has chosen to pursue a greater degree of financial integration under the ABIF initiative. Hence, there would potentially be a higher prospect of systemic risk in the banking sector in this sub-region. Effective regional safety nets would be necessary in order to ensure that the banking industry is resilient. Moreover, a cross-border resolution framework, through a single resolution regime, as well as a common

[108] Federico Lupo-Pasini and Ross Buckley, 'International Coordination in Cross-Border Bank Bail-ins: Problems and Prospects' (2015) 16 (2) European Business Organization Law Review, 31.

[109] Ana Corbacho and Shanaka J. Peiris (eds), *The ASEAN Way: Sustaining Growth and Stability* (International Monetary Fund 2018).

backstop (e.g., deposit insurance) could help reduce the prospect of using taxpayers' money to bail out financial institutions.[110] According to Moody's, the emphasis of authorities in ASEAN is still upon *crisis prevention* through sound supervision, macro-prudential measures and the implementation of stringent capital and liquidity requirements consistent with Basel III, rather than *resolution*.[111] Regulators in the region tend to view early action as preferable to addressing banking stress, rather than waiting for resolution and bail-in regimes to be triggered.[112] If a financial crisis happens, it is likely that national authorities in ASEAN countries will intervene to prop up banks in trouble.[113]

In my view, it is necessary for the ASEAN Member States to consider whether or not there is a need for an appropriate resolution regime for two main reasons. First, ASEAN states do not have the crucial degree of cooperation and coordination in resolution sufficient for coping with a financial crisis. For instance, there is no supranational legal framework ensuring that foreign decisions would be recognised in the Member States. Secondly, a national approach to bank failure utilised by the Member States may raise concern regarding the inequality of treatment of creditors. This issue could obstruct the financial integration agenda of ASEAN.

3.3.1.1 Cooperation and Coordination in Resolution during a Financial Crisis

The Key Attributes of the FSB have become a framework for creating resolution regimes in many countries, including the EU. However, the majority of the ASEAN states are not FSB members. The idea of bank resolution in ASEAN is still in its infancy. ASEAN states can be categorised into two groups: states which have a bank resolution regime, and states which have limited or no formal resolution frameworks and tools. The former group comprises Singapore, Malaysia and Indonesia

[110] Geert Almekinders et al., 'ASEAN Financial Integration' (February 2015) IMF Working Paper, https://www.imf.org/en/Publications/WP/Issues/2016/12/31/ASEAN-Financial-Integration-42727, accessed 4 June 2025.

[111] Moody's, 'Moody's: Asia Pacific Advances Cautiously on Bank Resolution and Bail-in' (24 July 2014), https://www.moodys.com/research/Moodys-Asia-Pacific-advances-cautiously-on-bank-resolution-and-bail--PR_304863, accessed 4 June 2025.

[112] Ibid.

[113] Chen et al. (n 109) 15.

and, arguably, Thailand;[114] the special resolution regimes of Malaysia and Singapore extend beyond their banking sector to the insurance industry. Concerning the latter group, states in this group are Brunei, Cambodia, Lao PDR, Myanmar, the Philippines and Vietnam. They have legal provisions which permit their authorities to assume control of a bank which is in distress.[115] Failing banks in these countries will be either under the control of the official, or liquidated under corporate insolvency law.[116] Bank insolvency regimes of the states in this group still rely on a court-based procedure in order to grant relief.

There are no specific provisions regarding a cross-border bank resolution in ASEAN. Cross-border cooperation will be conducted via home-host supervisory relationships and the establishment of a supervisory college.[117] Nevertheless, the existing cooperation in ASEAN may not be sufficient as recent experience in the EU has shown that a regional approach to financial stability is crucially important in a crisis. For example, an insolvency of a large bank could cause a significant uncertainty to creditors as well as create mistrust in the financial markets. This could lead to a liquidity crisis and collateral shortages as well as fire sales which could, in turn, dampen the financial markets in this sub-region. Utilising the principle of reciprocity and host control over foreign branches might not be sufficient to mitigate systemic risk.

In addition, the European experience has demonstrated that cross-border cooperation was most needed during the financial crisis when conflicting incentives of national interest protection was particularly high. Uncoordinated insolvency regimes may result in the authorities in each country conducting a ring-fencing of assets in order to satisfy the claims of their local creditors. For example, the Thai authorities could ring-fence assets of branches of foreign commercial banks in their territory, as Section 56 of the Deposit Protection Agency Act, B.E. 2551 (2008) (DPA) stipulates that those branches are deemed to be juristic persons

[114] Botes et al. state that Thailand has a separate bank resolution framework. Jacques Botes et al., 'Managing Banking Crises in Emerging Market Economies' (December 2021) FSI Insights on Policy Implementation No. 38, 15.

[115] Andrews (n 266) 477.

[116] Ibid.

[117] Ibid., 484.

under Thai laws.[118] This issue could be exacerbated by the fact that the attitude of ASEAN states has emphasised national interest.[119] Hence, it is possible that the national authorities might use public interest arguments in supporting their action to ring-fence assets.

Diverse Decisions and Non-Recognition of Orders of Foreign Authorities

Another worrying concern relating to the issue of cooperation and coordination is the possibility that national authorities might make inconsistent orders in a cross-border case. Diverse decisions of the courts and administrators in different states could exacerbate a financial crisis. For example, in the case of *Perpetual Trustee Company Limited and others v BNY Corporate Trustee Services*, judges in the UK and the US delivered conflicting decisions regarding substantive insolvency laws.[120] They held differently on the issue of Anti-deprivation rule (ADR).[121] ADR is a principle in insolvency law which prevents property of a bankrupt person from being passed to another person who is not his creditor.[122] In this case, creditors were left with an uncertain situation as to whether or not they could enforce their rights. In the UK, Lord Neuberger MR held that ADR had not been infringed as there was no deprivation of property. There was a mere change of priorities.[123] In addition, Lord Collins

[118] Section 11 of the Deposit Protection Agency Act (No. 2) B.E. 2560 (2017) has added a legal provision regarding the use of the host state rule in a cross-border case to the 2008 Act.

[119] The attitude of protecting national interest can be considered from, for example, the fact that in implementing the ABIF Indonesian government has to prioritise its national interests. Tri Handayani et al., 'Strengthening Indonesian Banking Industry to Comply with ASEAN Banking Integration Framework Concerning Reciprocity and Gap-Reduction Principles' (2018) 5 (2) Padjadjaran Journal of Law.

[120] *Perpetual Trustee Company Limited & another v BNY Corporate Trustee Services Ltd & another* [2009] EWCA Civ 1160.

[121] When the case went up to the UK Supreme Court the name of the case was *Belmont Park Investment Pty v BNY Corporate Trustee Services*.

[122] According to Mellish LJ in *Re Jeavons, ex parte Mackay* [1873] LR 8 Ch App 643, 'a person cannot make it a part of his contract that, in the event of bankruptcy, he is then to get some additional advantage which prevents the property being distributed under the bankruptcy laws'.

[123] Goode has argued on this point that a proposition that a change of priority is not a deprivation is not tenable. The reason is that a loss of priority might reduce or extinguish the party's interest in the asset. Goode (n 351).

was of the view that the contractual provision was freely entered into in good faith. It was not a deliberate evasion of the insolvency legislation.[124] In contrast, in the US, Judge Peck was of the view that the 'flip clause' contravened the US *ipso facto* rule. Hence, it was not saved by the 'safe harbour' provisions.[125]

In the case of ASEAN, there is no supranational legal framework ensuring that decisions of the authorities of other Member States would be recognised. The non-recognition of those decisions in a cross-border case could occur in many ways. First, a national court might not recognise a judicial order of a foreign court regarding a bank with cross-border operation. That is, in part, because conflict-of-law rules in ASEAN differ from jurisdiction to jurisdiction. In addition, there is no ASEAN conflict-of-law rule which is applicable to bank insolvency.[126] As a result of the non-recognition of foreign decision, there might be delays in liquidating a bank with assets in different states.[127]

[124] Roy Goode, 'Flip clauses: the end of the affair?' (2012) 128 Law Quarterly Review 171.

[125] Gabriel Moss, 'Anti-Deprivation, Flip Clauses, Ipso Facto Rules and the Dante Infero' (2017) 30 (2) Insolv. Int., 24.

[126] Malaysia, Brunei and Singapore are common law countries. The common law rules on the recognition and enforcement of foreign judgments in these three jurisdictions are largely derived from the English common law rules. In addition, these three states have similar statutory rules regarding the enforcement and recognition of foreign judgments in civil and commercial cases. The legal provisions in these jurisdictions ensure that judgments from the courts in reciprocating countries are mutually recognised. Nevertheless, the statutory rules do not apply to the winding-up and bankruptcy issues. For example, Section 2 of the Reciprocal Enforcement of Judgments Act 1958 (REJA) of Malaysia explicitly excludes bankruptcy and winding up of companies from the scope of application of the Act. Adeline Chong, Recognition and Enforcement of Foreign Judgments in Asia (Asian Business Law Institute 2017).

[127] There is a recent development regarding the recognition of foreign decision in ASEAN in a landmark decision by the Central Jakarta District Court on 27 July 2021. This case concerns the restructuring of an Indonesian conglomerate, PT. Pan Brothers Tbk. The Singapore High Court has granted the debtor a moratorium under Section 64 of the Insolvency, Restructuring and Dissolution Act 2018. The Singapore moratorium order has 'in personam' nature, which, in effect, makes foreign courts recognise an order of a Singaporean court. Catherine Shen, 'Landmark Indonesian Recognition of Singapore Moratorium' (17 August 2021) LexisPSL, https://www.lexisnexis.co.uk/legal/news/landmark-indonesian-recognition-of-singapore-moratorium-pt-pan-brothers-tbk, accessed 4 June 2025. Decision of the Central Jakarta District Court, dated 27 July 2021, PT Maybank Indonesia Tbk v PT Pan Brothers Tbk.

Secondly, a national court might not recognise a measure taken by a foreign resolution authority, if that measure contradicts its national laws. This issue could be considered from the English case of *Goldman Sachs International v Novo Banco, S.A.*[128] The dispute in this case was whether the Oak liability had been transferred to Novo Banco, a Portuguese bridge bank, despite the fact that Banco de Portugal issued its December decision providing effects to the contrary. The case went to the English High Court before Hamblen J who held that the liabilities were transferred to Novo Banco. Consequently, the English court would have a jurisdiction in accordance with the jurisdiction clause in the Facility Agreement. The judge was of the view that the claim concerned the issue of the repayment of a debt, which could not be determined by the Portuguese administrative court. As a result of the High Court decision, the decision of the home resolution authority would not be recognised and given effect in the UK.

Nevertheless, the Court of Appeal and the UK Supreme Court overturned the decision of the High Court. According to Lord Justice Moore-Bick in the Court of Appeal, the decision of the home Member State regarding reorganisation and winding up of credit institution within the EU should have universal recognition in accordance with the BRRD, the Reorganisation Directive[129] and Regulation 5 of the Credit Institutions (Reorganisation and Winding up) Regulations 2004. Similarly, Lord Sumption in the UK Supreme Court held that Article 3 of the Reorganisation Directive requires reorganisation measures of the home Member State to be applied and given full effect in accordance with the legal provisions and procedures of that Member State. Had this case not been pursued in the higher courts of England and Wales, the fundamental principle of universal recognition underlining reorganisation and winding up of financial institutions in the EU would have been compromised.

Thirdly, national administrators might not recognise measures of their foreign counterparts. Currently, bank resolution and bank insolvency regimes in some ASEAN states do not provide a power for their resolution authority to enforce or recognise foreign resolution measures. Moreover, states which have legal provisions enabling their authority to do so may

128 *Goldman Sachs International v Novo Banco, S.A.* [2015] EWHC 2371 (Comm).

129 European Parliament and Council Directive 2001/24/EC of 4 April 2001 on the reorganisation and winding up of credit institutions [2001] OJ L125/15.

require that some conditions have to be satisfied. For instance, the MAS will only recognise foreign resolution measures if such recognition would not constitute a widespread adverse effect on the financial system or economy of Singapore, discriminate against Singapore creditors or shareholders, be contrary to the national interest or public interest, or have material fiscal implications for Singapore.[130]

3.3.1.2 *Inequality of Treatment of Creditors in Different States*

Different rules and procedures in bank resolution, and insolvency in ASEAN countries could raise a concern regarding the inequality of treatment of creditors in a cross-jurisdictional case for some reasons. First, there is no common criterion in ASEAN regarding the resolution trigger. Therefore, an overseas branch of a bank might be subject to a resolution regime of the host state even though its financial position does not trigger a resolution by the home authority. For example, in Thailand, the BIS ratio is used to measure the trigger points of actions. In the case that a bank's capital falls below 60 per cent of the prescribed ratio in the Financial Institutions Businesses Act (FIBA),[131] the BOT will have a power to take control of the bank in trouble.[132] In this case, a control committee will be appointed by the BOT in order to manage the bank.[133] In addition, if a bank's capital fund is below 35 per cent of the required ratio, the BOT can issue an order to close it.[134] In the case that a bank ceases to operate, its right of claims might be transferred to an asset management company established under the Emergency Decree on Asset Management Company 1998.[135]

[130] In addition, such recognition should not be contrary to any regulations made under Section 126. The MASA 1970, s 94(3). Similarly, according to the FSMA, such recognition should not be contrary to any regulations under Section 135. The FSMA, s 103(3).

[131] The Act has been amended by the Financial Institution Business Act (No. 3), B.E. 2561 (2018).

[132] The FIBA, s 96.

[133] The FIBA, s 102.

[134] The FIBA, s 97.

[135] Jan Putnis, *The Banking Regulation Review* (Law Business Research Ltd 2012), 757. Some commentators are of the view that Thailand also utilises qualitative resolution triggers. According to Botes et al., other intervention grounds are, for example, the bank breaches any licensing condition and its condition or operation may cause damage to the public interest. Botes et al. (n 374) 24. However, in my view, those other intervention

Meanwhile, the resolution triggers in Singapore are based upon both quantitative and qualitative indicators. With respect to quantitative triggers, these indicators are, for example, balance sheet insolvency assessment as well as capital, liquidity and credit indicators. With regards to qualitative indicators, the Singaporean authorities could take into account various concerns (e.g., serious governance issues, risk management, control deficiencies, public or creditor confidence and conduct detrimental to public interest).[136] The combination of both quantitative and qualitative triggers allows the Singaporean authorities a larger discretion than the Thai counterparts regarding a decision to take a resolution action.

Secondly, ASEAN states have created their own approach in order to distinguish financial institutions which should be resolved under their resolution regime from those to be restructured or liquidated by NIPs. For instance, the Indonesian regime utilises the concept of 'systemic banks', in order to determine the applicable approach for restructuring a bank. If the Financial Services Authority and Bank Indonesia determine that a financial institution is a 'systemic bank', the bank could be resolved under the Indonesian resolution regime.[137] Article 1 of the Law on Prevention and Resolution of Financial System Crisis (Number 9 of 2016), defines a 'systemic bank' as follows:

> Banks that, due to the size of its assets, capital and liabilities; its network coverage or complexity of banking services transactions; and its interconnectedness with other financial sector, may trigger the failure of other partial or whole Banks or the financial services sector, either operationally or financially, if it is undergoing disruption of failure.

Meanwhile, in Thailand, Division 5/1 of Bank of Thailand Act (No.7), B.E. 2561 (2018) (BTA of 2018)) sets forth a criterion of 'damage on the economic and monetary system' in determining the applicable approach

grounds should not be considered as a resolution trigger in the strict sense as they are grounds which allow the BOT to use not only a resolution tool but also other measures to cope with the situation of the bank (e.g., remove any or all of its directors and managers, order the bank to reduce its capital and/or increase its capital etc.).

136 IMF, 'Financial Sector Assessment Program: Singapore' (July 2019) IMF Country Report No. 19/2016, 14.

137 Law on Prevention and Resolution of Financial System Crisis (Number 9 of 2016), A. 17(1).

to tackle a bank failure.[138] In the case that the condition or operation of a bank may harm the economic and monetary systems, the BOT has the authority to propose a plan for resolving the bank's problems to the Minister of Finance (MOF).[139] Then, the plan will be submitted to the Cabinet for approval. The approved plan will be implemented by the Financial Institutions Development Fund[140] in accordance with Section 43/2 of the BTA of 2018. As for banks that do not raise any concern regarding the stability of the economic and monetary systems, they shall be rehabilitated in accordance with Section 90 of the FIBA.

Nevertheless, in my view, it cannot be assumed that 'systemic banks' according to Indonesian law would be the same as banks which could cause 'damage on the economic and monetary system' under Thai law. If these criteria are not applied consistently across countries, creditors of the bank in different jurisdictions might not be treated on the same legal footing. For example, a bank with cross-border operation in one jurisdiction might be resolved under a resolution regime while its offices in another country might be rehabilitated or liquidated in accordance with the NIPs of that state.

In order to guarantee equal treatment before the law for creditors in a cross-jurisdictional case, ASEAN would need a bank resolution regime which provides common criteria for the resolution trigger and identification of systemic banks. In addition, it is important to ensure that those standards are applied consistently throughout the sub-region. A mere creation of guidelines and rules for the national authorities to follow might not be adequate, as rules are always subject to interpretation by those utilising them. Instead, ASEAN might consider centralising decision-making powers as in the case of the EU. In the Banking Union, discrepancies regarding the assessment of the resolution trigger

138 Teeranuntaraporn has argued that the legal provisions in Division 5/1 of Bank of Thailand Act (No.7), B.E. 2561 (2018) might have created a bank resolution regime. Puchong Teeranuntaraporn, 'Dose Thailand Has Bankruptcy Process for Financial Institution?' (2020) 9(2) Ramkhamhaeng Law Journal, 84 (*in Thai*). The 2018 Act has amended the Bank of Thailand Act 2008.

139 The BTA, s 43/1.

140 The Fund is established in the BOT.

(i.e., FOLTF) have been minimised by giving the ECB the authority to conduct it.[141]

After the ECB declares a bank FOLTF, the SRB will assess whether the bank satisfies all the remaining criteria regarding the triggering of resolution. Under the BRRD and SRMR regime, the presence of critical functions is key in determining whether a credit institution would be resolved under the resolution regime or liquidated by the NIPs.[142] According to Article 2(1)(35) of the BRRD I, critical functions are[143]:

> activities, services or operations the discontinuance of which is likely in one or more Member States, to lead to the disruption of services that are essential to the real economy or to disrupt financial stability due to the size, market share, external and internal interconnectedness, complexity or cross-border activities of an institution or group, with particular regard to the substitutability of those activities, services or operations.

However, it is unclear regarding which authority should make a decision about what are the critical functions of a bank for the purposes of the BRRD. On the one hand, banks conduct a self-assessment for their critical functions. The results of such assessment are included in the Recovery Plans, which are under the purview of the ECB. On the other hand, the SRB has conducted its own assessment of critical functions of banks. The SRB has developed a common approach for the assessment by creating

141 Article 18(1) of SRMR I states that the SRB may make a FOLTF assessment only if it has informed the ECB, and the ECB does not make such an assessment within 3 calendar days of receipt of that information. This power of the ECB has recently been announced by the CJEU in joined Cases C-551/19 P and C-552/19P. C-551/19 P *ABLV Bank AS and Others v European Central Bank* and C-552/19 P *Cassandra Holding Company SIA v European Central Bank* (CJEU, 6 May 2021), https://www.bailii.org/cgi-bin/format.cgi?doc=/eu/cases/EUECJ/2021/C55119P.html&query, 19 April 2023. According to the CJEU, the ECB's FOLTF assessments do not have a legal binding effect. The SRB still has the last word regarding whether or not to adopt a resolution regime. Hence, this ECB's power cannot be subject to a judicial review under Article 263 of the TFEU.

142 Single Resolution Board, 'Critical Functions: SRB Approach in 2017 and Next Steps', 10, https://srb.europa.eu/sites/default/files/critical_functions_final.pdf, accessed 4 June 2025.

143 Recital 114 of the BRRD I states that the Commission should be delegated the power to stipulate the criteria for determining critical functions in accordance with the Directive. Those criteria could be found in the Commission Delegated Regulation (EU) 2016/778.

the Critical Functions Template. The Template specifies five economic functions in accordance with the FSB assessment, in order to increase consistency in the identification of critical functions. These functions are (1) deposit taking; (2) lending; (3) payment, cash, settlement, clearing and custody (PCSCC) services; (4) capital markets; and (5) wholesale funding.[144] An assessment of critical functions is based on two main analyses: (1) impact on the real economy and financial stability; and (2) substitutability of critical functions.[145]

In addition, the issue concerning the inequality of treatment of creditors in resolution and insolvency is not completely eliminated in the Banking Union. That is, in part, because the harmonisation of rules and centralisation of decision-making powers are incomplete. The EU has created a two-tier framework for bank resolution and insolvency. The former is regulated by the BRRD while the latter is still governed by national insolvency laws. Recital 49 of the BRRD has made it explicit that NIPs are a default option in order to deal with bank failures. In other words, resolution tools could only be applied in limited circumstances where normal insolvency proceedings would cause a destabilisation of the financial system. Moreover, resolution measures must be necessary for the continuation of systemically important functions, and there is no other private solution available.

The inequality of treatment of creditors when failed banks are liquidated could be considered from the case of Banca Popolare di Vicenza[146]

[144] Financial Stability Board, 'Recovery and Resolution Planning for Systemically Important Financial Institutions: Guidance on Identification of Critical Functions and Critical Shared Services (July 2013), https://www.fsb.org/wp-content/uploads/r_130716a.pdf?page_moved=1, accessed 4 June 2025.

[145] SRB (n 402) 3.

[146] Banca Popolare di Vicenz is a small Italian commercial bank. 'As of 31 December 2016, Banca Popolare di Vicenza had around 500 branches and a market share in Italy of around 1% in terms of deposits and around 1.5% in terms of loans'. The bank had slightly below 35 billion euros of total assets. European Commission, 'State Aid: Commission Approves Aid for Market Exit of Banca Populare di Vicenza and Veneto Banca under Italian Insolvency Law, Involving Sale of Some Parts to Intesa Sanpaolo' (*Press Release*, 25 June 2017), https://www.europeansources.info/record/state-aid-commission-approves-aid-for-market-exit-of-banca-popolare-di-vicenza-and-veneto-banca-under-italian-insolvency-law-involving-sale-of-some-parts-to-intesa-sanpaolo/, accessed 4 June 2025.

and Veneto Banka.[147] The SRB concluded that a resolution action regarding these two banks was not necessarily in the public interest; these institutions did not carry out critical functions.[148] Consequently, the banks were broken up under an emergency decree of the Italian government.[149] The exclusion of these banks from the scope of the resolution regime, in effect, resulted in a leeway for Italy to escape the state aid control.

The objective of the state aid regime under Article 107 of the TFEU is to avoid the distortion of competition in the internal market.[150] However, an exceptional rule in Article 107(3)(b) was applied to Banca Populare di Vicenza and Veneto Banca. Article 107(3)(b) allows an aid which is to 'remedy a serious disturbance in the economy of a Member State'. As a consequence of this exception, the Italian banks were liquidated under a special liquidation procedure by means of a partial sale to Intesa Sanpaolo instead of a standard liquidation procedure.[151] Italy paid at least 5 billion euros to Intesa Sanpaolo, for it to take the best assets of Banca Populare di Vicenza and Veneto Banka.[152] The Italian government stated that the measures were necessary in order to prevent an economic disruption in the region of Veneto.[153] Eventually, the liquidation of these banks has

147 Veneto Banca is a small Italian commercial bank. 'As of 31 December 2016, Veneto Banca had around 400 branches and a market share in Italy of around 1% in terms of deposits and in terms of loans'. The bank had 28 billion euros of total assets. Ibid.

148 SRB, *Banca Popolare di Vicenza S.p.A.* (*Decision*, 23 June 2017) and *Veneto Banca S.p.A.* (*Decision*, 23 June 2017).

149 According to Binder, there was a sale of 'parts of their business to a competitor and the transfer of the unviable parts to a 'bad bank', and a generous compensation for those private investors who had purchased subordinated debt instruments issued by both banks'. Binder (n 297) 469–470.

150 As the European commission has clarified, financial stability is the overall goal in its assessment on state aid. European Commission, 'State Aid: Commission Adapts Crisis Rules for Banks' (*Press Release*, 10 July 2013), 2, https://ec.europa.eu/commission/presscorner/detail/en/IP_13_672, accessed 4 June 2025.

151 The special Decree of the Ministry of Economy and Finance No. 237/2016 (December 2016) and Act No. 15/2017 stipulate a special procedure which was used in this case. Aleksander Kowalski, 'Ethical Aspects of Bank Resolution' (2017) Ethics & Trust in Finance Global Edition 2018–1019, 152, http://www.obsfin.ch/wp-content/uploads/Document/2019-Gl-Kowalski.pdf, access 19 April 2023.

152 John O'Donnell, 'Italy Bank Rescue Divides Europe' *Reuters* (Frankfurt, 26 June 2017).

153 European Commission (n 406).

resulted in the irony that senior creditors were better off under the liquidation regime than they would have been in resolution. In other words, the measures effectively amounted to bailing out domestic lenders, which did not meet the public interest test.

Another important case which highlights the issue of inequality of treatment of creditors in a cross-border case is ABLV Bank. The parent entity in Latvia (ABLV Bank, AS) and its subsidiary in Luxembourg (ABLV Bank Luxembourg, SA) were declared FOLTF by the ECB. However, the SRB decided that their functions (e.g., deposit-taking) were not critical. In its Decisions, the SRB states that the discontinuance of those functions was not likely to lead to a financial instability in any Member State as their clients were mainly from non-EU countries.[154] Therefore, the SRB would not take a resolution action at the EU level.

Nevertheless, different national insolvency law frameworks in Luxembourg and Latvia have resulted in two conflicting decisions. The Luxembourg Commercial Court delivered an inconsistent decision with the ECB, the SRB and the national resolution authority that the subsidiary was not insolvent due to its strong financial standing.[155] Hence, the Luxembourg entity was to be sold to new investors while its parent entity in Latvia was subject to liquidation proceedings. Underlying the Luxembourg Court reasoning was the fact that national insolvency laws normally require present and actual illiquidity in order to liquidate an entity. This is in contrast to the FOLTF assessment under the BRRD/SRMR regime, which takes into account both present and future illiquidity.[156]

[154] Single Resolution Board, 'Decision of the Single Resolution Board of 23 February 2018 concerning the assessment of the conditions for resolution in respect of ABLV Bank, AS' (SRB/EES/2018/09). Single Resolution Board, 'Decision of the Single Resolution Board of 23 February 2018 concerning the assessment of the conditions for resolution in respect of ABLV Bank Luxembourg S.A.' (SRB/EES/2018/10).

[155] Dalvinder Singh, *European Cross-border Banking and Banking Supervision* (Oxford University Press 2020), 179.

[156] European Central Bank, Letter to Mr. Sven Giegold (Frankfurt, 3 May 2018), https://www.bankingsupervision.europa.eu/ecb/pub/pdf/ssm.mepletter180503_giegold.en.pdf, accessed 4 June 2025.

3.4 Conclusion

Cross-border banking could yield many benefits to the economy. Nevertheless, it could also increase the likelihood of systemic risk, which would, in turn, have adverse effects upon the economy. The promotion of financial integration in ASEAN raises concerns with respect to systemic risk and the readiness of ASEAN in coping with a financial crisis. In this chapter, I argue that ASEAN should consider building up measures which would help mitigate systemic risk, and ensure that the financial markets in this region are resilient. Bank resolution is one of those measures. In my view, ASEAN needs to centralise rules and decision-making power, as well as increase cooperation and coordination among the authorities dealing with the issue of bank failure. The experience of other countries and regions could provide some guidance in designing a bank resolution regime. For instance, ASEAN could learn from Europe's experience which has demonstrated some weaknesses in utilising resolution measures.

References

Almekinders G. et al., 'ASEAN Financial Integration' IMF Working Paper (February 2015)

Andres J-M et al, 'Optimizing the Banking Union: Proposals for Member States to Benefit from Private Risk Sharing within the Banking Union'

Andrews M, 'Effective Resolution Regimes for Financial Institutions in ASEAN + 3', in Iwan J Azis and Hyun S Shim (eds), *Global Shock, Risks and Asian Financial Reform* (Edward Elgar 2014)

Bank of England, 'The Bank of England's approach to resolution' (October 2017)

Binder J, 'Cross-border coordination of bank resolution in the EU: All problems resolved?', in Matthias Haentjens (ed), *Research Handbook on Cross-Border Bank Resolution* (Edgar Elgar 2019)

Binder J., 'Proportionality at the Resolution Stage: Calibration of Resolution Measures and the Public Interest Test' (2020) 21 European Business Organization Law Review

Bolton P. and Oehmke M., 'Bank Resolution and the Structure of Global Banks' (2018) Paul Wooley Centre Working Paper No. 59

Botes J. et al., 'Managing Banking Crises in Emerging Market Economies' (December 2021) FSI Insights on Policy Implementation No. 38

Buckingham S. et al., 'Study on the Differences between Bank Insolvency Laws and on Their Potential Harmonization: Final Report', Country Report: Spain (2019)

Chen V. et al., 'Cross-border Cooperation in Bank Resolution: A Framework for Asia' (2016) Singapore Journal of Legal Studies 1–28
Chong A, Recognition and Enforcement of Foreign Judgments in Asia (Asian Business Law Institute 2017)
Chong L., 'Legal Issues of Cross-border Bank Resolution in the EU Context: The Desirability and Feasibility of Having an EU Cross-border Bank Resolution Framework' (LLM. Thesis, Ghent University 2012)
Collins H., 'Flipping Wreck: Lex Mercatoria on Shoals of Ius Cogens', in Grundmann S. et al. (eds), Contract Governance: Dimensions in Law and Interdisciplinary Research (Oxford University Press 2015).
Corbacho A. and Peiris S. (eds), *The ASEAN Way: Sustaining Growth and Stability* (International Monetary Fund 2018)
Dell'Ariccia G. et al., 'Trade-offs in Bank Resolution' (February 2018) IMF Staff Discussion Note
De Grone W., 'Valuation Reports in the Context of Banking Resolution: What Are the Challenges?' (2018)
de Seriere V.P.G. and van der Houwen D.M., ''No Creditor Worse Off' in Case of Bank Resolution: Food for Litigation?' (2016) 31(7) Journal of International Banking Law and Regulation
EBA, 'Final Report: Draft Regulatory Technical Standards on the Contractual Recognition of Stay Powers under Article 71a(5) of Directive 2014/59/EU' (16 December 2020)
Enria A., 'Fragmentation in Banking Markets: Crisis Legacy and the Challenge of Brexit', 'Speech' (BCBS-FSI High Level Meeting for Europe on Banking Supervision, 17 September 2018)
European Banking Authority, 'Handbook on Valuation for Purposes of Resolution' (22 February 2019)
European Central Bank, Letter to Mr. Sven Giegold (Frankfurt, 3 May 2018)
European Commission, 'State Aid: Commission Adapts Crisis Rules for Banks' (*Press Release*, 10 July 2013)
European Commission, 'State Aid: Commission Approves Aid for Market Exit of Banca Populare di Vicenza and Veneto Banca under Italian Insolvency Law, Involving Sale of Some Parts to Intesa Sanpaolo' (*Press Release*, 25 June 2017)
Financial Stability Board, 'Cross-border Recognition of Resolution Action' Consultative Document (29 September 2004)
Financial Stability Board, 'Key Attributes of Effective Resolution Regimes for Financial Institutions: Revised Version' (25 April 2024)
Financial Stability Board, 'Recovery and Resolution Planning for Systemically Important Financial Institutions: Guidance on Identification of Critical Functions and Critical Shared Services (July 2013)
Finch V. and Milman D., *Corporate Insolvency Law: Perspectives and Principles* (Cambridge University Press 2017)

Gardella A., 'Bail-in and the Two Dimensions of Burden-sharing,' in From Monetary Union to Banking Union, on the Way to Captial Markets Union: New Opportunities for European Integration, ECB Legal Conference 2015 (1–2 September 2015)
Georgosouli A., 'Regulatory Incentive Realignment and the EU Legal Framework of Bank Resolution' (2016) 10 Brook. J. Corp. Fin. & Com. L.
Goode R., 'Flip clauses: the end of the affair?' (2012) 128 Law Quarterly Review 171
Goode R., Perpetual Trustee and Flip Clauses in Swap Transactions (2011) 127 Law Quarterly Review 1
Gordon G., 'Slapped in the Face by the Invisible Hand: Banking and the Panic of 2007' (2009) SSRN Paper
Gordon J. and Ringe W., 'Bank Resolution in the European Banking Union: A Transatlantic Perspective on What It Would Take' (2015) 115 Columbia Law Review
Hadjiemmanuil C, 'Bank Stakeholders' Mandatory Contribution to Resolution Financing: Principle and Ambiguities of Bail-in' in From Monetary Union to Banking Union, on the way to Captial Markets Union: New Opportunities for European Integration, ECB Legal Conference 2015 (1–2 September 2015)
Handayani T. et al., 'Strengthening Indonesian Banking Industry to Comply with ASEAN Banking Integration Framework Concerning Reciprocity and Gap-Reduction Principles' (2018) 5 (2) Padjadjaran Journal of Law
Huser A. et al., 'The Systemic Implications of Bail-in: A Multi-Layered Network Approach' (2017) European Central Bank Working Paper Series No. 2010/ February 2017
IMF, 'Financial Sector Assessment Program: Singapore' (July 2019) IMF Country Report No. 19/2016
ISDA, 'BRRD II Omnibus Jurisdictional Module – FAQs'
ISDA, 'ISDA Resolution Stay Jurisdictional Modular Protocol' (3 May 2016)
ISDA, 'ISDA Resolution Stay Jurisdictional Modular Protocol BRRD II Omnibus Jurisdictional Module' (14 September 2021)
ISDA, 'ISDA Resolution Stay Jurisdictional Modular Protocol 2020 UK (PRA Rule) Jurisdictional Module' (22 December 2020)
ISDA, 'ISDA 2015 Universal Stay Protocol' (4 November 2015)
Kleinheisterkamp J., 'Overriding Mandatory Laws in International Arbitration' (2018) I.C.L.Q. 67(4)
Kowalski A., 'Ethical Aspects of Bank Resolution' (2017) Ethics & Trust in Finance Global Edition 2018–1019
Lastra R, 'Northern Rock and Banking Law Reform in the UK', in Franco Bruni and David T. Llewellyn (eds), The Failure of Northern Rock: A Multi-dimensional Case Study (January 2009)

Lehmann M., 'Bail-in and Private International Law: How to Make Bank Resolution Measures Effective Across Borders' (2017) 66 (1) International & Comparative Law Quarterly

Lintner P., 'De/centralized Decision making Under the European Resolution Framework: Does Meroni Hamper the Creation of a European Resolution Authority?' (2017) 18 Eur Bus Org Law Rev (2017) 591

Lupo-Pasini F., The Logic of Financial Nationalism: The Challenges of Corporation and the Role of International Law (Cambridge University Press 2017)

Lupo-Pasini F. and Buckley R., 'International Coordination in Cross-Border Bank Bail-ins: Problems and Prospects' (2015) 16 (2) European Business Organization Law Review

Mahakhun W., *A Commentary on Insolvency and Business Rehabilitation Law* (Nitibannakarn Publishing 2016)

Malvagna U. and Alibrandi A., 'Misselling in Self-Placement and Bank Resolution under BRRD2' (2020) 17(5) European Company and Financial Law Review

Miskova M. and Orszaghova L., 'MREL: Gone Concern Loss Absorbing Capacity' (2015) Banking Regulation

Moody's, 'Moody's: Asia Pacific Advances Cautiously on Bank Resolution and Bail-in' (24 July 2014)

Moss G., 'Anti-Deprivation, Flip Clauses, Ipso Facto Rules and the Dante Infero' (2017) 30 (2) Insolv. Int. 24

Myles D., 'TLAC's Toll' (2016) 35 Int'l Fin. L. Rev. 24

Putnis J., *The Banking Regulation Review* (Law Business Research Ltd 2012)

PWC, 'Successfully Addressing Stay Regulations' (March 2015) RRP Viewpoint

Remolona E and Shim I, 'The Rise of Regional Banking in Asia and the Pacific' (September 2015) BIS Quarterly Review

Schoenmaker D., 'A Macro Approach to International Bank Resolution' (2017) Working Paper Series No. 56/ November 2017

Shen C., 'Landmark Indonesian Recognition of Singapore Moratorium' (17 August 2021) LexisPSL

Singh D., *European Cross-border Banking and Banking Supervision* (Oxford University Press 2020)

Single Resolution Board, 'Critical Functions: SRB Approach in 2017 and Next Steps'

Single Resolution Board, 'Decision of the Single Resolution Board in Its Executive Session of 23 June 2017, Concerning the Assessment of the Conditions for Resolution in Respect of Veneto Banca S.p.A.' (2017)

Single Resolution Board, 'Decision of the Single Resolution Board in its Executive Session of 23 June 2017, Concerning the Assessment of the Conditions for Resolution in Respect of Banca Popolare di Vicenza S.p.A.' (2017)

Single Resolution Board, 'Decision of the Single Resolution Board of 23 February 2018 concerning the assessment of the conditions for resolution in respect of ABLV Bank, AS' (SRB/EES/2018/09)
Single Resolution Board, 'Decision of the Single Resolution Board of 23 February 2018 concerning the assessment of the conditions for resolution in respect of ABLV Bank Luxembourg S.A.' (SRB/EES/2018/10)
Single Resolution Board, 'Framework for Valuation: Q&A
Single Resolution Board, 'Resolution Q & A'
Teeranuntaraporn P., 'Dose Thailand Has Bankruptcy Process for Financial Institution?' (2020) 9(2) Ramkhamhaeng Law Journal
Troger T, 'Why MREL Won't Help Much' (2018) SAFE Working Paper No 180
United Nations, UNCITRAL Model Law on Cross-Border Insolvency with Guide to Enactment and Interpretation (New York 2014)
Valiante D., 'Harmonising Insolvency Laws in the Euro Area: Rationale, Stock-taking and Challenges. What Role for the Eurogroup?' (2016)
Wihlborg C., 'Bail-ins: Issues of Credibility and Contagion' (January 2017) SUERF Policy Note Issue No. 10

Cases

Cases C-551/19 P and C-552/19P. C-551/19 P ABLV Bank AS and Others v European Central Bank and C-552/19 P Cassandra Holding Company SIA v European Central Bank (CJEU, 6 May 2021)
Decision of the Central Jakarta District Court, dated 27 July 2021, PT Maybank Indonesia Tbk v PT Pan Brothers Tbk
Goldman Sachs International v Novo Banco, S.A. [2015] EWHC 2371 (Comm)
Lehman Brothers Special Financing Inc. v. (1) National Power Corp; (2) Power Sector Assets and Liabilities Management Corp [2018] EWHC 487 (Comm)
Lomas v JFB Firth Rixon [2012] EWCA Civ 419
Perpetual Trustee Company Limited & another v BNY Corporate Trustee Services Ltd & another [2009] EWCA Civ 1160
Re Jeavons, ex parte Mackay [1873] LR 8 Ch App 643

CHAPTER 4

Cogs in the Wheel—Deposit Insurance Systems in ASEAN

4.1 Introduction

International agencies and standard setters have advocated that an explicit, limited insurance scheme is one of the important mechanisms in the financial system safety net which helps to alleviate systemic risk. Other components of the safety net are prudential regulation and supervision, bank resolution and the LOLR. Nevertheless, deposit insurance alone is not capable of coping with a systemic crisis or a significant bank failure. Instead, it has to operate with other safety-net participants in order to mitigate the effects of a crisis. The performance of the financial system safety net as a whole would increase, if the powers and mandate of the deposit insurance are seamlessly aligned with those of other safety-net components.

Currently, explicit deposit insurance systems (DISs) have been utilised by many counties around the world, including the majority of ASEAN countries. Those schemes have to be well-designed, effectively implemented and adequately understood by the public to be able to function properly and minimise moral hazard. In the case of ASEAN, the attributes of DISs vary from country to country. I argue that the increase in financial and banking integration in this sub-region warrants a consideration

© The Author(s), under exclusive license to Springer Nature Singapore Pte Ltd. 2025

W. Kun-amornpong, *The Financial Trilemma and Cross-border Bank Crisis Management in ASEAN*,
https://doi.org/10.1007/978-981-95-0512-8_4

for harmonising and improving those deposit insurance schemes in order to withstand the next crisis. In doing so, experiences of governance networks, international organisations, the EU and other countries could help shed some light on possible considerations for designing DISs in ASEAN.

This chapter proceeds in two parts. Part I will provide an overview regarding the relationship between 'the financial trilemma' thesis and deposit insurance. In addition, the context of ASEAN—which has raised some concerns regarding the need to harmonise DISs in this sub-region—will be explored. In Part II, I will discuss the issues about the designs and effects of deposit insurance, from the perspective of soft and hard law approaches. I will argue that the effects of deposit insurance regimes, which have utilised these two approaches, might not be significantly different, despite their dissimilar legal forms. The chapter will conclude by describing necessary considerations in designing and improving DISs in ASEAN.

4.2 Part I: Financial Trilemma and the Need for a Harmonisation of Deposit Insurance Schemes

According to the financial trilemma thesis, increasing cross-border banking and financial integration in ASEAN with a high degree of the utilisation of national approach could jeopardise financial stability in this sub-region. Deposit insurance, which is one of the vital mechanisms of the financial system safety net, has a pertinent role to play in maintaining financial stability. Nonetheless, not all ASEAN Member States have set up an explicit DIS. In addition, a deposit insurance scheme in some countries might not be well-designed to minimise systemic risk, as well as support cross-border cooperation and coordination in a crisis. These concerns, as well as the relationship between financial stability and deposit insurance, will be elaborated in this part.

4.2.1 *Financial Stability and Deposit Insurance*

In the history of banking crises, the beginning of many financial instabilities has been marked by depositor runs on banks (e.g., Venezuela in 1993 and Argentina in 2001).[1] Commercial banks are prone to liquidity risks, because they conduct a business of maturity transformation. In other words, banks borrow short in the forms of savings and demand deposits, which could be withdrawn at short notice. Meanwhile, they lend at longer maturities by creating loans.[2] The liquidity risks are likely to increase markedly in the case that there is a bank run in a financial crisis (e.g., the Northern Rock saga in 2007). As LaBrosse and Mayes explain, the rate of time preference of depositors would be altered when they lose a

[1] According to Reinhart and Rogoff, banking problems often caused by the deterioration of the quality of assets, which stems from either a price collapse of real estates or a significant rise in insolvencies manifested from the non-financial sector (e.g., non-performing loans). Carmen M. Reinhart and Kenneth S. Rogoff, *This Time is Different: Eight Centuries of Financial Folly* (Princeton University Press 2009), 9. In addition, the recent bank failures in the US (i.e., Silicone Valley Bank and Signature Bank) have demonstrated that the uninsured depositors' incentives to run on their banks are still present. Marco Cipriani et al., 'Mitigating the Risk of Runs on Uninsured Deposits: the Minimum Balance at Risk' (*Liberty Street Economics*, 14 April 2023), https://libertystreeteconomics.newyorkfed.org/2023/04/mitigating-the-risk-of-runs-on-uninsured-deposits-the-minimum-balance-at-risk/, accessed 4 June 2025.

[2] In the modern economy, commercial banks create the majority of money in society by lending money to households and businesses. In making a loan, a commercial bank will create an equivalent amount of money in the form of deposit to the account of the borrower. There are only exceptional circumstances when the central bank creates new money. The Bank of England will only do so when it cannot lower the interest rates as they are at the effective lower bound. In these circumstances, the Bank may decide to use 'Quantitative Easing' (QE) in order to boost the amount of money directly. The Bank will buy financial instruments held by non-financial institutions (e.g., government bonds) and inject money into the economy by requesting commercial banks to create deposits into the accounts of those non-financial institutions. Deposits account for a large portion of total amount of money in circulation. For example, in the UK notes and coins account for only three per cent, while bank deposits make up ninety-seven per cent of the total amount of money in circulation. Michael McLeay et.al., 'Money Creation in the Modern Economy' (Q1 2014) Bank of England Quarterly Bulletin, https://www.bankofengland.co.uk/quarterly-bulletin/2014/q1/money-creation-in-the-modern-economy, accessed 4 June 2025.

confidence in their banks. They would rush for more secure assets; therefore, there would be a downward spiral of asset prices and circle of debt inflation.[3]

Withdrawing deposits is the low-cost option for depositors in response to their fears about the financial status of their banks.[4] According to Payne, the inherent problems of information asymmetry and coordination costs have resulted in depositor behaviour of running on their banks.[5] As for the issue of information asymmetry, the ability of depositors to consider a bank's assets are limited, since these assets are opaque. In addition, providing more information to depositors would not solve this problem, since it is still costly for them to monitor the performance of their banks.[6] With regard to coordination costs, depositors are a large group of individuals; therefore, forming a collective response to the bank's problems could be a challenging task.[7]

[3] John Raymond LaBrosse and David G. Mayes, 'Promoting Financial Stability through Effective Depositor Protection: The Case for Explicit Limited Deposit Insurance' in Andrew Campbell and others (eds), ***Deposit Insurance*** (Palgrave Macmillan 2007), 2.

[4] Jennifer Payne, 'The Reform of Deposit Guarantee Schemes in Europe' (2015) 12 ECFR 539, 542. Deposits are not risk-free investment. Unlike a 'proprietary claim' of an investor against his or her investment company, bank deposits are 'debt claims'. According to Foley v Hill (1848), banks are debtors while their depositors are creditors. In other words, a depositor has an 'unsecured contractual personal claim against the bank' which 'does not attach to the proceeds of the deposit itself'. This legal position of a depositor could be troublesome in the case that his/her commercial bank faces an insolvency problem. That is because a depositor as an unsecured creditor would occupy a low rank in the hierarchy of claims. In the event of insolvency, a depositor was likely to receive nothing. Nevertheless, most bank depositors might not be aware of their legal relationship with their banks. They might consider that their banks look after their savings. Nikoletta Kleftouri, 'Meeting the Rationale of Deposit Protection System' (2014) 22(4) Journal of Financial Regulation and Compliance 300, 302–304.

[5] Payne (n 420).

[6] Eugene White, 'Deposit Insurance' (1995) Policy Research Working Paper 1541, https://elibrary.worldbank.org/doi/abs/10.1596/1813-9450-1541, accessed 4 June 2025. In addition, depositors could not rely on fund managers or other institutional investors to conduct the monitoring. Institutional investors, who are rationally apathetic as other shareholders, might not actively monitor the managers of the firms. They might consider that the cost of active monitoring of financial institutions would outweigh the opportunity cost and benefits gained from so doing. The exception may be that of hedge fund managers, who have strong incentive to be active as their compensation is tied to the performance of financial institutions (typically 20 per cent of any value generated above the benchmark).

[7] Payne (n 420) 542.

In the case that there are many credit institutions which encounter bank runs, they might not be able to borrow from other private banks. This scenario could be considered from the US experience, during the subprime crisis in 2007, when financial institutions lost trust in their counterparts.[8] In such circumstances, deposit insurance could help maintain financial stability by ensuring depositors would not lose some or all of their savings.[9] This utility of deposit insurance has been famously elaborated by Diamond and Dybvig's model.

According to Diamond and Dybvig, deposit insurance provided by the government could produce superior contracts to an agreement which could suspend the convertibility of deposits to currency.[10] Deposit insurance can eliminate bank runs, while still allowing banks to transform assets.[11] In addition, unlike an insurance provided by a private insurance company, the governmental deposit insurance is not constrained by its reserves in the scale of unconditional guarantees. This view is also supported by Anginer et al's (2014) study of the effects of deposit insurance on bank risk and systemic fragility, prior to and during the GFC.

[8] Reinhart and Rogoff (n 417) 144–145. The Global financial crisis did not originate from the classic depositor run at their banks. It was caused by a 'financial institution run' when financial institutions did not trust each other. They decided not to roll over their short-term debts. As a result, many financial institutions had to sell their assets at fire sale prices. This inevitably exacerbated the situation.

[9] The legal nature of a deposit insurance is a 'guarantee' that a bank receives from the state. The latter will undertake the obligations of the former in the case that the former defaults on its debts. Moreover, the latter will subrogate for the rights of depositors regarding claims against the bank. Payne (n 420) 541. A contract of guarantee differs from an insurance agreement in some respects. For example, the liability of the surety of a guarantee contract is a secondary obligation to that of the principal. In other words, the liability of the guarantor arises only if and when the principal defaults. Joanna Benjamin, *Financial Law* (Oxford University Press 2007), 52. Meanwhile, an insurance contract is a tool of risk mitigation that the insurer has a primary obligation, which does not depend on a default on the part of the policyholder. According to case law, there are two types of an insurance contract: indemnity insurance and contingency insurance. The former provides an indemnity for the insured loss while the latter pays a sum, which is determined by the contractual terms, on a contingent event. Benjamin (n 425) 58.

[10] Douglas W. Diamond and Philip H. Dybvig, 'Bank Runs, Deposit Insurance, and Liquidity' (1983) 91(3) Journal of Political Economy 401.

[11] Ibid., 404.

Anginer et al. find that 'generous' financial safety nets have a stabilisation effect during the crisis, which results in lower bank risk and greater systemic stability in countries where a deposit insurance coverage exists.[12]

However, deposit insurance has a major downside, in that its existence could also generate a destabilisation effect due to moral hazard. The research result conducted by Anginer et al. in the same study highlights that generous financial safety nets accelerate bank risk and systemic fragility in the years prior to the crisis. They conclude that the destabilisation effect due to moral hazard was greater than the stabilisation effect during the crisis. In the case of ASEAN, the research results of a study by Suhal Kusairi et al. demonstrate that deposit insurance policy in ASEAN countries has a negative effect, in that bank managers are likely to take a higher risk in order to enhance their returns and make up for the cost of deposit insurance. This adverse effect outweighs the improved level of confidence of depositors, which would, in turn, increase the total deposit. Besides this, the research concludes that deposit insurance policy indirectly escalates the risk of moral hazard in the banking industry.[13]

Meanwhile, a recent study by Abu Hanifa Md Noman et al. (2022) has further explored the relationship between the existence of an explicit deposit insurance scheme and bank risk-taking in ASEAN-5 states, by investigating the mediating role of competition during economic crises. The results show that Thai banks are subject to the highest level of competition, while Singaporean banking institutions encounter the lowest competition among banks in ASEAN-5 countries. Moreover, their findings highlight that in the absence of competition, deposit insurance does reduce both credit and insolvency risks of banks.

In contrast, in a highly competitive market, deposit insurance increases bank risk as well as weakens bank stability.[14] In other words, the effect of moral hazard exceeds that of bank stability in a highly competitive market. According to Abu Hanifa Md Noman et al., this result could be explained by the fact that competition may influence the increase in the

[12] Deniz Anginer et al., 'How Does Deposit Insurance Affect Bank Risk? Evidence from the Recent Crisis' (2014) 48 Journal of Banking and Finance 312.

[13] Suhal Kusairi et al., 'Impact of Deposit Insurance on Banking Industry of ASEAN Countries: In Quest of Stability' (2015) 10(4) Banks and Bank Systems, 49.

[14] Abu Hanifa Md. Noman et al., 'The Mediating Role of Competition on Deposit Insurance and the Risk-taking of Banks in ASEAN Countries' (2022) 59 Research in International Business and Finance 59, 1.

level of loan interest rate, which is adjusted in order to maintain interest rate spread, as well as to compensate for the cost of deposit insurance premium.[15] Nonetheless, deposit insurance diminishes instability in the banking system of a competitive market during a financial crisis.[16]

Despite the complexity of the interplay between deposit insurance, moral hazard, and financial stability, I argue that the benefits of deposit insurance in maintaining financial stability could outweigh its moral hazard downside for two main reasons.[17] First, legal and institutional infrastructures and arrangements could help mitigate the adverse impacts of moral hazard and systemic risk. Secondly, an explicit deposit insurance could minimise the risk-taking of banks by limiting a de facto scope of implicit insurance and blanket guarantee. As a consequence, moral hazard of credit institutions would be lowered.

4.2.1.1 Mitigating the Moral Hazard by Utilising Legal and Institutional Infrastructures and Arrangements

Concerning the first argument, some research studies have shown that legal and institutional infrastructures and arrangements could help alleviate the risk of moral hazard associated with deposit insurance. For instance, according to Anginer et al., deposit insurance has not resulted in a significant negative impact in non-crises years, in the case that the quality of bank supervision is high.[18] In addition, Demirguc-Kunt and Detragiache find that deposit insurance may not increase bank instability in countries where there is a strong institutional setting (i.e., regulatory and legal environment). They argue that the results were due to the fact that regulators in these countries can negate the moral

[15] Ibid., 13.

[16] Ibid., 1.

[17] Deposit insurance enables credit institutions to provide greater liquidity transformation which has a desirable welfare-enhancing effect. As Franklin Allen et al. have argued, banks might generate too little liquidity when facing the risk of bank run. Thus, the reduction of a run risk by deposit insurance might induce financial institutions to expand the scope of liquidity transformation activities. Franklin Allen et al., 'Government Guarantees and Financial Stability' (2017) ECB Working Paper 2032, 4, https://www.ecb.europa.eu/pub/pdf/scpwps/ecbwp2032.en.pdf, accessed 4 June 2025.

[18] Anginer et al. (n 428) 319–320.

hazard more effectively.[19] Their study utilises proxies, consisting of many indexes of institutional quality and legal environment. These proxies are the prevalence of the rule of law (law and order), quality of contract enforcement, quality of bureaucracy, bureaucratic delay and the degree of corruption. Demirguc-Kunt and Detragiache put forth an argument that these institutional indexes may have effects on the relationship between deposit insurance and bank stability, notwithstanding the fact 'they are not accurate proxies for prudential regulation and supervision' per se. In their view, there 'may be more opportunities for gambling with insured deposits' in a society in which the legal protection for economic agents such as creditors and investors is not well-established.[20]

Nevertheless, the proxies used in the study by Demirguc-Kunt and Detragiache might not be able to sufficiently capture the effects of legal and regulatory measures in reducing the risk of moral hazard caused by deposit insurance. Appendix A of the article provides data sources for the variables used in the regressions of this study. Law and order, quality of bureaucracy and corruption are data created by the International Country Risk Guide (ICRG). Meanwhile, Business Environment Risk Intelligence (BERI) produces data about bureaucratic delay and contract enforcement utilised in this study. The purposes of data from both ICRG and BERI are for companies conducting international business or other organisations to use ratings, analyses or forecasts, for example, to allocate country exposure and manage risk. However, an analysis regarding financial stability and deposit insurance requires data specifically focused on these issues rather than general information about political, economic and financial risks prevalent in a country. Besides, this type of analysis requires experienced regulators and supervisors who have an expertise about, for instance, macro-prudential policies. It is doubtful whether analysts working for an investment risk company possess expertise and understanding necessary for analysing this matter.

In my view, legal and institutional infrastructures and arrangements—which could help mitigate the risk of moral hazard and systemic risk—could be considered from the structure and authorities of a DIS, as well as its power and organisation structure vis-à-vis other safety-net

[19] Asli Demirguc-Kunt and Enrica Detragiache, 'Does Deposit Insurance Increase Banking System Stability? An Empirical Investigation' (2002) 49 Journal of Monetary Economics 1373, 1403.

[20] Ibid., 1390.

players. With respect to a deposit insurer's structure and authorities, the design features, such as funding approach and mandates, need regulatory and supervisory mechanisms to support their functions in minimising moral hazard problems. For example, a pricing system such as risk-based premiums could, in principle, discourage insured banks from taking excessive risk.[21] The risk-based premiums would incentivise a bank manager to take into account the true cost of risk when he or she balances the trade-off between risk and return of the optimal portfolio.[22] In ASEAN, Malaysia was a pioneer in introducing the Differential Premium Systems framework in 2008, to provide incentives for insured banks to adopt sound risk management practices.[23] The Malaysian Deposit Insurance Corporate (MDIC) utilises both quantitative and qualitative criteria in order to classify deposit-taking members according to their risk profiles. Apart from Malaysia, only Brunei Darussalam and Singapore have used a risk-sensitive scheme. Meanwhile, Indonesia, Lao PDR, the Philippines, Thailand and Vietnam have chosen to use a flat-rate regime.

Nonetheless, there are inherent problems as to the limitation in the ability of the deposit insurer to assess the risk characteristics of a bank's investment portfolio (e.g., asset valuation, credit and off-balanced sheet exposures, loan-loss provisionings, and NPLs etc.). This constraint could, in turn, generate significant subsidies via deposit insurance premiums, as the expected deposit insurance payout is greater than the premium payment.[24] Besides this, risk-based insurance premiums could not eliminate a specific type of moral hazard, as banks still have an incentive to

[21] Risk could be defined as the 'variance of the expected future returns on the bank's asset portfolio'. Mark D. Flood, 'Deposit Insurance: Problems and Solution' (1993) Federal Reserve Bank of St. Louis, 29, https://files.stlouisfed.org/files/htdocs/publications/review/93/01/Flood_Jan_Feb1993.pdf, accessed 4 June 2025. George Shoukry finds that deposit insurance premiums provide strong incentives to mitigate moral hazards although differentials in premiums have led to distortion (e.g., regulatory arbitrage) George Shoukry, 'Insurance Pricing, Distortions, and Moral Hazard: Quasi-experimental Evidence from Deposit Insurance' (2020) FDIC CFR Working Paper 2020–08, 1.

[22] Flood (n 437) 32.

[23] Perbadanan Insurans Deposit Malaysia, 'Guideline on the Differential Premium Systems for Deposit Insurance System' (2020), 1, https://www.pidm.gov.my/pidm2022/files/a2/a25f2a2c-5eb5-4eb2-ac4e-23c1253d9370.pdf, accessed 4 June 2025.

[24] George Pennacchi, 'Deposit Insurance, Bank Regulation, and Financial System Risks' (2006) 53(1) Journal of Monetary Economics 1, 14.

provide loans and create contracts with high systematic risk.[25] Hence, regulation and supervisory activities are needed in supporting risk-based premiums to achieve the objective of controlling moral hazard.

According to Prescott, supervisory monitoring could reduce the problem of a transaction with 'private information', where one party (i.e., the bank) possesses information that the other party does not (i.e., the deposit insurer). These measures are, for example, safety and soundness exams, audits, balance sheet observations, as well as on-site and off-site surveillances.[26] Besides this, according to Cartwright, a system of prior approval and constant supervision could minimise the need for consumers' monitoring of banks, as well as reduce the likelihood of a market failure caused by information disclosure to consumers.[27]

Concerning the mandates of a deposit insurance, its roles and responsibilities can be categorised into four groups: paybox, paybox plus, loss minimiser and risk minimiser. According to the FSB, paybox systems merely take responsibility for premium assessment, fund management, and depositor reimbursement.[28] Meanwhile, a deposit insurance scheme with paybox plus mandates has further responsibilities (e.g., being the liquidator of failed banks).[29] Many DISs have the mandates of either loss minimiser or risk minimiser, depending on the policy of each country.

With respect to loss minimiser mandates, the deposit insurer will select appropriate least-cost-resolution options.[30] In some jurisdictions, deposit insurers with loss-minimiser mandates might have a responsibility in resolution, by deciding on how a failing bank should be dealt with. As for risk minimiser mandates, the responsibilities of the deposit insurer would include prudential oversight in addition to resolution options, as

[25] Ibid., 17.

[26] Edward S. Prescott, 'Can Risk-based Deposit Insurance Premiums Control Moral Hazard?' (2002) 88(2) Federal Reserve Bank of Richmond Economic Quarterly 87, 97–98, https://www.richmondfed.org/-/media/RichmondFedOrg/publications/research/economic_quarterly/2002/spring/pdf/prescott.pdf, accessed 4 June 2025.

[27] Peter Cartwright, 'Understanding, Awareness and Deposit Insurance' in John R. Labrosse and others (eds), *Financial Crisis Management and Bank Resolution* (Informa Law 2009), 146.

[28] Eg, Australia, Hong Kong, India and Singapore.

[29] Eg, Argentina, Brazil and the United Kingdom.

[30] Eg, Canada, Indonesia, Japan, Mexico, Russia and Turkey.

in Korea and US.[31] According to Kryzanowski, a deposit insurance with a 'loss minimisation' mandate fares better than those with other types of mandates in controlling the moral hazard problems. This is especially so in the case that a deposit insurance is proactive and independent.[32] An insurer with a loss minimiser mandate needs sufficient authority and power in order to elicit information necessary for conducting an independent risk monitoring, including an ability to conduct on-site examinations on demand.[33] A well-designed legal framework could help safeguard the independence of the deposit insurer by preventing undue interference from other entities or political actors. In addition, the legal framework could provide sufficient power and authority to the insurer to obtain adequate and up-to-date information from the banking industry.

With regard to the power and organisation structure vis-à-vis other financial safety-net members, there must be mechanisms enabling a deposit insurer to coordinate with other participants in a seamless way. This is crucial for the former to be able to deal with a systemic crisis effectively, as a deposit insurance scheme alone is normally able to cope with only single failures.[34] For example, the DIS would need support from a strong bank supervision, well-functioning resolution, and efficient liquidation proceedings. In the case that a bank faces a financial difficulty, a bank supervisor should be able to identify the issue and help the bank to avoid a worsened situation speedily, by using measures such as prompt corrective action. In addition, a timely resolution of failing banks would minimise a disruption of critical functions and restore liquidity to the economy.[35] The legal framework, if properly designed, could help promote certainty and trust in the system, by ensuring that property rights of stakeholders would be adequately protected and creditors—including

[31] Financial Stability Board, 'Thematic Review on Deposit Insurance Systems:' (Peer Review Report 2012), https://www.fsb.org/wp-content/uploads/r_120208.pdf?page_moved=1, accessed 4 June 2025.

[32] Lawrence Kryzanowski, 'Organizational Design and Positioning of the Deposit Insurance Function in the Financial System Safety Net' in Andrew Campbell and others (eds) (n 419) 93.

[33] Ibid., 108.

[34] Dalvinder Singh and David Walker, 'The European Deposit Guarantee Directive: An Appraisal of the Reforms' in John R. Labrosse and others (eds) (n 443) 157.

[35] Nicholas Ketcha Jr, 'Deposit Insurance System Design and Considerations' (1999), 235–236, https://www.bis.org/publ/plcy07o.pdf, accessed 4 June 2025.

depositors—would be fairly treated. This would, in turn, contribute to the improvement of public confidence in the financial system. Moreover, the need for using resources of the deposit insurance scheme would be minimised, if a liquidation regime is able to maximise the values in the event of liquidation for stakeholders.

There is no one-size-fits-all approach for prescribing deposit insurance function within a country's financial safety net, in order to achieve seamless coordination. The design of those mechanisms would depend on 'informational, ethical, legal, historical, political and economic features' of a particular country.[36] For example, Canada separates the functions of deposit insurance and supervision, on the basis that deposit insurer and supervisor might have different incentives in making a decision with respect to intervention. While a deposit insurer with a loss minimiser mandate is more concerned with the costs of bank failure, a supervisor could focus more on maintaining financial stability.[37]

4.2.1.2 Minimising the Moral Hazard from an Implicit Insurance and Blanket Guarantee by Establishing a Credible Explicit DIS

With regard to the second argument, an explicit deposit insurance could minimise the risk-taking of banks by limiting a de facto scope of implicit insurance and blanket guarantee. As a consequence, the moral hazard problems of credit institutions would be lowered. For example, according to Gropp and Vesala (2001), 'European banking systems may have been characterised by a strong implicit insurance' that the governments would rescue banks in distress. In their study, banks which have lower charter values and more subordinated debts reduce their risk taking when an explicit deposit insurance has been established.[38]

In addition, in the case of ASEAN—prior to the burst of the AFC—Indonesia, Malaysia and Thailand had not established any explicit deposit insurance scheme. The AFC revealed that the lack of an explicit deposit insurance coupled with the weaknesses in supervisory and regulatory

[36] Kryzanowski (n 448) 101.

[37] LaBrosse and Mayes (n 419) 16.

[38] Reint Gropp and Jukka Vesala, 'Deposit Insurance and Moral Hazard: Does the Counterfactual Matter' (2001) ECB Working Paper No. 47, 5. However, Gropp and Vesala find that large banks do not change the level of their risk-taking.

framework worsened the crisis.[39] Accordingly, explicit blanket guarantees were utilised in Thailand, Malaysia and Indonesia in order to prevent bank runs and a collapse of the financial system.[40] Nonetheless, a blanket guarantee is no antidote to the problem, as it can produce unfavourable effects by diminishing market disciplines and magnifying moral hazards.[41] In other words, it generates an expectation that the government will always honour guarantees and might rescue even badly-managed financial institutions.

Moreover, an extension of blanket guarantees to creditors could add substantial fiscal outlays to bank restructuring programme when the guarantees are used in addition to substantial liquidity support.[42] According

[39] David Walker, 'A Survey of Deposit Insurance in East Asia: Post-Asian Financial Crisis' in Andrew Campbell and others (eds) (n 419) 123–124.

[40] ibid. In Malaysia, liquidity support slowed down after the announcement that a blanket guarantee would be utilised. Meanwhile, in the case of Thailand, liquidity support decelerated significantly following the introduction of a blanket guarantee. However, this result should be considered by taking into account the fact that the guarantee was used in the same month that the IMF programme was approved. In contrast, liquidity support rose rapidly in Indonesia following the announcement of a blanket guarantee. A possible explanation for the Indonesian experience is that there were 'severe market turbulence occurred due to the release of an unrealistic new state budget, the nomination of Habibi.e.,as Vice President, and the virtual reopening of a previously closed bank by one of the President's sons'. Luc Laeven and Fabian Valencia, 'The Use of Blanket Guarantees in Banking Crises' (2008) IMF Working Paper WP/08/250, 7–10.

[41] In the aftermath of the AFC, many ASEAN states embarked on introducing an explicit deposit insurance into the financial system. ASEAN countries created an explicit deposit insurance after the AFC: Brunei Darussalam in 2011, Indonesia in 2004, Lao PDR in 1999, Malaysia in 2005, Singapore in 2006, Thailand in 2008 and Vietnam in 2000. The Philippines already has an explicit DIS since 1963. Kevin Davis, 'Asian Banking Integration, Depositor Preference, and Deposit Insurance' (2015), 5, http://www.kevindavis.com.au/secondpages/workinprogress/Asian%20Banking%20Depositor%20Preference%20and%20Deposit%20Insurance.pdf, accessed 4 June 2025. Concerning Myanmar, it has recently established a deposit insurance scheme administered by Myanmar Insurance Agency, which is a state-owned enterprise. However, Myanmar has not promulgated any rules or regulations regarding its deposit insurance scheme. IADI, 'Systems under Development', https://www.iadi.org/en/about-iadi/deposit-insurance-systems/systems-under-development/, accessed 4 June 2025.

[42] Laeven and Valencia (n 456) 4. For instance, in Thailand, there were fiscal costs of over 1.4 trillion bahts (around 42 billion US dollars) as a result of the blanket guarantee used during the AFC. Taweesak Manakul et al., 'Executive Summary: Does A Deposit Insurance System Strengthen the System of Financial Institutions and Stabilise the Financial System?' *RYT9* (Bangkok, 22 September 2008) (in Thai), https://www.ryt9.com/s/mof/436620, accessed 4 June 2025.

to Honohan and Klingebiel, fiscal costs could be reduced to one-half without the use of blanket guarantees.[43] Furthermore, foreign liabilities of banks might not be susceptible to the use of blanket guarantees. A research study by Laeven and Valencia finds that non-resident investors continue moving their funds out of the country facing significant banking distress in spite of the announcement of a blanket guarantee.[44] This is especially so in the case that currency pressures are high.[45]

However, an explicit deposit insurance must be well-designed, effectively implemented, and adequately understood by the public for it to be able to minimise the risk of moral hazard and prevent unwarranted bank runs.[46] Otherwise, a country might need to resort to an implicit guarantee. The failure of Northern Rock is telling, in that it suggests an explicit DIS which lacked those attributes could fail to deliver its expected benefits. According to Singh and LaBrosse, the UK DIS at that time was not well-designed; it relied on an inadequate coverage of compensation system and co-insurance.[47] In other words, a full coverage was only available for the amount of £2000 of deposits, while merely 90 per cent of deposits above £2000 and up to £33,000 were covered.[48] Besides this, depositors were not well aware of the existence of the co-insurance

[43] Patrick Honohan and Daniela Klingebiel, 'The Fiscal Cost Implications of an Accommodating Approach to Banking Crises' (2003) 27(8) Journal of Banking and Finance 1539.

[44] Laeven and Valencia (n 456) 4. In the case of Thailand and Malaysia, the study finds that 'capital outflows subside for some time, but this period only lasts at most two months'. As for Indonesia, 'foreign liabilities decline sharply after the announcement of a guarantee'. Laeven and Valencia (n 456) 9.

[45] Ibid., 10.

[46] LaBrosse and Mayes (n 419) 8. Dalvinder Singh and John R. LaBrosse, 'Northern Rock, Depositors and Deposit Insurance Coverage: Some Critical Reflections' (2010) 2 Journal of Business Law 55, 62. According to Adema et al., in general not more than 50 per cent of the total population have some awareness regarding the existence of a DIS. Joop Adema et al., 'Deposit Insurance: System Design and Implementation across Countries' (2019) 17 ifo DICE Report, 44.

[47] Singh and LaBrosse (n 462) 64. One of the main objectives of co-insurance is to provide an incentive to monitor bank risk-taking as well as market discipline to the insured depositors as they risk bearing small losses. Ketcha Jr. (n 451) 229.

[48] Singh and LaBrosse (n 462) 64.

rules; they considered deposits to be risk-free financial products.[49] Consequently, the UK explicit deposit insurance neither reduced moral hazard nor obviated a bank run.[50]

This is not surprising, as surveys in 2017 have shown that 'only around 55 per cent of Dutch and 40 per cent of German citizens know what a deposit insurance entails'. Another survey, conducted in New Zealand in 2014, reveals that three-fourths of the term-deposit account holders misunderstood that their deposits were protected by the state. This is despite the fact that there was no deposit insurance scheme in New Zealand at that time.[51] In some ways, bank regulation and supervision could contribute to raise public awareness regarding a deposit insurance scheme. For example, the UK Prudential Regulation Authority regulations have required banks to display the Financial Services Compensation Scheme (FSCS) stickers in branches and on other communications channels (e.g., posters, leaflets, websites, mobile banking applications, and information sheets, etc.) in order to increase customer awareness of deposit protection.[52]

In addition, it is crucially important to introduce an explicit DIS when the financial system is stable. Otherwise, a transition from a blanket guarantee to a limited guarantee system could result in 'bank fragility',

[49] Singh and Walker (n 450) 169.

[50] In response to the Northern Rock collapse, the UK Government introduced a blanket guarantee as well as increased the level of compensation. It was only when there was a government announcement to provide a full guarantee of deposits that the bank run was stopped. Singh and LaBrosse (n 462) 59–60. Furthermore, the EU policymakers realised that the EU Deposit Guarantee Schemes Directive 1994 might have gone wrong in utilising co-insurance. This mistake was corrected in the Deposit Guarantee Schemes Directive 2009 which no longer had a co-insurance mandate. Singh and Walker (n 450) 168.

[51] Adema et al. (n 462) 46. New Zealand has established its first explicit deposit insurance scheme–the Depositor Compensation Scheme (DCS), which covers deposits of up to $100,000 starting from 1 July 2025. Reserve Bank of New Zealand, *'Deposit Takers that Offer DCS-Protected Deposits'* (22 April 2025), https://www.rbnz.govt.nz/regulation-and-supervision/cross-sector-oversight/registers-of-entities-we-regulate/deposit-takers-that-offer-dcs-protected-deposits, accessed 4 June 2025.

[52] Financial Services Compensation Scheme, 'Ground-breaking New Industry Wide Agreement to Raise Awareness of Deposit Protection for Consumers' (Media Information 2017), https://www.fscs.org.uk/globalassets/press-releases/20170920---fscs-badge-agreement-press-release---final.pdf, accessed 4 June 2025.

'capital flight', 'moral hazard' and other 'agency problems'.[53] According to Walker and Hoontrakul, the relevant authorities should assess a suitable time for the transition by taking into consideration stability triggers (e.g., the 'containment of systemic risks', 'sustained increases in credit and deposit growth' as well as 'improving confidence levels', 'capital adequacy' and 'asset quality').[54]

4.2.2 A Call for Harmonising Deposit Insurance Schemes in Response to Increasing Interconnected Financial Markets in ASEAN

4.2.2.1 DISs in ASEAN States

The majority of ASEAN states have established a deposit insurance scheme. For example, there has been a DIS in the Philippines since 1963.[55] Other ASEAN states have taken lessons from the AFC which highlighted the importance of a deposit insurance scheme. For instance, Malaysia has set up the Perbadanan Insurans Deposit Malaysia (PIDM) under the Malaysia Deposit Insurance Corporation Act in 2005.[56] Similarly, Thailand has created its Deposit Protection Agency in 2008 in accordance with the Deposit Protection Agency Act.[57] However, deposit insurance design features in ASEAN states are various since there has not been any regional effort in harmonising deposit insurance schemes proposed by an ASEAN organ or a Member State.

As illustrated in Chapter 1, cross-border banking and financial integration in ASEAN have increased due to factors such as QAB scheme.

[53] David Walker and Pongsak Hoontrakul, 'Transitioning from Blanket to Limited Deposit Guarantees: Thailand Policy Considerations' (2001) SSRN Paper, 1, https://papers.ssrn.com/sol3/papers.cfm?abstract_id=292924, accessed 4 June 2025.

[54] Ibid., 8.

[55] Philippine Deposit Insurance Corporation, http://www.pdic.gov.ph/, accessed 4 June 2025.

[56] Philippine Deposit Insurance Corporation, 'About PIDM FAQS', https://www.pidm.gov.my/en/for-public/soalan-soalan-lazim/about-pidm-faqs/, accessed 4 June 2025.

[57] This Act together with the Bank of Thailand Act 2008 and the Financial Business Institutions Act 2008 were drafted since the early years after the AFC broke out. However, they were opposed by the government and the Ministry of Finance until the military coup was staged in 2006. In 2007, the military-appointed legislature accomplished these pieces of legislation.

In addition, an improvement in the banking sector integration could be considered from the fact that ASEAN-5 banking sectors have switched from being completely segmented during the AFC to partially segmented during the GFC.[58] According to Saheruddin and Soedarmono, a long-running relationship regarding systemic risk has existed in the banking systems in ASEAN-5 countries. By utlilising bilateral cointegration tests, their study demonstrates that three groups of ASEAN countries (i.e., Indonesia and Malaysia, Malaysia and Singapore, and Malaysia and Thailand) were already 'cointegrated' during the 2008 crisis.[59] In my view, the increasing financial integration in this sub-region warrants a harmonisation of deposit insurance schemes to enable those systems to work seamlessly with other financial safety-net components for some reasons.

First, the disparity in respect of deposit protection among ASEAN states could result in the relocations of cross-border bank deposits. This concern is particularly worrying in a systemic banking crisis, since deposit relocations and depositor runs on banks could destabilise the liquidity position of banks and contribute to a contagion in the sub-region. According to Qi et al. (2020), the existence of a deposit insurance and its detailed features could result in massive relocations of cross-border deposits.[60] During a stable time, cross-border depositors conduct a regulatory arbitrage by searching for a deposit insurance scheme which has a relatively more credible design.[61] The absence of a deposit insurance in their home country as well as the weak power of regulatory authorities act as the main push factors for the regulatory arbitrage.[62] Meanwhile, cross-border depositors search for countries which provide the most attractive deposit insurance schemes during systemic crises.[63] As the experience

[58] Herman Saheruddin and Wahyoe Soedarmono, 'Financial Crisis and Cointegration of Systemic Risk in Southeast Asian Banking' (2019) 23(4) Jurnal Keuangan dan Perbankan 479, 481.

[59] Ibid., 484.

[60] Shusen Qi et al., 'The Travels If a Bank Deposit in Turbulent Times: The Importance of Deposit Insurance Design for Cross-border Deposits' (2020) 58(2) Economic Inquiry 980, 980.

[61] Ibid., 991.

[62] Ibid.

[63] Ibid., 980.

during the GFC has demonstrated, emergency actions taken by some governments led to tremendous relocations of cross-border deposits.[64]

Secondly, the current deposit insurance regimes in ASEAN have left a large degree of legal risk and unequal protection to depositors in cross-border banking. None of the ASEAN states has provided a legal protection for deposit accounts located outside its territory. Accordingly, depositors of overseas subsidiaries and branches of ASEAN headquartered banks have to rely on a protection provided by their local deposit insurers. This concern could be alarming when considering the fact that Cambodia has not established an explicit deposit insurance scheme. Although Cambodia provides an explicit 100 per cent guarantee from its central banks for all deposits,[65] the success of the blanket guarantee depends on its credibility, accompanying policy actions, and the severity of the crisis.[66] Experiences from other countries have shown that there are many circumstances which could render a blanket guarantee ineffective (e.g., Turkey's political turmoil, Ecuador's financial transaction tax, and weak political commitments of Indonesian politicians).[67] This could be exacerbated by the fact that Cambodia does not have the capacity to insure dollar deposits, which constitute around 90 per cent of bank deposits in the country.[68]

Therefore, in the circumstance that there are bank failures in Cambodia, depositors of branches and subsidiaries of banks headquartered in another ASEAN state might not have any effective deposit protection. This is despite the fact that there are deposit insurance schemes in the home ASEAN states of those banks. For example, Bangkok Bank, a Thai bank, has one branch in Cambodia. According to Section 51 of the Thai DPA, protected deposits must be denominated in Thai baht and located in accounts opened in Thailand. As a consequence, deposits of the branch of Bangkok Bank in Cambodia would not be protected by the Thai Deposit Protection Agency.

[64] Ibid.

[65] Walker (n 455) 123.

[66] Laeven and Valencia (n 456) 18.

[67] Ibid., 10.

[68] Cam McGrath, 'Deposit Protection Scheme Edges Closer to Reality' *The Phom Phenh Post* (Phnom Phenh, 26 September 2016), https://www.phnompenhpost.com/supplements/deposit-protection-scheme-edges-closer-reality, accessed 4 June 2025.

The number of credit institutions that could fall into this situation is not negligible. According to Fig. 1.1 of Chapter 1, Cambodia is the host state for a total number of 85 subsidiaries and branches of banks headquartered in Malaysia, Thailand and Vietnam. The majority of the five largest commercial banks by assets in Cambodia, according to data from Orbis Bank Focus, are not home-grown credit institutions.[69] For instance, the fourth largest commercial bank in the country, Cambodian Public Bank Limited, is a wholly-owned subsidiary of Public Bank Group, which is headquartered in Malaysia.

It could be argued that Cambodia has depositor preference rules in place which should help safeguard the interests of the depositors. Depositor preference rules would give priority to depositors' claims on the assets of a failed bank over those of other unsecured creditors. According to the IMF, depositor preference rules could be classified into three groups: insured depositor preference (i.e., deposits which are eligible and within the limit of deposit protection will be given preferential treatment over other ordinary, senior unsecured creditors),[70] tiered depositor preference (i.e., insured deposits are given the top priority while uninsured eligible deposits receive a preference after the insured deposits),[71] and general depositor preference.[72] Cambodia uses general depositor preference rules.[73] In other words, all deposit liabilities, regardless of their eligibility and coverage under deposit insurance scheme (which has not been established in Cambodia), are given a more senior position over other senior unsecured creditors.[74] However, Article 64 of the Cambodian Law on Banking and Financial Institutions (1999) has put depositors' claims at a relatively low position in the creditor hierarchy. Their claims would be met after administration and liquidation expenses,

[69] These top five banks are Canadia Bank Plc, Acleda Bank Plc, Advanced Bank of Asia Limited (a subsidiary of National Bank of Canada), Cambodian Public Bank Limited, and Sathapana Bank Plc (ultimate parent is MARUHAN Corporation of Japan).

[70] Marc Dobler et al., 'The Case for Depositor Preference' IMF Technical Notes and Manuals 2020/002, 9.

[71] In addition, both insured and uninsured eligible deposits are given preference over other senior unsecured creditors. Ibid., 8.

[72] Ibid., 8–9.

[73] Chan et al. (n 15) 237–238. See Article 64 of Law on Banking and Financial Institutions 1999 of Cambodia.

[74] Dobler et al. (n 486) 9.

taxes and fee to the Treasury, staff's salaries, and preferential or secured claims of sureties are paid in full. Therefore, depositors of Cambodian branches of banks headquartered in other ASEAN states might recover only a small part of their deposits or nothing at all in liquidation.

In addition, the mere existence of deposit preference rules would not be adequate to maintain depositor confidence and mitigate the risk of bank runs. There is still a need to establish a deposit insurance and other components of the financial safety net for some reasons.[75] For example, depositor preference does not guarantee that uninsured depositors will recover their funds speedily.[76] Hence, those depositors might still have an incentive to withdraw their resources in order to avoid the loss of access to their deposits.[77] Moreover, depositor preference as a stand-alone measure could intensify the moral hazard problems because it could mislead depositors to consider their deposits as risk-free investments.[78] Therefore, a better approach is to utilise depositor preference rules, in combination with other tools, to support the functioning of the financial system safety net. For instance, depositor preference could help reduce the risk of litigations under the no-creditor-worse-off rule when resolution measures are utilised. Depositor preference rules would provide a legal justification in the case that the resolution authority transfers only deposits to another bank or excludes deposits from the pool of assets subject to a bail-in.[79]

Lastly, there is a cross-border issue with respect to national preference rules. These rules give priority to the claims of home jurisdiction's depositors over those of depositors in branches of a bank headquartered in foreign jurisdiction. National preference rules could not only produce unequal treatment of depositors but also reduce an incentive of the host state officials to cooperate and coordinate with the home state authorities. The former might decide to ring-fence assets or require subsidiarisation in order to protect their local depositors.[80] Currently,

[75] Ibid., 16.

[76] Kumudini Hajra and Ramadhian Moetomo, 'Depositor Preference and Implications for Deposit Insurance' (2020) IADI Briefs No. 4, 3.

[77] In addition, in the case of a tiered depositor preference, the amount of funds that unsecured creditors could recover might be negligible, especially if there are insufficient unsecured creditors to absorb losses. Ibid., 5.

[78] Ibid.

[79] Ibid., 4.

[80] Dobler et al. (n 486) 11. Chan et al. (n 15) 237.

some ASEAN countries have implemented national preference rules. For example, Section 205 and Section 206(3)(a)(ii) of Financial Services Act 2013 of Malaysia state that assets of an insolvent bank shall be available to meet all liabilities concerning its (Islamic) deposits in Malaysia in priority to all other unsecured liabilities.[81]

4.3 Part II: Harmonising DISs in ASEAN—Soft or Hard Law Approach?

In order to harmonise deposit insurance schemes, as well as create seamless financial system safety nets in ASEAN, it is worth considering the forms of legalisation used for this purpose by the international community and other countries. These legal measures could be considered as two main forms: soft and hard law. Nevertheless, the demarcation line between soft law and hard legal commitment is sometimes blurred, as the degrees of 'softness' of soft law are varied. In the words of Abbott and Snidal, the 'realm of 'soft law' begins once legal arrangements are weakened along one or more of the dimensions of obligation, precision, and delegation'.[82] By relaxing one or more elements of legalisation, a 'rough consensus' could be more easily achieved.[83] For instance, a state might be more reluctant to agree on an agenda which provides a strong delegation of power to a supranational organisation. In addition, soft legalisation would allow a larger degree of flexibility for a state to adapt its arrangement when circumstances are fundamentally uncertain.[84]

Moreover, as argued in Chapter 1, soft law might possess a disciplinary power and generate effects similar to those of hard legal instruments. That is, in part, because regulators in a close-knit community can encounter

[81] Other ASEAN states which have national preference rules are Singapore (Section 62(1) of Banking Act (Revised Edition 2008)) and Brunei Darussalam (Section 101(1) of Banking Order 2006 and Section 2012(1) of Islamic Banking Order 2008).

[82] Kenneth Abbott and Duncan Snidal, 'Hard and Soft Law in International Governance' (2000) 54 International Organization 421, 422.

[83] Ibid., 423. See Gralf-Peter Calliess and Peer C Zumbansen, *Rough Consensus and Running Code: A Theory of Transnational Private Law* (Hart Publishing 2010). The authors of this book analyses law-making regimes in transnational private law where rule-creators cannot be clearly described as either the state or the market. In addition, both hard and soft laws play an important role in the regulatory landscape.

[84] Abbott and Snidal (n 498) 444.

a social criticism from their counterparts for their failure to behave in accordance with the group's programme.[85] In the following sections, I will reflect on the arguments made in Chapter 1 regarding the similarities between soft law and hard legal measures, by using DISs as a concrete illustration.

4.3.1 Soft Legal Instrument: The IADI Core Principles for Effective Deposit Insurance Systems

International standard setters and governance networks have played an important role in using 'soft law' to harmonise rules governing deposit protection in order to enhance financial stability. These legal instruments are soft law, in the sense that they are not legally binding. In addition, they merely establish a framework which could be tailored to specific circumstances and the context of a particular country.[86] Moreover, states do not delegate their national power to the international organisations or networks which create those soft legal tools. Besides this, there is no specialised procedure operated by legal professionals which could adjudicate disputes and address questions of interpretation arising as a result of the use of soft law.

The most important soft law utilised in harmonising DISs is the BCBS-IADI *Core Principles for Effective Deposit Insurance Systems (2009)* (Core Principles). The BCBS, in cooperation with the International Association of Deposit Insurers (IADI), developed the Core Principles which were based on the IADI Core Principles for Effective Deposit Insurance Systems (February 2008). The designers of the Core Principles aimed at creating a device which was adaptable to different contexts of various jurisdictions. The Core Principles were not intended to cover every aspect of every banking system.[87] Instead, national authorities were allowed to

[85] See Brummer (n 99).

[86] IADI, 'Core Principles for Effective Deposit Insurance Systems' (2014), 5, https://www.iadi.org/en/assets/File/Core%20Principles/cprevised2014nov.pdf, accessed 4 June 2025.

[87] BCBS and IADI, 'Core Principles for Effective Deposit Insurance Systems' (Consultative Document 2009), 2, https://www.bis.org/publ/bcbs151.pdf, accessed 4 June 2025.

set up necessary supplementary measures in their own jurisdictions.[88] In the 2009 Core Principles, there was no emphasis on the home country control in dealing with issues which could arise in cross-border cases.

In addition, the Core Principles factored in consideration about the broader characteristics of safety net measures as a deposit insurance scheme needs to function within a well-designed financial safety net to be able to reduce moral hazard.[89] Principle 6 stated that there should be a framework for the close coordination and information sharing among the deposit insurer and other components in the financial safety-net. Moreover, cross-border issues were addressed in Principle 7, that there should be cooperation and information exchange between a deposit insurer and other foreign safety-net participants. For instance, there should be a recognition of the deposit insurance provided by the home country system in determining levies and premiums.[90] Furthermore, Principle 15 and Principle 16 recognised the importance of the effectiveness of other financial safety-net entities in bank resolution. Principle 15 described that a deposit insurer should be part of the system which provided early detection as well as timely intervention and resolution of banks. Meanwhile, Principle 16 emphasised that a deposit insurer needs effective resolution processes which could facilitate the insurer's ability to fulfil its obligations in the event of bank failures. Besides this, the Core Principle embraced the lesson learnt from the Northern Rock debacle by emphasising the importance of public awareness as to the benefits and limitations of the DIS in Principle 12.

In 2010, the BCBS, the IADI, the European Forum of Deposit Insurers (EFDI), the European Commission, the IMF and the World Bank issued *Core Principles for Effective Deposit Insurance Systems: A Methodology for compliance assessment* (Core Principles Methodology) to assist a deposit insurer and an outside party in conducting a fully objective assessment of compliance with the Core Principles.[91] After the GFC occurred, the IADI and its internal Steering Committee took important

[88] BCBS and IADI, 'Core Principles for Effective Deposit Insurance Systems: A Proposed Methodology for Compliance Assessment' (Consultative Document 2010), 1, https://www.bis.org/publ/bcbs182.pdf, accessed 4 June 2025.

[89] BCBS and IADI (n 503) 1.

[90] Ibid., 3.

[91] BCBS and IADI (n 504) 2. The Core Principles Methodology was replaced in 2016 with an Assessment Handbook.

lessons from the crisis, as well as international regulatory developments and their experience using the Core Principles. Thus, in 2014, the IADI issued a revised version of the Core Principles.

The 2014 Core Principles place more emphasis on ensuring that the deposit insurer has operation independence to fulfil its mandate as well as raising the bar for more effective DISs.[92] For instance, Core Principle 2 prescribes that the deposit insurer has a power to transfer deposits to another bank.[93] In addition, the deposit insurer should be able to obtain information directly from banks in order to fulfil its mandate[94] as well as compel those institutions to comply with their obligations to the deposit insurer.[95] Moreover, Core Principle 9 spells out that the deposit insurer should be funded on an *ex ante* basis in order to ensure prompt reimbursement to depositors.[96] Besides this, the deposit insurer can exercise the option to authorise the utilisation of its funds for resolution of banks.[97]

Concerning the functions of the deposit insurer in relation to those of its foreign counterparts and other safety-net players, Core Principle 5 sets forth that there should be 'formal' information sharing and coordination arrangements among depositors in relevant jurisdictions. In addition, Core Principle 6 specifies that the deposit insurer be a member of the national crisis management arrangements, and that all financial safety-net agencies have a role in developing a crisis preparedness strategies and management policies.

Moreover, in the case that there is a high level of capital mobility or a regional integration policy, Core Principle 8 stipulates that a deposit insurer should consider the effects of protection levels and related polices of relevant jurisdictions in lowering the level and scope of deposit coverage.[98] Besides this, according to Core Principle 14, there should

[92] IADI (n 502) 6.

[93] Essential Criteria 4(b).

[94] Essential Criteria 4(d).

[95] Essential Criteria 4(f).

[96] Essential Criteria 1. Core Principle 15 also strengthens the reimbursement function of deposit insurers by stating that there should be a 'clear and unequivocal trigger for insured depositor reimbursement'.

[97] Essential Criteria 8.

[98] Essential Criteria 10(d).

be a special resolution regime which treats relevant depositors equally, regardless of their nationality or residence. Decisions of this resolution regime should not be reversible by any court. Furthermore, the resolution regime should shorten the period between depositors losing access to their deposits and the implementation of a resolution tool(s) as much as possible.

4.3.1.1 Hard Disciplining Powers of Soft Law

Soft law, by its nature, does not have any legally binding effect. However, in the case of the Core Principles, I argue that they could produce a strong impact in securing compliance of a particular state in some ways. First, a country where there is a state entity which is an IADI member would be more likely to follow the Core Principles. According to the IADI Annual Survey in 2021, DISs in IADI member states can be categorised into 'government legislated and administered', 'government legislated and administered by central bank', 'government legislated and privately administered', and 'privately established and administered'.[99]

In the case that a state has established a DIS which is legislated and administered by the government,[100] or legislated and administered by the central bank,[101] the DIS as a state or public institution would participate in the transnational norm-making through the IADI forum.[102] The entity is likely to act as an intermediary which brings the norms of the IADI (e.g., the Core Principles) into the local setting. The DIS could support or accommodate the IADI norms, which might later become part

[99] IADI, '2021 Annual Survey 15 Key Features' (8 November 2021).

[100] E.g., the DISs of Indonesia, Malaysia, the Philippines and Thailand.

[101] E.g., the DIS of Vietnam.

[102] Despite the fact that most international organisations have a neutral view regarding whether DISs should be run by the government, the industry, or a hybrid system, the IMF has proposed the public administration as the best practice. Bruno M. Salama and Vicente P. Braga, 'The Case for Private Administration of Deposit Guarantee Schemes' (2023) 24 The Journal of Banking Regulation 51, 53.

of state law.[103] In ASEAN, the DISs in Indonesia, Malaysia, the Philippines, Thailand and Vietnam, which are IADI members, fall into these types of DISs.

In addition, I argue that in the case of an IADI member which is a 'government legislated and privately administered' DIS (e.g., Brunei Darussalam's DIS), the influence of the IADI norms in the country in which the DIS is situated might not be significantly different from that of the first two categories.[104] That is, in part, because a 'government legislated and privately administered' DIS might still have a close tie with the government. A DIS can be incorporated as a private entity in spite of the fact that the government appoints its directors or officials.[105] Moreover, a DIS has to coordinate its activities closely as well as share information on an ongoing basis with other financial safety net members regardless of whether it is publicly or privately managed. In doing so, the DIS has to share regulatory space and authority with other financial safety net agencies. This could, in turn, lead to a dissemination of the IADI norms to other state entities even in the case of a DIS which is privately established and run.

Secondly, the Core Principles can have an influence in countries where their DISs are not an IADI member. This is especially the case where the Core Principles are utilised by governance networks (e.g., the FSB) and the IFIs (i.e., the IMF and the World Bank) as a benchmark for international best practice. For instance, the FSB completed a peer review

[103] See Gregory Shaffter and Terence Halliday, 'With, Within, and Beyond the State: The Promise and Limits of Transnational Legal Ordering' in Peer Zumbansen (ed), *The Oxford Handbook of Transnational Law* (Oxford University Press 2021) for the arguments that states remain central to transnational processes through their state officials participating in transnational norm-making.

[104] Deposit insurers in Singapore and Lao PDR are 'government legislated and privately administered' but they are not IADI members.

[105] For instance, the UK's FSCS is self-identified as a 'government legislated and privately administered' deposit guarantee scheme (DGS). However, according to s. 212(4) of the Financial Services and Markets Act 2000, the chairman, chief executive and other board members are subject to the appointment and removal by the regulator, with the approval of the Treasury. Salama and Braga (n 518) 55.

of DISs by employing the Core Principles as a benchmark of best practices.[106] The FSB has encouraged all of its member countries, including Singapore, to establish a DIS which operates consistently with the Core Principles of the IADI.

Moreover, the World Bank and the IMF deployed the Core Principles in assessing compliance under the programmes of ROSCs and FSAPs.[107] Besides this, the World Bank, in providing financial and technical assistance to its clients, uses the Core Principles as a benchmark against which recipient countries are assessed. For instance, the World Bank has provided a loan and technical assistance to Lao PDR regarding financial safety net strengthening by using Investment Project Financing (IPF) with disbursement linked indicators (DLIs).[108] The purpose of this project is to 'strengthen the financial and institutional capacity of the Deposit Protection Office to fulfil its deposit insurance mandate'.[109] In doing so, the Deposit Protection Office (DPO) of Lao PDR has to improve its legal mandate in order to undertake reforms necessary to comply with the Core Principles. Furthermore, the DPO has to complete a self-assessment, with the World Bank's support, on the extent of compliance with the Core Principles, as well as identify gaps and create action plan to move towards full compliance.[110]

The World Bank's approach, which enables the recipient state to act as the implementing agency, has twofold advantages: providing a legitimacy

[106] FSB (n 447). IADI, 'Enhanced Guidance for Effective Deposit Insurance Systems: Mitigating Moral Hazard' (Guidance Paper 2013), 6. The FSB has recommended all of its members which do not have an explicit deposit insurance to establish one.

[107] FSB (n 447) i. IADI (n 502) 5.

[108] IPF is one the World Bank's instruments. It is an investment lending for specific projects. The nature of these projects covers various types of reforms including institution building, increasing social capacity, and social development. Other main instruments are Program-for-Results Financing (PforR) and Development Policy Financing (DPF). The use of these programmes will be selected in accordance with the nature of the project. For example, a project with a macro-economic impact will be conducted by using a DPF. Meanwhile, PforRs provide assistance to government programmes to achieve results; the World Bank uses the achievement of programme results as a measure for disbursing funds. World Bank Group, 'Products' (May 2018).

[109] World Bank, 'Lao PDR Financial Sector Safety Net Strengthening' (Project Information Document, 10 February 2020), 2, https://policycommons.net/artifacts/1264264/project-information-document/1839634/, accessed 4 June 2025.

[110] World Bank, 'Lao PDR Financial Sector Safety Net Strengthening' (Project Appraisal Document, 9 March 2020), 22.

to the Bank's rule-of-law enterprise and strengthen the effects of soft law. On the one hand, this approach has protected the World Bank's reputation from being criticised as interfering with the political affairs of its clients.

According to Article IV, Section 10 of the International Bank for Reconstruction and Development (IBRD) Articles of Agreement, the World Bank should not interfere in the political affairs of any member.[111] The World Bank and its twin sister the IMF were and are still criticised by Third World scholars as practicing, in the word of Pahuja, 'technologies of colonial governance'.[112] In other words, the practice of the IFIs is the same as that of the colonial powers in the colonisation period. The South or developing countries are translated and represented by the North or developed countries. According to this thesis, the IFIs have increased their authority by shifting power from 'hard' to 'soft' international law. This, in effect, allows the IFIs to have a legitimate purview of issues in the Third World countries.[113]

In the case of Lao PDR, by enabling the DPO to have an implementing power and ownership in the project, the World Bank has turned its recipient state and their relevant agents into a self-regulating person.[114] The self-regulating person has autonomy to make his or her own decision but still acts in accordance with specified norms.[115] For example, the Project Implementation Unit (PIU) in the DOP takes charge of monitoring project implementation, taking fiduciary oversight, as well as cooperating closely with the Bank of Lao PDR and the Ministry of Finance

[111] IBRD, 'IBRD Articles of Agreement: Article IV', https://www.worldbank.org/en/about/articles-of-agreement/ibrd-articles-of-agreement/article-IV, accessed 4 June 2025. The IBRD is a global development cooperative which supports the World Bank Group's mission. World Bank, 'International Bank for Reconstruction and Development', https://www.worldbank.org/en/who-we-are/ibrd, accessed 4 June 2025.

[112] Sundhya Pahuja, 'Global Formations: IMF Conditionality and the South as Legal Subject' in Peter Fitzpatrick and Patricia Tuitt (eds), *Critical Being* (Ashgate Publishing Limited 2004).

[113] Ibid.

[114] Peter Miller, 'Governing by Numbers: Why Calculative Practices Matter' (2001) 68(2) Social Research 379, 381.

[115] Ibid., 380. Miller calls the use of calculative practices which could alter capacities of agents 'technologies of government'. The ultimate goal of using the 'technologies of government' is ensuring that the regulated industry/actors behave in accordance with specified economic objectives.

regarding the implementation of the performance-based conditions.[116] However, the DPO has to liaise with the World Bank in respect of project progress,[117] and provide information as may be reasonably requested by the Bank. In this way, the World Bank can master the functioning of the recipient state's project without the need to impose an overly intrusive form of control.

On the other hand, the World Bank's strategy has minimised the major disadvantages of soft law instruments, which are the lack of legal enforcement and legally binding power. The implementing agency is under a legal obligation to comply with the Bank's financing agreement. A failure by the DPO to ensure compliance in carrying out the Bank's programme could result in a sanction from the World Bank.

The Bank has several ways to ensure compliance with covenants in its agreements, despite the fact that it does not normally take a collateral from the borrowing states.[118] For example, the Bank could suspend the unwithdrawn amount of loan or cancel the suspended disbursement under existing loans. In addition, the Bank could utilise its right of cross suspension for the rest of the loan portfolio that is still disbursing. Moreover, in an extreme case, the Bank could exercise its right of acceleration by demanding an immediate repayment of the loan in full.[119] In the case that a state is subject to any of these sanctions, its reputation in the eyes of other lending organisations could be severely damaged. As a result of this market stigma, the state could find it very difficult to secure a loan from other international organisations in the future.[120]

[116] World Bank (n 526) 69.

[117] Ibid.

[118] There may be circumstances in which the Bank takes a collateral, for example, when it provides a guarantee.

[119] World Bank, 'The World Bank: Legal Aspects' (2011), 26, https://documents1.worldbank.org/curated/ru/713951468349810804/pdf/326020REVISED00egalAspects2011Final.pdf, accessed 4 June 2025. The Bank has never used the right of acceleration.

[120] The World Bank's loans are attractive to developing countries as it is more concessional when compared with other lending organisations. For example, the World Bank's 'most concessional loans are provided with 1.54% fixed interest rates, 10-year grace periods, and 40-year maturities'. In contrast, 'Chinese Government loans to low-income countries typically have a 2% interest rate, 6-year grace periods, and 20-year maturities'. Scott Morris et al., 'Chinese and World Bank Lending Terms: A Systematic Comparison Across 157 Countries and 15 Years' (2020) CGD Policy

4.3.2 *Hard Law Approach: The European Union Experience*

Concerning efforts in harmonising DISs by utilising hard legal instruments, the EU is a pioneer in establishing laws and regulations in order to enhance cross-border cooperation. Prior to the European sovereign debt crisis in 2009, the EU passed the Directive 94/19/EC on deposit guarantee schemes[121] which aimed at two main objectives: increasing the banking system stability and protecting depositors.[122] It was based on the principles of minimum harmonisation[123] and mutual recognition.[124] Nevertheless, the 1994 Directive yielded an insufficient level of harmonisation as DGSs in the EU still provided various coverage levels, depositor eligibility, funding mechanisms and payout procedures.[125] In addition, national authorities were empowered with complete mandates in dealing with deposit insurance.

The need for revising the Directive came into the spotlight when the GFC and the European sovereign debt crisis occurred. In 2009, the EU moved towards a greater degree of harmonisation by recasting the 1994 Deposit Guarantee Schemes Directive.[126] The 2009 Directive embraced the recommendations of de Larosiere report for further harmonisation of the DGSs as well as setting up pre-funded arrangements of the DGSs by the private sector.[127] The de Larosiere report also recommended reviewing powers of host states with respect to branches of foreign banks

Paper 170, 3–5, https://www.cgdev.org/sites/default/files/chinese-and-world-bank-lending-terms-systematic-comparison.pdf, accessed 4 June 2025.

[121] European Parliament and Council Directive 94/19/EC of 30 May 1994 on deposit-guarantee schemes [1994] OJ L135/5.

[122] Maria Gerhardt and Karel Lannoo, 'Options for Reforming Deposit Protection Schemes in the EU' (2011) ECRI Policy Brief No. 4, 2.

[123] Recital 6 of European Parliament and Council Directive 2014/49/EU of 16 April 2014 on deposit guarantee schemes (recast) [2014] OJ L173/149.

[124] Marco Bodellini, 'The Optional Measures of Deposit Guarantee Schemes: Towards a New Bank Crisis Management Paradigm? (2021) 13(1) European Journal of Legal Studies, 348.

[125] Gerhardt and Lannoo (n 538) 2.

[126] European Parliament and Council Directive 2009/14/EC of 11 March 2009 amending Directive 94/19/EC on deposit-guarantee schemes as regards the coverage level and the payout delay [2009] OJ L68/3.

[127] Gerhardt and Lannoo (n 538) 2. European Commission, 'The High-Level Group on Financial Supervision in the EU Chaired by Jacques de Larosiere' (Report 2009). See Recommendation 14 in 'Brief Summary of the de Larosiere Report',

in order to provide equal protection to all bank customers across the EU.[128] In 2014, the 2009 Directive was recast and the Directive 2014/49/EU (hereafter, the DGSD) was adopted.[129] The goals of the DGSD are to provide a consistent level of depositor protection across the Union and ensure that the DGSs have the same level of stability. Moreover, the DGSD aims to contribute to the completion of the internal market by setting common requirements for all the DGSs to eliminate market distortions.[130]

4.3.2.1 Weaknesses of the Harmonised Deposit Guarantee Schemes in the EU

According to Abbott and Snidal, hard law provides credible commitments to future behaviour in order to enhance welfare-improving cooperation.[131] For example, legalisation constrains 'self-serving auto-interpretation' by giving the authority to interpret legal issues to legal institutions (e.g., the judiciary). As judicial reviews allow disputes to be resolved by using legal standards and procedures, relevant parties would find the cost of non-performance of their legal obligations is higher.[132] In addition, when international legal commitments are incorporated into domestic law, the national courts and administrative authorities could apply domestic law in order to uphold those commitments.[133]

As for the DGSD regime, the Member States have to transpose the Directive into their national laws. Consequently, the EU rules are applicable in each member country. For example, the deposit coverage for each depositor across the Union is set at EUR 100,000.[134] In addition, all DGSs of the Member States have mandatory tasks of repayment to

11, https://www.europarl.europa.eu/meetdocs/2009_2014/documents/deea/dv/2110_09/2110_09en.pdf, accessed 4 June 2025.

[128] Ibid.

[129] Directive 2014/49/EU (n 539).

[130] Recital 6 (n 539).

[131] Abbott and Snidal (n 498) 426.

[132] Ibid., 427.

[133] Ibid., 428.

[134] Recital 21 of the DGSD. This level of coverage was first stipulated in Recital 3 of the 2009 Directive.

depositors of a failed bank[135] and financing a resolution.[136] Moreover, conducts of national and supranational authorities are subject to legal reviews by the national courts, the EU General Court and the CJEU. Nevertheless, the current regime still has some weaknesses which reveal soft aspects of hard legal commitments. I will discuss these issues from the perspectives of the synchronisation of the DGSD system with other regimes, and the EU incomplete vertical network which could lead to problems about cooperation and coordination among relevant authorities.

Inconsistencies and Tensions Between the DGSD and Other Regimes

Hard legal instruments could provide the advantage of creating an internally consistent system. However, in the case of the DGSD regime, this benefit is doubtful. That is, in part, because the effectiveness of a DIS depends not only on its own functioning but also its synchronisation with other mechanisms of the financial safety net. More importantly, the hard law systems which involve in dealing with bank crisis management are not necessarily designed and promulgated in a way which yield consistent frameworks. Inconsistencies and tensions between the operation of the DGSD system and those of other regimes could arise from the use of the deposit guarantee funds for non-traditional functions of deposit insurance. These non-traditional roles of the DGSs are 1) financing a resolution to preserve continuous access to deposits (Article 11(2) of the DGSD); 2) failure prevention if it is allowed by national laws (Article 11(3) of the DGSD); and 3) preserving the access of depositors to covered deposits in insolvency proceedings which is optional for the Member States (Article 11(6) of the DGSD).[137] I will elaborate these issues in turn.

Financing a Resolution: Doubts About the Adequacy in Protecting the DGS Funds

There are three possible main sources which can be used in financing a resolution: the Single Resolution Fund (SRF), national resolution funding

[135] Article 11(1) of the DGSD.

[136] Article 11(2) of the DGSD. Previously, the DGSs of Germany and the Netherlands had 'paybox' mandate. FSB (n 447) 16.

[137] EBA, 'Guidelines on Stress Tests of Deposit Guarantee Schemes under Directive 2014/49/EU' (24 May 2016), 15.

arrangements (NRFAs), and national DGS funds. With respect to the SRF, it is the Banking Union's mechanism which is available for 19 Eurozone Member States and participating non-Eurozone Member States.[138] The participating non-Eurozone Member States are Bulgaria and Croatia: they have established a close cooperation with the European Central Bank in accordance with Article 7 SSMR in 2020. Bulgaria and Croatia have also transferred and mutualised their resolution financing arrangements with the SRF.[139]

In addition, a financial institution has to provide critical functions and obtain a positive PIA in order to be resolved and eligible for accessing the SRF. The SRB can use the SRF when utilising resolution tools and resolution powers.[140] The Fund is responsible for facilitating resolution and acting as a fiscal backstop to the SRM.[141] It is to be used as a primary source of any additional funding support in resolution after the failed bank's shareholders and creditors have borne the cost associated with the resolution process.[142]

Concerning the NRFAs, they are established by the Member States in accordance with Article 100 of the BRRD I. The NRA can utilise them when applying the resolution tools and exercising the resolution powers. According to Article 101 of the BRRD II, the purposes for which the NFRAs can be applied are limited to, for example, purchasing assets of the credit institution under resolution, making contributions to a

[138] Recital 15 of SRMR I states that the SRMR 'applies only in respect of banks whose home supervisor is the ECB or the national competent authority in Member States where currency is the euro or in Member States whose currency is not the euro which have established a close cooperation in accordance with Article 7 of Regulation (EU) No 1024/2013'.

[139] Maria J. Nieto and Dalvinder Singh, 'Incentive Compatible Relationship Between the ERM II and Close Cooperation in the Banking Union: The Case of Bulgaria and Croatia' (2021) Banco de Espana Occasional Paper No. 2117, 24, https://papers.ssrn.com/sol3/papers.cfm?abstract_id=3882611, accessed 4 June 2025.

[140] Article 67 of the SRMR I. However, the SRB does not have a legal authority to access national DGS funds in resolution. Atilla Arda and Marc Dobler, 'The Role for Deposit Insurance Funds in Dealing with Failing Banks in the European Union' (2022) IMF Working Paper WP22/2, 9–10.

[141] The SRF is the single financing arrangement for the Member States which participate in the SSM and the SRM.

[142] Central Bank of Ireland, 'Central Bank of Ireland Technical Views on Topics Raised in the European Commission's Targeted Questionnaire on the CMDI Review' (Memorandum 2021), 9.

bridge bank and an asset management vehicle, and paying compensation to shareholders or creditors in pursuance of the NCWO principle.[143]

With regard to the DGS funds, according to Recital 14 of the DGSD, their primary role is to repay depositors (i.e., the 'paybox' mandate) in order to protect them 'against the consequences of the insolvency of a credit institution'.[144] In addition, Recital 15 of the DGSD stipulates that the DGSs 'should also assist in the financing of the resolution of credit institutions' (i.e., a 'paybox plus' mandate). Nevertheless, the DGSD does not state that the DGS funds are to be used as a primary source for funding a resolution.

Moreover, Article 11(2) of the DGSD has provided safeguards to protect depositors as well as prevent the DGS funds from being depleted in resolution by requiring that the DGS's contribution must be made in accordance with Article 109 of the BRRD I.[145] Pursuant to Article 109, the DGS's contribution in resolution must not be greater than the amount of the hypothetical exposure of the DGS in liquidation. Besides this, Article 109 specifies that the contribution of the DGS is limited to the amount equal to 50 per cent of its target level, which is 0.8 per cent of the amount of the covered deposits of its members (Article 10 of the DGSD). Furthermore, the resolution authority has to consult with the DGS when determining the amount by which the DGS is liable (A. 11(2) of the DGSD).

Nonetheless, the BRRD regime could create a massive burden on a DGS capacity in financing a resolution process. For example, the use of NRFAs and the SRF is subject to strict constraints; these limitations could effectively put the national DGSs under great pressure in financing a resolution during a crisis. According to Article 101(2) of the BRRD I and Article 76(3) of the SRMR I, the NRFAs and the SRF can neither be used directly to absorb the losses nor to recapitalise an institution or entity. As a result of this restriction, the scope of utilising these funds

[143] See further A. 101(1)(a)-(h) for the purposes which the NRFAs can be utilised.

[144] A traditional task of deposit insurance is the repayment function or 'paybox' mandate (Article 11(1) of DGSD). However, given the harmonisation agenda of the DGSD, functions of the DGSs across the Union have expanded to include a 'paybox plus' mandate, which is financing a resolution to preserve continuous access to deposits (Article 11(2) of the DGSD).

[145] Directive 2014/59/EU (n 539).

would be extremely narrow.[146] It would exclude many circumstances such as a transfer of uninsured deposits by the SRB prior to the initiation of insolvency proceedings.

In addition, the NRFAs and the SRF can only support a failed bank, 'in exceptional circumstances, where the bail-in tool is applied' and the losses that would have been borne by excluded liabilities 'have not been passed on fully to other creditors'. In order to do so, two key conditions must be satisfied.[147] First, there has been a bail-in of at least eight per cent of total liabilities including own funds of the institutions.[148] Secondly, the contribution does not exceed five per cent of the total liabilities including own funds of the credit institutions.[149]

Concerning the first limb of the conditions, this requirement could exclude many medium-sized banks from the scope of permitted contributions of the NRFAs and the SRF. This is despite the fact that some of those financial institutions could pose significant systemic threats, as exemplified by the Northern Rock collapse. Those medium-sized institutions might lack a reputation which is necessary to attract sophisticated investors to buy their MREL-eligible instruments and/or to issue their debt securities on a regulated market. Hence, they might not be able to gain access to an adequate funding in order to satisfy the requirement for the use of the NRFAs and the SRF. Besides this, the eight per cent loss-absorbing requirement neither covers 'historical' losses already absorbed by shareholders and creditors prior to the declaration of FOLTF nor losses which are not yet reflected in CET1 at the point of failure. As a consequence, the condition could exclude some credit institutions which have utilised a large part of their loss absorption capacity (i.e., MREL) during the recovery period.[150]

Moreover, the BRRD implicitly suggests the use of the DGS funds, rather than a resolution tool. The BRRD allows a resolution action to

[146] As Gleeson has argued, 'almost any intervention in a bank resolution is at least arguably for the purpose of avoiding losses'. Simon Gleeson, 'The Single Resolution Mechanism and the EU Crisis Management Tools' in Gianni Lo Schiavo (ed), *The European Banking Union and the Role of Law* (Elgar Financial Law Series 2019).

[147] See Articles 44(3), 44(4) and 44(5) of the BRRD I and Articles 27(5), 27(6) and 27(7) of the SRMR I.

[148] Article 44(5)(a) of the BRRD I and Article 27(7)(a) of the SRMR I.

[149] Article 44(5)(b) of the BRRD I and Article 27(7)(b) of the SRMR I.

[150] Central Bank of Ireland (n 558) 9–10.

be taken only in limited circumstances in which the public interest test is satisfied. Otherwise, a liquidation under normal insolvency proceedings should be the norm (Recital 45 and Article 32(b) of the BRRD I). This interpretation of the BRRD, in effect, renders resolution an exception and insolvency a default mode. Since the NRFAs and the SRF can only be used in resolution, it is more likely that the DGSs will be under an obligation to provide an assistance to a failed bank.

Apart from the above-mentioned arguments, there are some limitations in protecting the DGS funds which do not apply to both the NRFAs and the SRF. For instance, in the Banking Union, A. 79 of the SRMR I prohibits the circumstance in which the DGS incurs its losses in resolution more than it would have been the case in a winding up under national insolvency proceedings. Meanwhile, it is possible under the BRRD framework for the DGS to do so. In this instance, the DGS will be entitled to receive the difference of payment from the NRFA. However, the NRFA will only pay the difference to the DGS if the valuer determines that the latter has to bear a greater amount than the net losses in a winding up under normal insolvency proceedings (Article 109 (1) of the BRRD I). As discussed in Chapter 3, valuation could lead to inaccurate results as the valuer has to complete the task within a very short timeframe. Accordingly, the extent to which the DGS funds would be adequately protected in resolution outside the jurisdiction of the Banking Union is questionable.

Furthermore, the SRF has its own limitations and conditions for using it which raise a question regarding whether the SRF is a credible source to fund a resolution during a systemic crisis. As Nicolaides and O'Connor have stated, the size of the SRF is much smaller than some national resolution funds (e.g., Germany and Sweden).[151] Similarly, the IMF has commented that the SRF's target level at 55 billion euros by 2023 is relatively small when compared with the size of the largest significant financial institutions and the possibility of contagion which could prevent the use of bail-in tool.[152] Besides its small size, the Member States could exercise their right to object an access to the SRF for a failing institution. Article

[151] Phedon Nicolaides and Tony O'Connor, 'Is the Bank-Sovereign Link Truly Severed?' (2016) Bruges European Economic Policy Briefings 43/2016, 5.

[152] IMF, 'Euro Area Policies. Financial Sector Assessment Program. Technical Note-Bank Resolution and Crisis Management' (2018) IMF Country Report No. 18/232, 19.

7(4) of the Intergovernmental Agreement[153] enables a Member State to utilise a veto power regarding a temporary transfer of the funds from their own national contribution.[154] In the case that this right is exercised in a crisis, it could distort the incentive of the Member States to coordinate and cooperate with each other.

Failure Prevention Functions: Legal Risk Due to State-aid Rules

A soft aspect of the EU hard law-based deposit insurance regime could be considered based on the fact that the Member States may choose to implement some or all national options and discretions (NODs).[155] One of these NODs is for the deposit guarantee funds to support preventative measures. According to the European Forum of Deposit Insurers, taking preventative measures costs less than reimbursing depositors.[156] In addition, it might be more efficient for the DGSs to contribute to a restructuring of a bank in difficulty at an early stage than to await until the bank's problems become out of control.[157] Pursuant to Article 11(3) of the DGSD, national DGSs are allowed to do so provided that some conditions have been satisfied. For example, there has not been any resolution action taken by the resolution authority,[158] and the costs of the measures

153 Council of the European Union, 'Agreement on the transfer and mutualisation of contributions to the Single Resolution Fund' (14 May 2014) 8457/14, https://data.consilium.europa.eu/doc/document/ST-8457-2014-INIT/en/pdf, accessed 4 June 2025.

154 Napoleon Xanthoulis, 'Single Resolution Fund and Emergency Liquidity Assistance: Status Quo and Reform Perspectives on Emergency Financial Support in the Banking Union' in Gianni Lo Schiavo (ed), *The European Banking Union and the Role of Law* (Elgar Financial Law Series 2019), 281.

155 The Member States could do so if they deem the implemenation appropriate to reflect their national circumstances. European Commission, 'Options and National Discretions under the Deposit Guarantee Scheme Directive and Their Treatment in the Context of a European Deposit Insurance Scheme' (Final Report 2019), 9.

156 European Forum of Deposit Insurers, 'Deposit Guarantee Schemes' Alternative Measures to Pay-out for Effective Banking Crisis Solution' (2019) EFDI State of Play and Non-Binding Guidance Paper, 29.

157 Bodellini (n 540) 353.

158 Article 11(3)(a) of the DGSD.

must not exceed those of the DGS in fulfilling its statutory or contractual mandate.[159] Currently, only nine Member States have transposed this NOD.[160]

Nevertheless, the scope of permitted use of the DGS funds on preventative measures could be uncertain due to the operation of the EU state aid framework. As noted in Chapter 3, the objective of the state aid control under article 107 of the TFEU is to avoid the distortion of competition in the internal market. The distortion could occur where a state grants any selective advantage through state resources for certain undertakings or the production of certain goods.[161]

The EU state aid rules are susceptible to different national applications. For example, various legal structures of national DGSs (e.g., private or public legal nature) could lead to different decisions as to whether or not the concerned measures constitute state aid.[162] In the case that a preventative measure might be considered state aid, the Member State must wait for the European Commission's decision before the measure can take effect. This legal risk could be considered from the case of *Banca Tercas*. In *Tercas*, the Italian mandatory deposit guarantee scheme, Fondo Interbancario di Tutela dei Depositi (FITD), was found by the Commission in

[159] Article 11(3)(c) of the DGSD. Baudino et al. have argued that it is ambiguous whether the cap means 'the total amount of covered deposits or the expected net costs of payout in the event the bank failed and was liquidated'. Patrizia Baudino et al., 'Bank Failure Management – The Role of Deposit Insurance' (2019) FSI Insights on Policy Implementation No. 17, 32.

[160] European Commission (n 571) 124. The Member States which have transposed NOD 13 are Austria, Croatia, France, Germany, Ireland, Italy, Malta, Poland and Spain.

[161] According to paragraph 133 of *Tercas* case, 'the concept of intervention 'through State resources', within the meaning of A. 107(1) TFEU, is intended to cover, in addition to advantages granted directly by the State, those granted through a public or private body appointed or established by that State to administer the aid'. In addition, financial means need not be permanent state assets. They may be assets which are under public control and available to the competent national authorities (C-656/15P *Commission v TV2/Denmark* [2017] (ECJ, 9 November 2017)).

[162] Kathrin Blanck, 'State Aid and Bank Resolution Law before the European Court of Justice' in Chiara Zilioli and others (eds), *Judicial Review in the European Banking Union* (Edward Elgar Publishing Limited 2021), 483–484.

2015 to act contrary to the state aid rules.[163] Its conduct was decided to be beyond pay-out functions to depositors. The FITD provided funding for the benefit of Banca Tercas in order to cover losses of the bank as well as facilitate its sale to Banca Populare di Bari. According to the Commission, the FITD had acted on behalf of the Italian State.[164]

The Commission's state aid decisions and procedures are subject to judicial review by the EU General Court and the CJEU (Article 263 of the TFEU). Its decision in Tercas was challenged before the EU General Court; the latter delivered its judgement in 2019 which annulled the Commission's Decision.[165] The General Court held that the Commission had to prove, among other things, that Italian public authorities controlled resources used in order to establish that an intervention was adopted under the influence or control of public authorities.[166] In this case, the FITD was 'a consortium of banks governed by private law'; it acted in the interests of its members. Besides this, the Bank of Italy did not have an influence on the decision of the FITD to intervene in favour of Banca Tercas. Hence, it could not be concluded that 'as a result of the control exercised by the public authorities, the resources used by the FITD to finance the intervention measures are 'State resources' within the meaning of Article 107(1) TFEU'.[167]

[163] A. 108(3) of the TFEU. Commission Decision of 23 December 2015 on the State aid SA. 39451 (2015/C) (ex 2015/NN) implemented by Italy for Banca Tercas. The FITD is a 'government legislated and privately administered' DGS according to the IADI Annual Survey in 2021. IADI (n 515).

[164] European Commission, 'State aid: Commission Finds Italy Provided Incompatible State Aid to Banca Tercas and Welcomes Plans of Private Funds to Step In' (Press Release. 23 December 2015).

[165] Joined cases T-98/16, T-196/16 and T-198/16 *Italy and Others v Commission* [2019].

[166] The Court stated that 'Where that entity is governed by private law or is autonomous, including, as regards the management of its funds, by comparison with intervention by public authorities and with public funds, in the strict sense, the Commission is, subject to full review by the EU Courts, under an even more important obligation to specify and substantiate the reasons which justify its conclusion that the resources used are under public control and the measures are imputable to the State and, consequently, that there is aid within the meaning of Article 107(1) TFEU'. Ibid., paragraph 67.

[167] Ibid., paragraph 144.

In 2021, the CJEU dismissed the Commission's appeal.[168] One of the grounds of appeal raised by the Commission was that the General Court imposed on the Commission a more onerous burden of proof than that which case-law of the CJEU requires. On this issue, the CJEU ruled that the burden of proof regarding the imputability of an aid measure depends on the circumstances and the context in which the measure was utilised. The General Court merely applied case-law rather than imposed a different standard of proof. The CJEU also clarified that the Commission had to demonstrate that there was a clear capital connection between the FITD and the State for the measures taken by the former to be held imputable to the latter (s. 73).[169]

However, the decisions in *Tercas* have raised a concern about the extent to which judicial reviews could provide credible commitments to future behaviour, increase the cost of reneging, and create consistency of the relevant legal frameworks. For instance, the scope of legal matters that are subject to judicial review is limited. The CJEU in *Tercas* has explained that according to Article 256(1) TFEU and Article 58(1) of the Statue of the Court of Justice of the European Union, an appeal is merely allowed on points of law which do not include an assessment of facts and evidence. It is only when the General Court has found or appraised facts, as well as decided on their legal nature and legal consequences, that the CJEU has a jurisdiction to conduct a review.[170]

Moreover, the CJEU in *Tercas* did not take the opportunity to provide consistency to the incoherent EU legal frameworks. It did not explicitly state the criteria which would differentiate measures adopted by the DGS which are imputable to the State from those which are not. Therefore,

[168] Case C-425/19 P *Commission v Italy and Others* [2021].

[169] Mario Siragusa et al., 'EU Court of Justice Confirms that Italian Deposit Guarantee Scheme Intervention in Support of Banca Tercas Did Not Cconstitute State Aid' (*Cleary Gottlieb*, 2 April 2021), https://www.clearygottlieb.com/news-and-insights/publication-listing/eu-court-of-justice-confirms-that-italian-deposit-guarantee-scheme, accessed 4 June 2025.

[170] The Court of Justice normally demonstrates deference to the administrative authorities in complex assessment. As Ioannidis has noted, the EU authorities enjoy a broad discretion while the role of the EU courts is not to replace the former's analysis regarding complex facts with their own judgement. Michael Ioannidis, 'The Judicial Review of Discretion in the Banking Union: From 'Soft' to 'Hard(er)' Look?' in Zilioli and others (eds) (n 578) 133.

the inconsistency between the resolution rules, DGSs' optional intervention and state aid framework are still present. This incongruity stems from the fact that Article 32(4)(d) of the BRRD I states that a bank is deemed to be FOLTF if there is a need for the use of an extraordinary public financial support. Article 2(1)(28) of the BRRD I defines extraordinary public financial support as 'State aid within the meaning of Article 107(1) TFEU or any other public financial support at supranational level, which, if provided at national level, would constitute State aid'. In other words, if the utilisation of an alternative measure is a form of state aid within the meaning of Article 107(1) TFEU, the credit institution would be deemed to be FOLTF. Then, a resolution action, which was eschewed by using alternative measures in the first place, would be triggered.[171] To circumvent this discrepancy, Marco Bodellini has advocated that the DGS's measures which comply with the least cost principles should not breach state aid rules, irrespective of their governance structures and decision-making process.[172]

This inconsistency between the resolution, DGS and state aid frameworks should be alleviated when the CMDI legislation enters into force. Currently, the Commission, the Parliament and the Council—during the ongoing trilogue—are of the view that an extraordinary financial support, which complies with the conditions and requirements of the state aid framework, should not result in an institution being deemed as FOLTF under Article 32(4)(d) of the BRRD I.[173]

Furthermore, it is doubtful whether the utilisation of judicial reviews in *Tercas* has promoted a welfare-improving cooperation. Preventative measures were likely to minimise losses to the DGS by solving the bank's problems promptly.[174] However, this case took six years to reach

[171] The resolution action would be triggered provided that the public interest assessment was satisfied and there is no reasonable prospect that any alternative private sector measures or supervisory action would prevent the failure within a reasonable timeframe (A. 32(1)(b) BRRD I).

[172] Bodellini (n 540) 375.

[173] Article 32c(1) of the Proposal for a Directive of the European Parliament and of the Council amending Directive 2014/59/EU as regards early intervention measures, conditions for resolution and financing of resolution action and Directive 2014/24/EU as regards services needed for the preparation, application and exercise of resolution tools and powers.

[174] Abstaining from using those measures was contrary to the long practice of the DGS in Italy. According to Bodellini, the Italian DGS used optional measures more frequently

a final decision regarding the status of the measures. The delay, in effect, deprived Italy of its right to use preventative measures while the case was still pending in the EU Courts. Besides this, the *Tercas* case could give rise to an undesirable incentive on the part of a Member State to strategically establish a DGS with a similar legal structure to the FITD in order to avoid the state aid control. This could, in turn, jeopardise a genuine cooperation among the Member States.

Contribution to Insolvency Scenario: Striking the Right Balance Between Protecting Depositors and Maintaining Financial Stability

As for funding alternative measures in accordance with Article 11(6) of the DGSD, these tools are intended to preserve the access of depositors to covered deposits in insolvency.[175] Article 11(6) or NOD 14 has been transposed by only 10 Member States so far.[176] The measures laid out in Article 11(6) cover transfers of assets and liabilities including deposit book transfers of an insolvent bank to a healthy credit institution. Deposit guarantee funds could be utilised to back a transfer in the case that there is a shortfall in assets of a failed bank.[177] In performing such intervention, the DGSs would help ensure the depositors that their deposits are fully protected. Thus, the risk of bank run and potential disruption to the real economy would be minimised.

Article 11(6) has stipulated a condition for using the funds that 'the costs borne by the DGS do not exceed the net amount of compensating covered depositors' of the failed bank. Nonetheless, the financial cap might not be able to help maintain financial stability in some instances. As Restoy has criticised, the financial cap is too restrictive on the use

than its pay-box function as the former were considered by the DGS to provide more effectiveness than the latter. Bodellini (n 540) 362.

[175] Fernando Restoy et al., 'Bank Failure Management in the European Banking Union: What's Wrong and How to Fix It' (2020) Financial Stability Institute Occasional Paper No. 15, 10.

[176] These Member States are Belgium, Denmark, Finland, Greece, Ireland, Italy, Luxembourg, Lithuania, Malta and Poland. European Commission (n 571) 139.

[177] Restoy et al. (n 591) 10.

of the deposit guarantee funds in insolvency.[178] The effect of the financial cap has to be considered with the super-preference rule for covered deposits[179] (i.e., covered deposits would be paid out in priority to non-covered deposits) under the BRRD's tiered depositor preference.[180] As the DGS will subrogate for insured depositors' rights in the assets of the failed bank, the risk of the DGS suffering losses will be significantly diminished. Losses will be shifted to uninsured depositors and other senior unsecured creditors.[181] Consequently, the financial cap coupled with the super-preference rule would largely limit the amount of deposit guarantee funds which can be used for the alternative measures.[182] This limitation could lead to financial instability concerns in the case that the DGS funds are not adequate to fund transfers, especially those of mid-sized banks with a negative PIA.[183]

The Incomplete Vertical Network of the EU Deposit Guarantee Schemes

The current DGS systems in the EU are conducted mainly at the national level. The EU supranational authorities have taken only some duties in respect of deposit insurance schemes. For example, the EBA is responsible

[178] ibid. According to Restoy et al., the 'expected recoveries from subrogation to the depositors' claims in insolvency' have to be factored in when calculating the net amount of compensating the holders of covered deposits.

[179] With regard to the super-preference rule, the CMDI framework has introduced certain changes in order to broaden the scope of funding available for resolution. However, at the time of writing, the three institutions involved in trilogue negotiations remain divided. The Commission proposes a single-tier depositor preference approach, under which all deposits rank equally in a higher position than the claims of ordinary unsecured creditors. The Parliament, by contrast, advocates for a two-tier structure of depositor preference, whereby covered deposits, DGS claims, eligible deposits, and deposits held by branches located outside the Union that would otherwise qualify as eligible deposits rank above other deposits. Concerning the Council's proposal, it supports a general depositor preference consisting of four tiers. According to this approach, covered deposits and DGS claims would rank highest among all deposits. Council of the European Union, *'CMDI Trilogue'* (16 January 2025).

[180] Some EU Member States have utilised general depositor preference rules instead of a tier depositor preference approach under Article 108 of the BRRD I (e.g., Germany and Italy). Chan et al. (n 15) 251.

[181] Hajra and Moetomo (n 492).

[182] Restoy et al. (n 591) 10.

[183] Ibid., 18.

for publishing a peer review based on the DGS stress tests performed by national authorities across the European Economic Area (EEA). The national DGSs as well as relevant authorities have to comply with the Revised EBA Guidelines on DGS stress tests,[184] or provide reasons for non-compliance in accordance with Article 16(3) of Regulation (EU) No 1093/2010. In addition, in reporting to the EBA with respect to the legal functions assessed in the core tests, the DGSs have to grade their resilience against their ability to fulfil their functions in accordance with Directives 2014/49/EU and 2014/59/EU.[185]

Concerning the home-host cooperation, the Revised Guidelines states that the DGSs of both home and host states should 'assess their ability to efficiently and securely communicate with each other', including the ability necessary for accessing and exchanging data for repayment.[186] In addition, DGSs should test systems for repaying depositor at branches of their member banks in other Member States.[187] Moreover, the home and host DGSs should collaborate with each other to specify the deadline that the former will transfer funds to the latter. These funds will be used by the host DGS in making repayments to bank branches' depositors.[188] With regard to cooperation between DGSs and other authorities, in the case that a stress test is carried out on a stand-alone basis, the EBA encourages the DGSs to consult resolution authority for the purposes of designing the scenario and conducting the test. Besides this, the resolution authority should be invited to take part in the test; it should also provide the DGSs with necessary information in designing and running the tests.[189]

I argue that the incomplete vertical network of EU authorities and national deposit insurance officials might not be able to deliver a sufficient level of legal certainty as well as maintain financial stability in a

[184] The Revised Guidelines repeal and replace the 2016 Guidelines on the DGS stress tests. EBA, 'Final Report on the Revised Guidelines on Stress Tests of Deposit Guarantee Schemes under Directive 2014/49/EU Repealing and Replacing Guidelines EBA/GL/2016/04 (Revised Guidelines on DGS Stress Tests)' (2021) EBA/GL/2021/10.

[185] Ibid., 46. DGS functions which are covered by core tests are functions under Articles 11(1), 11(2), 11(3), 11(6), 14 and 109 of the DGSD. Ibid., 19.

[186] Ibid., 34.

[187] Ibid., 33.

[188] Ibid., 36.

[189] Ibid., 21.

cross-border case for some reasons. First, the bifurcation of responsibilities between the supranational and national authorities is cumbersome in controlling and mitigating a contagion risk, which could spread from one country to another. For example, the costs of activating national deposit guarantees and using liquidation measures as a result of a bank failure in a Member State might not be taken into account by the supranational authorities (e.g., the SRB).[190] Similarly, national authorities may not sufficiently factor in the effects of their decisions in other Member States. As Gerhardt and Lannoo have argued, the incentive for national supervisors or deposit insurers to intervene in the case of deposits located in other countries or activities of foreign branches in their territory could be lower.[191]

In addition, the current system does not provide power for national deposit insurance authorities to take a more active supervisory role with respect to foreign branches of banks headquartered in their countries. This is despite the fact that the home DGS is responsible for funding the liquidation of those branches. In my view, the home DGS needs to be constantly informed about financial standings of its member financial institutions in order to effectively perform this task.

According to Article 84(4) of the BRRD I, the Directive does not prevent resolution authorities and other competent officials from sharing information with deposit insurers. Similarly, Article 88(6) of the SRMR I allows the ECB, NCAs and other authorities to share information with the DGSs. In addition, Article 4(10) of the DGSD states that the DGSs should be informed immediately if the competent authorities detect that there are problems which are likely to lead to the intervention of a deposit insurer. However, the DGSD does not stipulate that the Member States shall put in place formal and explicit arrangements with other members of the financial safety net. Hence, this would allow a large discretion on the part of the national and supranational authorities in interpreting and implementing the rules as well as setting up an arrangement.[192] This is in contrast to the practice of some Member States, such as Italy, where

[190] Joao Valle e Azevedo and Diana Bonfim, 'Deposit Insurance and Cross-border Banks' (2019) 17(1) ifo DICE Report 14.

[191] Gerhardt and Lannoo (n 538) 9.

[192] The IADI has commented on Article 4(10) that it has created some mismatching with Core Principle 4. According to the *Handbook for the Assessment of Compliance with the Core Principles for Effective Deposit Insurance Schemes* (2015), there should be

the law has allowed the central bank to share information with the FITD and foreign DGSs. According to Salama and Braga, the Bank of Italy provides information about business profile and contribution basis to the FITD tri-annually as well as promptly informs the DGS at the start of crisis management procedures.[193]

Moreover, a mere information sharing between the DGSs and the home and host supervisors or the ECB might not be adequate in the case of a liquidation or resolution of foreign branches of a bank. For instance, bank supervisors in one country might be willing to keep the problem bank alive as its failure might lead to financial instability in the country. Meanwhile, a national DGS of another state might be of the view that closing the bank in trouble as soon as possible is necessary in order to avoid worse situations and greater losses to the DGS funds. In such instance, the national supervisory authorities might not share all the important information with the DGS of another state. This practice could impact the functioning of the DGS in carrying out its tasks. For example, a timely access to information is crucially important for the home DGS which has to complete a payment decision as well as operational arrangements within a short timeframe before the resolution weekend.

Secondly, the current DGSD regime which allows for varied national features and rules could exacerbate a crisis. The regime leaves a large amount of discretion to the Member States in transposing the Directive, which could dilute its intended effects. According to the European Commission, the progress in transposing 22 NODs of the DGSD and the established national requirements are various among the Member States.[194]

'explicit, formal arrangements' in order to ensure that the deposit insurers receive necessary information constantly, especially in the case that supervisory authorities are taking important actions. IADI, "Mind the Gap!' A Comparative Analysis Between the IADI CPs and the DGSD' (2017), 23, https://www.iadi.org/en/assets/File/Papers/Regional%20Papers/Mind_the_Gap__Final.pdf, accessed 4 June 2025.

193 Salama and Braga (n 518) 28.

194 European Commission (n 571) 3.

In addition, the heterogeneity of national rules could allow problems relating to the link between the sovereign state and their credit institutions[195] to spread from one country to another.[196] For instance, the non-transposition of Article 15(1) of the DGSD or NOD 20 could result in a situation in which a crisis in a non-EU state spreads into the EU through their foreign branches located in the host EU state.[197] According to Article 15(1) of the DGSD, the Member States may require branches

[195] The sovereign-bank nexus occurs where high indebtedness of a national government could harm the stability of its banking system, and vice versa. There could be the 'doom loop' where the affected system further weakens the financial strength of the originating sector of the problem, be that a sovereign government or the banking industry. Andreas Dombret, 'A Way to a Viable Level Playing Field' in Andreas Dombret and Patrick S. Kenadjian (eds), *EDIS, NPLs, Sovereign Debt and Safe Assets* (De Gruyter 2020), 194. The circumstance in which a crisis originating in the sovereign indebtedness later affects the banking sector could be considered from the case of Greece. Greece encountered a sovereign debt crisis in the aftermath of the GFC. Consequently, the problem of the state's public finances resulted in a financial distress for banks in the country. Patirick Kenadjian, 'What Do Sovereign Debt and 'Safe Assets' Have to Do with EDIS?' in Dombret and Kenadjian (n 611), 253. With regard to a scenario where an initial shock starting from the banking sector, this could be considered from the case of Ireland. In 2008, the Irish banking system became a serious issue; therefore, the government provided bailouts in order to rescue failing financial institutions. As a consequence of bank bailouts, the Irish government had to request a financial assistance from the IMF.

[196] The role of a national government which provides deposit guarantee in the emergence of debt and sovereign debt crises have been studied by some scholars. For example, according to Leonello (2018), public guarantees or deposit insurance arrangements to financial institutions have a large effect on the sovereign-bank nexus. That is because a government must rely on resources, which are subject to investors' roll-over decisions of sovereign bonds, in contributing to state guarantees. In the case that there are few investors rolling over their investment or the government has to transfer a large amount of money to the banking sector, the state would become more fiscally-constrained. In such circumstance, the expected repayment to sovereign creditors would decrease and there is a greater possibility that a sovereign would default. Consequently, there is a sovereign risk that the state might not be able to pay the insured deposits. Hence, a low-cost response of depositors would be to withdraw their savings from a bank in difficulty. Agnese Leonello, 'Government Guarantees and the Two-way Feedback between Banking and Sovereign Debt Crises' (2018) 130 Journal of Financial Economics 592, 594. National deposit insurance typically has 'a fund that accounts for only a small portion of deposits they insure and rely on explicit support from the government to guarantee their obligations in case one or more banks default'. Diana Bonfim and Joao A.C. Santos, 'The Importance of Deposit Insurance Credibility' (2020) Working Paper, 5, https://www.bportugal.pt/en/paper/importance-deposit-insurance-credibility, accessed 4 June 2025.

[197] There are, currently, 23 Member States which have transposed this NOD. There countries are Belgium, Bulgaria, Croatia, Cyprus, Czechia, Denmark, Estonia, France, Germany, Greece, Hungary, Ireland, Italy, Lithuania, Luxembourg, the Netherlands,

of a bank headquartered outside the EU to join a national DGS. Most of the Member States which have done so require those branches to join their national DGSs only in the case that the home DGS is not deemed equivalent.[198] Meanwhile, a minority of the Member States (Austria, Finland, Latvia and Malta) do not allow branches of third country banks to join their national DGSs.[199]

However, the home state DGSs of those third country branches might not offer an equal level of deposit protection when compared with the protection provided by the DGSD framework. For instance, Malta has third country branches; one of them is Akbank TAS which is headquartered in Turkey. The deposit in this institution would not be protected by the Depositor Compensation Scheme of Malta. Besides this, the Savings Deposit Insurance Fund of Turkey provides a deposit coverage for only up to TRY 150,000 or around EUR 15,240, which is far below the level of coverage of EUR 100,000 provided by the DGSD.

In an extreme circumstance, in which there are significant third-country branches in the EU, the non-transposition of Article 15(1) could put EU Member States in a similar position to those of the UK and the Netherlands during the Icelandic crisis in 2008. The crisis involved the collapses and bank runs of three major credit institutions: Kaupthing, Landsbanki and Glitnir. The total assets of these three banks equal to more than 11 times of the GDP of Iceland in 2007. The Icelandic deposit insurance scheme could not solve this problem as it was underfunded. In addition, the Central Bank of Iceland could not provide LOLR support, due to the enormous size of the financial system relative to the country's economy.

There were many customers of the failed banks through their foreign branches in the UK and the Netherlands. Hence, the UK and Dutch governments decided to compensate the depositors in order to protect local depositors and pursued a litigation against the Icelandic government. Nevertheless, the EFTA Court delivered a decision in 2013 that Iceland's obligations under the Directive on deposit-guarantee schemes[200] were

Poland, Portugal, Romania, Slovakia, Slovenia, Spain and Sweden. European Commission (n 607) 179.

[198] Ibid., 180.

[199] Within this group, Malta is the only country which has third country branches. Ibid., 180.

[200] European Parliament and Council Directive 94/19/EC (n 573).

limited to establishing a deposit guarantee scheme.[201] Those obligations did not cover how Iceland would fund the scheme.[202] As a consequence of this ruling, Iceland's bank debts were effectively transferred to the UK and Dutch governments, as well as their taxpayers.[203]

Thirdly, the utilisation of the network of DGSs with a harmonised level of deposit protection might not be adequate in order to increase financial stability and prevent bank runs. The EU would also need to establish a common fiscal backstop and European deposit guarantee system in order to pursue these objectives. The DGSD considers the coverage level of deposits as an important factor in maintaining confidence of depositors, obtaining a greater extent of financial stability, and completing the Banking Union.[204] Recital 19 of the DGSD states that the 'uncoordinated increases in coverage' of the Member States have resulted in deposits being transferred to banks located in states which provided deposit guarantees at a higher coverage level. The differences in the level of protection have caused competitive distortions in a tranquil time and a liquidity flight in a crisis. This view is consistent with some studies such as research by Qi et al. (2020), which finds that a one per cent increase in the coverage limit has led to an increase in cross-border deposits by 0.68 per cent.[205]

However, depositors might not only take into consideration a higher level of coverage but also credibility of the sovereign state behind a deposit protection scheme. That is because a national deposit insurance

[201] EFTA stands for European Free Trade Association. The EFTA Court is responsible for three members of the European Free Trade Association: Iceland, Liechtenstein and Norway.

[202] Case E-16/11 *EFTA Surveillance Authority v Iceland* [2013]. Anna Gelpern, Sovereign Debt and Banking Crises: An 'Arial View' in Rosa Lastra (ed), *Sovereign Debt Management* (Oxford University Press 2014), 210.

[203] Recital 45 of the 2014 Directive reaffirms the EFTA's Court ruling in this case. Ivan Lazarov, 'Deposit Insurance in the EU: Repetitive Failures and Lessons from Across the Atlantic' (2017) 54 Common Market Law Review 1, 28.

[204] The 1994 and 2009 Directives on deposit guarantee schemes also consider the level of coverage as an important factor. For example, the 1994 Directive stipulates that a 'harmonised minimum level of deposit protection' is necessary for completing 'a single banking market'. In addition, Recital 3 of the 2009 Directive stipulates that the minimum coverage should be increased to 100,000 euros in order to 'maintain depositor confidence and attain greater stability on the financial markets'.

[205] Qi et al. (n 476) 989.

scheme relies on a trust that the government will reimburse depositors.[206] According to Bonfim and Santos (2020), the success of deposit insurance schemes in eliminating bank runs goes beyond the level of deposit coverage. Instead, it is closely related to the credibility of the arrangements and the certainty of protection. Besides this, a large increase in the 'perceived risk of sovereign debt' could lead to the transfers of deposits to other countries and the reduction of the DIS's effectiveness.[207] In their study, which focuses on the risk of bank runs in Portugal, Portuguese depositors relocated their deposits to bank subsidiaries, which were converted into branches. This is especially the case for branches of banks headquartered in countries with high credit ratings, regardless of their lower level of deposit coverage.[208]

4.4 A Final Thought: Considerations in Improving the DISs in ASEAN

Both international and regional efforts in harmonising deposit insurance schemes as well as synchronising the powers and mandates of deposit insurers with those of other safety-net entities can provide lessons for ASEAN. As elaborated in this chapter, soft legalisation and hard law approaches utilised by the IADI, the EU, IFIs and other governance networks do not produce significantly different effects in practice. For example, in spite of the fact that the IADI Core Principles are soft legal instruments, they could generate strong disciplining effects, especially when they are used by the IFIs and international organisations. Meanwhile, the hard legal instruments employed by the EU leave a large discretion on the part of the Member States and their national authorities as to their transposition and implementation. In addition, the benefits which the hard law approach is expected to bring about (e.g., legal certainty) could be reduced in the case that hard law regimes are not designed to function consistently with each other.

Thus, factors which ASEAN should take into account in selecting measures and tools in order to improve the functioning of DISs should

[206] The deposit insurance fund is very small relative to the size of the covered deposits (at least 0.8% of covered deposits in the EU by 2024).

[207] Bonfim and Santos (n 612) 4.

[208] Ibid., 3.

not be restricted to a consideration about their legal forms. Instead, an appropriate tool should be the one which yields a higher level of legitimacy and gains a larger degree of acceptance from the Member States. That is because harmonising and improving deposit insurance measures in a cross-border context could raise politically sensitive issues of 'loss allocation and burden sharing'.[209]

In addition, in my view, there are three main issues which ASEAN states should prioritise in improving their DISs. First, Cambodia should consider establishing an explicit DIS in order to provide a sufficient and equal protection to depositors in cross-border banking. In formulating the scope of powers and mandates of a DIS for Cambodia, designers should take into due consideration the country's level of economic and financial development, readiness for setting up an explicit DIS, and the synchronisation of the DIS with other safety-net players.

Secondly, ASEAN countries should put in place mechanisms which would increase cross-border cooperation and coordination among financial system safety-net participants beyond information sharing. As argued in this chapter, relying on the network of DISs and information-sharing systems between the DISs and the home and host supervisors might be a sub-optimal strategy in dealing with a systemic crisis. This is especially so in the case that a liquidation or resolution of foreign branches of a credit institution is required.

Thirdly, a harmonisation of the DISs in ASEAN could help minimise the problems of deposit flights to other countries as well as systemic risk. For example, ASEAN states might consider eliminating national preference rules in order to promote cooperation and coordination among the home and host state authorities. Moreover, the method for levying deposit insurance premiums could be harmonised in order to curb the moral hazard problems more effectively. Currently, only a minority of ASEAN states have used risk-based adjustments to the contribution of their DISs. This is despite the fact that risk-based premiums could help enhance the ability of the deposit insurer in restructuring the financial sector to prevent systemic risk, especially where a highly interconnected credit institution could be adversely affected by it.[210]

[209] Chan et al. (n 15) 250.

[210] Pilar Gómez-Fernández-Aguado et al., 'Moving toward Risk-based Deposit Insurance Premiums in the European Union: The Case of Spain' (2014) 46(13) Applied Economics 1547, 1563.

References

Abbott K and Snidal D, 'Hard and Soft Law in International Governance' (2000) 54 International Organization 421

Adema J et al., 'Deposit Insurance: System Design and Implementation across Countries' (2019) 17 ifo DICE Report

Allen F et al., 'Government Guarantees and Financial Stability' (2017) ECB Working Paper 2032

Anginer D et al., 'How Does Deposit Insurance Affect Bank Risk? Evidence from the Recent Crisis' (2014) 48 Journal of Banking and Finance 312

Arda A and Dobler M, 'The Role for Deposit Insurance Funds in Dealing with Failing Banks in the European Union' (2022) IMF Working Paper WP22/2

Azevedo JV and Bonfim D, 'Deposit Insurance and Cross-border Banks' (2019) 17(1) ifo DICE Report 14

Baudino P et al., 'Bank Failure Management – The Role of Deposit Insurance' (2019) FSI Insights on Policy Implementation No. 17

BCBS and IADI, 'Core Principles for Effective Deposit Insurance Systems' (Consultative Document 2009)

BCBS and IADI, 'Core Principles for Effective Deposit Insurance Systems: A Proposed Methodology for Compliance Assessment' (Consultative Document 2010)

Benjamin J, Financial Law (Oxford University Press 2007)

Blanck K, 'State Aid and Bank Resolution Law before the European Court of Justice' in Chiara Zilioli and others (eds), *Judicial Review in the European Banking Union* (Edward Elgar Publishing Limited 2021)

Bodellini M, 'The Optional Measures of Deposit Guarantee Schemes: Towards a New Bank Crisis Management Paradigm? (2021) 13(1) European Journal of Legal Studies

Bonfim D and Santos J, 'The Importance of Deposit Insurance Credibility' (2020) Working Paper

Brummer C., 'Why Soft Law Dominates International Finance-and not Trade' (2010) 13 (3) Journal of International Economic Law 623

'Brief Summary of the de Larosiere Report'

Calliess G and Zumbansen P, Rough Consensus and Running Code: A Theory of Transnational Private Law (Hart Publishing 2010)

Cartwright P, 'Understanding, Awareness and Deposit Insurance' in Labrosse J and others (eds), Financial Crisis Management and Bank Resolution (Informa Law 2009)

Central Bank of Ireland, 'Central Bank of Ireland Technical Views on Topics Raised in the European Commission's Targeted Questionnaire on the CMDI Review' (Memorandum 2021)

Chan A et al, 'Depositor Preference and Deposit Insurance Schemes – Challenges for Regulatory Convergence and Regulatory Coordination in Asia' (2018) Law and Financial Markets Review 12 (2)

Cipriani M. et al., 'Mitigating the Risk of Runs on Uninsured Deposits: The Minimum Balance at Risk' (*Liberty Street Economics*, 14 April 2023)

Council of the European Union, 'Agreement on the transfer and mutualisation of contributions to the Single Resolution Fund' (14 May 2014) 8457/14

Council of the European Union, 'CMDI Trilogue' (16 January 2025)

Davis K, 'Asian Banking Integration, Depositor Preference, and Deposit Insurance' (2015)

Demirguc-Kunt A. and Detragiache E., 'Does Deposit Insurance Increase Banking System Stability? An Empirical Investigation' (2002) 49 Journal of Monetary Economics 1373

Diamond D and Dybvig P, 'Bank Runs, Deposit Insurance, and Liquidity' (1983) 91(3) Journal of Political Economy 401

Dobler M et al., 'The Case for Depositor Preference' IMF Technical Notes and Manuals 2020/002

Dombret A, 'A Way to a Viable Level Playing Field' in Andreas Dombret and Patrick S. Kenadjian (eds), EDIS, NPLs, Sovereign Debt and Safe Assets (De Gruyter 2020)

EBA, 'Guidelines on Stress Tests of Deposit Guarantee Schemes under Directive 2014/49/EU' (24 May 2016)

European Commission, 'Options and National Discretions under the Deposit Guarantee Scheme Directive and Their Treatment in the Context of a European Deposit Insurance Scheme' (Final Report 2019)

European Commission, 'State aid: Commission Finds Italy Provided Incompatible State Aid to Banca Tercas and Welcomes Plans of Private Funds to Step In' (Press Release, 23 December 2015)

European Commission, 'The High-Level Group on Financial Supervision in the EU Chaired by Jacques de Larosiere' (Report 2009)

European Forum of Deposit Insurers, 'Deposit Guarantee Schemes' Alternative Measures to Pay-out for Effective Banking Crisis Solution' (2019) EFDI State of Play and Non-Binding Guidance Paper

Financial Services Compensation Scheme, 'Ground-breaking New Industry Wide Agreement to Raise Awareness of Deposit Protection for Consumers' (Media Information 2017)

Financial Stability Board, 'Thematic Review on Deposit Insurance Systems:' (Peer Review Report 2012)

Flood M, 'Deposit Insurance: Problems and Solution' (1993) Federal Reserve Bank of St. Louis

Gelpern A, Sovereign Debt and Banking Crises: An 'Arial View' in Rosa Lastra (ed), Sovereign Debt Management (Oxford University Press 2014)

Gerhardt M and Lannoo K, 'Options for Reforming Deposit Protection Schemes in the EU' (2011) ECRI Policy Brief No. 4

Gleeson S, 'The Single Resolution Mechanism and the EU Crisis Management Tools' in Gianni Lo Schiavo (ed), The European Banking Union and the Role of Law (Elgar Financial Law Series 2019)

Gómez-Fernández-Aguado P et al., 'Moving toward Risk-based Deposit Insurance Premiums in the European Union: The Case of Spain' (2014) 46(13) Applied Economics 1547

IADI, 'Core Principles for Effective Deposit Insurance Systems' (2014)

IADI, 'Mind the Gap!' A Comparative Analysis Between the IADI CPs and the DGSD' (2017)

IADI, 'Systems under Development'

IADI, '2021 Annual Survey 15 Key Features' (8 November 2021)

IMF, 'Euro Area Policies. Financial Sector Assessment Program. Technical Note-Bank Resolution and Crisis Management' (2018) IMF Country Report No. 18/232

Hajra K and Moetomo R, 'Depositor Preference and Implications for Deposit Insurance' (2020) IADI Briefs No. 4

Honohan P and Klingebiel D, 'The Fiscal Cost Implications of an Accommodating Approach to Banking Crises' (2003) 27(8) Journal of Banking and Finance 1539

Ketcha Jr N, 'Deposit Insurance System Design and Considerations' (1999)

Gropp R and Vesala J, 'Deposit Insurance and Moral Hazard: Does the Counterfactual Matter' (2001) ECB Working Paper No. 47

Ioannidis M, 'The Judicial Review of Discretion in the Banking Union: From 'Soft' to 'Hard(er)' Look?' in Zilioli C and others (eds), Judicial Review in the European Banking Union (Edward Elgar Publishing Limited 2021)

IBRD, 'IBRD Articles of Agreement: Article IV'

Kenadjian P, 'What Do Sovereign Debt and 'Safe Assets' Have to Do with EDIS?' in Dombret A and Kenadjian P (eds), EDIS, NPLs, Sovereign Debt and Safe Assets (De Gruyter 2020)

Kleftouri N, 'Meeting the Rationale of Deposit Protection System' (2014) 22(4) Journal of Financial Regulation and Compliance 300

Kryzanowski L, 'Organizational Design and Positioning of the Deposit Insurance Function in the Financial System Safety Net' in Campbell A and others (eds), Deposit Insurance (Palgrave Macmillan 2007)

Kusairi S et al., 'Impact of Deposit Insurance on Banking Industry of ASEAN Countries: In Quest of Stability' (2015) 10(4) Banks and Bank Systems

LaBrosse J and Mayes D, 'Promoting Financial Stability through Effective Depositor Protection: The Case for Explicit Limited Deposit Insurance' in Campbell A and others (eds), Deposit Insurance (Palgrave Macmillan 2007)

Laeven L and Valencia F, 'The Use of Blanket Guarantees in Banking Crises' (2008) IMF Working Paper WP/08/250

Lazarov I, 'Deposit Insurance in the EU: Repetitive Failures and Lessons from Across the Atlantic' (2017) 54 Common Market Law Review 1

Leonello A, 'Government Guarantees and the Two-way Feedback between Banking and Sovereign Debt Crises' (2018) 130 Journal of Financial Economics 592

Manakul T et al., 'Executive Summary: Does A Deposit Insurance System Strengthen the System of Financial Institutions and Stabilise the Financial System?' *RYT9* (Bangkok, 22 September 2008) (in Thai)

McGrath C, 'Deposit Protection Scheme Edges Closer to Reality' *The Phom Phenh Post* (Phnom Phenh, 26 September 2016)

McLeay M et.al., 'Money Creation in the Modern Economy' (Q1 2014) Bank of England Quarterly Bulletin

Miller P, 'Governing by Numbers: Why Calculative Practices Matter' (2001) 68(2) Social Research 379

Morris S et al., 'Chinese and World Bank Lending Terms: A Systematic Comparison Across 157 Countries and 15 Years' (2020) CGD Policy Paper 170

Nicolaides P and O'Connor T, 'Is the Bank-Sovereign Link Truly Severed?' (2016) Bruges European Economic Policy Briefings 43/2016

Nieto M and Singh D, 'Incentive Compatible Relationship Between the ERM II and Close Cooperation in the Banking Union: The Case of Bulgaria and Croatia' (2021) Banco de Espana Occasional Paper No. 2117

Noman AHM et al., 'The Mediating Role of Competition on Deposit Insurance and the Risk-taking of Banks in ASEAN Countries' (2022) 59 Research in International Business and Finance 59

Pahuja S, 'Global Formations: IMF Conditionality and the South as Legal Subject' in Fitzpatrick P and Tuitt P (eds), Critical Being (Ashgate Publishing Limited 2004)

Payne J, 'The Reform of Deposit Guarantee Schemes in Europe' (2015) 12 ECFR 539

Pennacchi G, 'Deposit Insurance, Bank Regulation, and Financial System Risks' (2006) 53(1) Journal of Monetary Economics 1

Perbadanan Insurans Deposit Malaysia, 'Guideline on the Differential Premium Systems for Deposit Insurance System' (2020)

Philippine Deposit Insurance Corporation, 'About PIDM FAQS'

Prescott E, 'Can Risk-based Deposit Insurance Premiums Control Moral Hazard?' (2002) 88(2) Federal Reserve Bank of Richmond Economic Quarterly 87

Qi S et al., 'The Travels If a Bank Deposit in Turbulent Times: The Importance of Deposit Insurance Design for Cross-border Deposits' (2020) 58(2) Economic Inquiry 980

Reinhart C and Rogoff K, This Time is Different: Eight Centuries of Financial Folly (Princeton University Press 2009)

Restoy F et al., 'Bank Failure Management in the European Banking Union: What's Wrong and How to Fix It' (2020) Financial Stability Institute Occasional Paper No. 15

Saheruddin H and Soedarmono W, 'Financial Crisis and Cointegration of Systemic Risk in Southeast Asian Banking' (2019) 23(4) Jurnal Keuangan dan Perbankan 479

Salama B and Braga V, 'The Case for Private Administration of Deposit Guarantee Schemes' (2023) 24 The Journal of Banking Regulation 51

Shaffter G and Halliday T, 'With, Within, and Beyond the State: The Promise and Limits of Transnational Legal Ordering' in Zumbansen Z (ed), *The Oxford Handbook of Transnational Law* (Oxford University Press 2021)

Shoukry G, 'Insurance Pricing, Distortions, and Moral Hazard: Quasi-experimental Evidence from Deposit Insurance' (2020) FDIC CFR Working Paper 2020–08

Singh D and LaBrosse JR, 'Northern Rock, Depositors and Deposit Insurance Coverage: Some Critical Reflections' (2010) 2 Journal of Business Law 55

Singh D and Walker D, 'The European Deposit Guarantee Directive: An Appraisal of the Reforms' in Labrosse J and others (eds), *Financial Crisis Management and Bank Resolution* (Informa Law 2009)

Siragusa M et al., 'EU Court of Justice Confirms that Italian Deposit Guarantee Scheme Intervention in Support of Banca Tercas Did Not Cconstitute State Aid' (*Cleary Gottlieb*, 2 April 2021)

Reserve Bank of New Zealand, 'Deposit Takers that Offer DCS-Protected Deposits' (22 April 2025)

Walker D, 'A Survey of Deposit Insurance in East Asia: Post-Asian Financial Crisis' in Campbell A and others (eds), *Deposit Insurance* (Palgrave Macmillan 2007)

Walker D and Hoontrakul P, 'Transitioning from Blanket to Limited Deposit Guarantees: Thailand Policy Considerations' (2001) SSRN Paper

White E, 'Deposit Insurance' (1995) Policy Research Working Paper 1541

World Bank Group, 'Products' (May 2018)

World Bank, 'International Bank for Reconstruction and Development'

World Bank, 'Lao PDR Financial Sector Safety Net Strengthening' (Project Information Document, 10 February 2020)

World Bank, 'Lao PDR Financial Sector Safety Net Strengthening' (Project Appraisal Document, 9 March 2020)

World Bank, 'The World Bank: Legal Aspects' (2011)

Xanthoulis N, 'Single Resolution Fund and Emergency Liquidity Assistance: Status Quo and Reform Perspectives on Emergency Financial Support in the Banking Union' in Schiavo G (ed), *The European Banking Union and the Role of Law* (Elgar Financial Law Series 2019)

Cases

Case C-425/19 P Commission v Italy and Others [2021]

Case C-656/15P Commission v TV2/Denmark [2017] (ECJ, 9 November 2017)

Case E-16/11 *EFTA Surveillance Authority v Iceland* [2013]

Foley v Hill (1848) 2 HLC 28

Joined cases T-98/16, T-196/16 and T-198/16 Italy and Others v Commission [2019]

CHAPTER 5

Increasing Legal Cooperation in Bank Crisis Management—Implications for the Public Assistance and Fiscal Backstops in ASEAN

5.1 Introduction

In the previous chapters, the roles of the horizontal and vertical government networks have been discussed. It has been argued that those networks have played a crucial role in bank crisis management by increasing cooperation and coordination among relevant authorities across borders, as well as formulating soft law which governs the national players. In this chapter, selected major interventions and fiscal backstops in dealing with a crisis provided by the states and their national organs, as well as the horizontal government network (i.e., the network of central banks and finance ministries) will be explored. I argue that there is an important role played by the government network in addition to that of the states: it has the potential to minimise the financial trilemma and cope with a systemic crisis. For instance, the government network could indirectly assist problem banks by providing a fiscal backstop to the states in which those banks operate.

Governments typically undertake a responsibility in providing urgent measures, which could contain or prevent a crisis, in order to protect the public goods in the society (e.g., economic growth and financial stability). For instance, during the COVID-19 pandemic, governments around the world have intervened and provided supporting measures to prop up the economy. Moreover, in a systemic crisis, governments often

© The Author(s), under exclusive license to Springer Nature Singapore Pte Ltd. 2025

W. Kun-amornpong, *The Financial Trilemma and Cross-border Bank Crisis Management in ASEAN*,
https://doi.org/10.1007/978-981-95-0512-8_5

'play a much more active role and call upon' the financial safety net entities to 'undertake extraordinary measures'.[1] According to Singh and LaBrosse (2012), the measures concerning bank crisis management could involve crisis containment policies and government supports in various forms (e.g., LOLR,[2] recapitalisation, asset purchase, good or bad banks, nationalisation,[3] and state guarantee, etc.).[4]

The Singh and LaBrosse framework was later adopted in 2022 by the Financial Stability Coordination Council (FSCC) of the Philippines, in its decision tree on managing systemic risks and possible crises. The FSCC's framework recognises that shocks could be both endogenous (i.e., manifests from the financial market) and exogenous (i.e., stems from the macroeconomy).[5] With regards to exogenous shocks, COVID-19 pandemic created shocks which are exogenous not only to the banking system but also to 'economic policy', as it was caused by neither 'unsustainable macroeconomic' nor 'financial imbalances'.[6]

In addition, the FSCC's framework has incorporated cyber risks and risks associated with climate change as 'specific risks' which could cause a systemic concern.[7] According to the FSCC, systemic risks could lead to, on the one hand, a systemic crisis which would trigger the FSCC's measures in accordance with its decision tree. On the other hand, systemic

[1] Dalvinder Singh and John Raymond LaBrosse, 'Developing a Framework for Effective Crisis Management' (2012) (2) OECD Journal: Financial Market Trends 2011, 3.

[2] There is no universal accepted definition of the term 'lender of last resort'. Stanley Fischer, 'On the Need for an International Lender of Last Resort' (*IMF*, 3 January 1999) https://www.imf.org/en/News/Articles/2015/09/28/04/53/sp010399#11 Accessed 4 June 2025.

[3] Nationalisation of banks in a systemic crisis has a specific meaning. The authorities will 'takeover an insolvent bank and recapitalise it', rather than takeover a solvent private bank, with a view that they would privatise the nationalised bank as soon as possible. Carl-Johan Lindgren et al., 'Financial Sector Crisis and Restructuring: Lessons from Asia' (1999) IMF Occasional Paper 188, 17.

[4] Singh and LaBrosse (n 627) 10.

[5] Financial Stability Coordination Council, 'Systemic Risk Crisis Management Framework' (2022), 6–7.

[6] World Bank Group, 'Evaluation of the World Bank Group's Early Response in Addressing the Economic Implications of COVID-19' (2021) Approach Paper, 1 < https://reliefweb.int/report/world/approach-paper-evaluation-world-bank-group-s-early-response-addressing-economic > accessed 4 June 2025.

[7] Financial Stability Coordination Council (n 631) 21–30.

risks could merely result in a lesson learned from the FSCC's 'ongoing assessments, interventions, and communication efforts to enhance the resiliency of the financial system'.[8]

As elaborated by Singh and LaBrosse, the efforts of the government, according to Laeven and Valencia (2008) and Acharya et al (2021), could be categorised into four main groups: (1) liquidity support; (2) guarantees[9]; (3) recapitalisation (i.e., 'all measures involving government-funded capital increases and conversions of existing capital or hybrid instruments into higher-order capital instruments')[10] or capital injection; and (4) 'troubled asset relief' (i.e., 'government interventions targeted at removing impaired or defaulted assets from a bank's balance sheets by means of asset sales or guarantees').[11,12] I will elaborate the financial trilemma and limitations which result from those government supports and interventions in dealing with cross-border banking in turn. In addition, this chapter seeks to support Schoenmaker's argument that a greater level of integration could help reconcile the three objectives of financial stability, financial integration and national financial policies, using bank crisis management measures in ASEAN and regional efforts in Asia as an illustration.[13]

5.2 Liquidity Support: LOLR

In a financial crisis, liquidity of banks could be one of the most important issues to be tackled by the authorities. Central banks are formally responsible for providing liquidity support to troubled banks as a LOLR in order

[8] Ibid 6.

[9] According to Acharya et al., guarantees exclude deposit guarantees. Viral V. Acharya et al., 'Kicking the Can Down the Road: Government Interventions in the European Banking Sector' (2021) The Review of Financial Studies 34, 4097.

[10] Ibid 4097.

[11] Ibid.

[12] Luc Laeven and Fabian Valencia, 'Systemic Banking Crises: A New Database' (2008) IMF Working Paper WP/08/224. ibid.

[13] Schoenmaker states that one of the solutions to the financial trilemma is to 'move powers for financial policies (regulation, supervision and stability)' as well as 'crisis management operations' to the supranational level. Schoenmaker (n 4) 59.

to safeguard financial stability.[14] According to Lastra, central banks are the most appropriate institution to perform this function as they can create 'high-powered money'.[15] Nonetheless, there are diverse and inconsistent views regarding what a LOLR should do.[16] Those views might differ from the theory regarding the function of a central bank as a LOLR laid down by Thornton (1802) and Bagehot (1873).[17] The Thornton-Bagehot principles have four main components: (1) central banks should prevent illiquid bank from closing; (2) central banks should charge a penalty rate for their loans which are lent freely; (3) central bank should take good collaterals against their loans or advances; and (4) the principles to which the LOLR are subject should be made clear in advance.[18]

The disagreements are that, in a modern system and in time of crisis, the Thornton-Bagehot principles might not correspond to the practice of a central bank for some reasons. First, a central bank might be able to distinguish solvent banks from insolvent institutions merely imperfectly

[14] Fischer has argued that the function of LOLR could also be performed by other agents or institutions (e.g., the US Treasury). In addition, LOLR comprises two main roles: (1) crisis lender and (2) crisis manager or coordinator. Neither of these two roles can only be conducted by central banks. Fischer (n 628). LOLR could generate negative effects in that 'it potentially creates moral hazard on massive scale, exposes central bank to large financial risks, and blurs the boundary with fiscal policy'. Dietrich Domanski and Vladyslav Sushko, 'Re-thinking the Lender of Last Resort: Workshop Summary' in *Re-thinking the Lender of Last Resort*, BIS Papers No 79 (September 2014), 1 < https://www.bis.org/publ/bppdf/bispap79.htm > accessed 4 June 2025.

[15] Rosa M. Lastra, *International Financial and Monetary Law* (2nd edn, OUP 2015) 150. Nevertheless, Fischer has argued that 'panics caused by a demand for currency are rare'. Normally, there would be a shift of deposits from banks which are considered to be in trouble to the institutions which are seemed to be sound. Hence, in Fischer's view, 'the key was not the legal right to create high-powered money, but the effective ability to provide liquidity to those who wanted it'. Fischer (n 628).

[16] Fischer (n 628).

[17] Sara Elisa Dietz, 'The ECB as Lender of Last Resort in the Eurozone? An Analysis of an Optimal Institutional Design of Emergency Liquidity Assistance Competence within the Context of the Banking Union' (2019) 26(5) Maastricht Journal of European and Comparative Law, 632. According to Lastra, LOLR has two forms. 'The first form is the traditional Thornton-Bagehot ' LOLR model: collateralised lines of credit to individual illiquid, but solvent, banks'. The 'second form (emergency liquidity assistance, ELA) is the 'market liquidity assistance' provided 'via ordinary open market operations and via extraordinary or unconventional measures'. Lastra (n 641) 151.

[18] Rosa M. Lastra, 'Emergency Liquidity Assistance and Systemic Risk' in Anita Anand, *Systemic Risk, Institutional Design, and the Regulation of Financial Markets* (OUP 2016), 227–228.

due to the existence of 'multiple equilibria'[19] or 'imperfect information'.[20,21] This is especially the case in a crisis in which information is limited, and central banks have to make a prompt decision. In addition, as Giannini states, 'most central banks have been willing to extend last-resort assistance at market or even at subsidised rates'.[22] In other words, it is not common practice for the central banks to charge a penalty rate for their liquidity support. This is due to the fact that doing so could intensify the crisis by creating a contagion, as banks might have to raise their funds and sell their assets at fire-sale prices.[23]

Nevertheless, it could be argued that the ability of a central bank to differentiate insolvent banks from healthy institutions has been improved by the use of Recovery and Resolution Planning. With regards to Recovery Planning, it aims at providing necessary information for supervisors regarding the safety and soundness of banks.[24] The recovery plan analyses preparatory measures in order to, for example, minimise the risk profile of a bank, respond to liquidity shocks, and facilitate a debt restructuring.[25]

[19] According to Freixas and Parigi, the multiple equilibria could include, for example, one in which 'banks are solvent and liquid' and the other one where 'banks are insolvent precisely because of the expectations that they are illiquid'. Xavier Freixas and Bruno M. Parigi, 'Lender of Last Resort: A New Role for the Old Instrument' in Allen N. Berger et al., *The Oxford Handbook of Banking* (3rd edn, OUP 2019), 610.

[20] E.g., due to the opacity of the banks' balance sheets. ibid.

[21] Ibid. 'There was broad consensus that distinguishing between insolvent and illiquid institutions was difficult in practice for at least three reasons': (1) 'illiquidity tended to develop into insolvency crises the longer a crisis lasted'; (2) 'illiquidity and insolvency were not independent from the judgment of the authorities'; and (3) 'solvency assessments by supervisors or analysts might be biased'. Domanski and Sushko (n 640) 4.

[22] Curzio Giannini, ''Enemy of None but a Common Friend of All'? An International Perspective on the Lender-of-Last-Resort Function' (1999) IMF Working Paper, 12.

[23] Dietrich Domanski et al., 'Central Banks as Lender of Last Resort: Experiences during the 2007–10 Crisis and Lessons for the Future' in BIS (n 640) 46.

[24] Clive Briault, 'Recovery Planning' (2020) Toronto Centre Note, 6 < https://www.torontocentre.org/index.php?option=com_content&view=article&id=194:recovery-planning&catid=13&Itemid=101 > accessed 4 June 2025. According to Recital 15 of the Commission Delegated Regulation (EU) 2016/1075, the 'objective of recovery planning, as set out in Directive 2014/59/EU, is to identify options to maintain or restore the viability and financial position of an institution or group when it is subject to severe stress'.

[25] EBA, 'EBA Final Draft Regulatory Technical Standards on the Content of Recovery Plans under Article 5(10) of Directive 2014/59/EU Establishing a Framework for the

In the context of the EU, a recovery plan is drafted by a bank in accordance with the RTS[26] and Guidelines[27] of the EBA. According to the final draft RTS, a recovery plan contains five main components: (1) summary of recovery plan (Article 4); (2) information regarding governance (Article 5); (3) strategic analysis (Article 6); 4) communication and disclosure plan (Article 7); and (5) preparatory measures (Article 8).[28] Then, the supervisory authority will verify whether or not the plan is in compliance with the law.[29] Within the Banking Union, the ECB is responsible for assessing and conducting benchmarking analyses of the plans of significant banks under its supervision.[30]

Concerning a resolution plan, it is designed to perform three main functions: (1) furnishing information about the 'structure and operation' of banks to resolution and supervisory authorities; (2) reducing opacity and enhancing market discipline; and (3) encouraging banks to streamline their corporate structures.[31] It is drafted by the resolution authority in cooperation with the supervisory authority. For example, the SRB will consult the ECB before it approves the plans for significant banks.

However, in the case of cross-border banking group, there might be some limitations of recovery plan in providing essential information regarding the solvency of banks to a central bank. For example, the home supervisory authority might not share a recovery plan of the banking group with the host authority.[32] As mentioned in Chapter 2, it is not

Recovery and Resolution of Credit Institutions and Investment Firms' EBA/RTS/2014/11 (2014), 6.

[26] Ibid. EBA RTS is published in Commission Delegated Regulation (EU) 2016/1075 of 23 March 2016.

[27] EBA, 'Guidelines on the Range of Scenarios to be Used in Recovery Plans' EBA/GL/2014/06 (2014) < https://www.eba.europa.eu/regulation-and-policy/recovery-and-resolution/guidelines-on-the-range-of-scenarios-to-be-used-in-recovery-plans > accessed 4 June 2025.

[28] European Banking Authority (n 651) 3.

[29] Marilena Rispoli Farina and Luigi Scipione, 'Recovery and Resolution Planning' in Mario P. Chiti and Vittorio Santoro (eds), *The Palgrave Handbook of European Banking Union Law* (Palgrave Macmillan Cham 2019), 276–277.

[30] European Central Bank, 'Recovery and Resolution: Banks Need to be Prepared' < https://www.bankingsupervision.europa.eu/press/publications/newsletter/2017/html/ssm.nl171115_4.en.html > 19 April 2023.

[31] Farina and Scipione (n 655) 288.

[32] Briault (n 650) 12.

obligatory for the former to transfer information to the latter. In addition, the recovery plan might be drafted based on the information at the group level, rather than that of each local group entity.[33] Hence, some specific information of a subsidiary might not be taken into account in drafting the plan.

Secondly, the Bagehot's principle might not be applicable, because a central bank is likely to lend to a solvent bank against a wider range of assets than high-quality collateral. Some central banks may provide uncollateralised liquidity supports as in the case of the Bank of Japan in 1997.[34] This practice could be explained, in part, by the fact that the central banks would be under a great pressure to abate the negative externalities, which could stem from bank failures.[35] Thirdly, the doctrine of 'constructive ambiguity' has redefined the central bank theory and practice regarding the last condition of the Bagehot's principle. According to this doctrine, central banks should retain a discretion regarding whether or not, and on what terms and conditions, to provide a LOLR facility in order to avoid the problems of moral hazard.[36]

Concerning the policy and practice regarding LOLR of the central banks in ASEAN, during the AFC, the central banks of both countries which were heavily hit by the AFC (i.e., Indonesia and Thailand) and those of states which experienced a less severe crisis (i.e., Malaysia and the Philippines[37]) provided liquidity assistance through emergency lending and LOLR to contain the crisis.[38] The policy regarding LOLR was and

[33] Ibid 5.

[34] Giannini (n 648) 12.

[35] Paul Tucker, 'The Lender of Last Resort and Modern Central Banking: Principles and Reconstruction' in BIS (n 640) 26.

[36] Dietz (n 643) 633. Giannini (n 648) 14. Even the doctrine of constructive ambiguity might not be universally applicable for all central banks. For example, the Bank of Japan found that 'constructive ambiguity can become counter-productive in periods of stress'. BIS (n 640) 4. In addition, Lastra is of the view that there should be clear rules with respect to 'who is in charge and how the assistance will be provided'. Lastra (n 641) 160.

[37] The Philippines provided 'fully-collateralised emergency loans' in the case that there was a bank run. Ben Fung et al., 'Public Asset Management Companies in East Asia—Case Studies', BIS (2005), 46 < https://www.semanticscholar.org/paper/Public-asset-management-companies-in-East-Asia-Case-Fung-George/676e76ab6810f76f10443 19d045b66bcf346b7fd > accessed 4 June 2025.

[38] Lindgren et al. (n 629) 18.

has remained within the purview of the national central banks of each country.

Nevertheless, when considering the fact that the financial integration in ASEAN has increasingly deepened (as discussed in Chapter 1), a failure of a regional SIFI or a significant part of the banking systems in this sub-region, could increase the need for every element of a regional financial safety net, including LOLR. As Schoenmaker has argued, relevant states do not normally factor in a consideration regarding externalities of a bank failure arising outside their territory; they are likely to backstop only their domestic institutions.[39] For example, in the case of a failure of a banking group which operate in multiple jurisdictions, relevant LOLR authorities need to consider whether such a failure would have damaging impacts, or cause systemic problems in their countries, so as to justify an official intervention.

Issues could arise where a perception regarding the systemic impact of the group's failure on a particular country of the relevant central banks is different from each other. Besides this, some central banks might not consider themselves as an appropriate LOLR to a banking group.[40] For instance, if there is no MOU between the home and the host authorities in place, the latter might not possess sufficient information to assess the financial position of the parent entity or that of the local branches.[41] As D'Hulster has stated, without an existing agreement about burden-sharing mechanisms, the incentives of national supervisory authorities to cooperate and communicate with those of other jurisdictions will decrease when the financial situation of a bank worsens. They will prioritise the problem in their own jurisdiction over those of other countries.[42] In the case that there is no guidance, this could, in turn, cause uncertainty and

[39] Dirk Schoenmaker, 'Is Burden Sharing Needed for International Financial Stability? in Philipp Hartmann et al., *The Changing Fortunes of Central Banking* (Cambridge University Press 2018), 209.

[40] Garry J. Schinasi and Pedro Gustavo Teixeira, 'The Lender of Last Resort in the European Single Financial Market' (2006) IMF working paper WP/06/127, 15.

[41] Marc Dobler et al., 'The Lender of Last Resort Function after the Global Financial Crisis' (2016) IMF Working Paper WP/16/10, 31.

[42] D'Hulster (n 70) 14.

reduce effectiveness in conducting crisis management measures for the cross-border group.[43]

Moreover, different practices and policies of central banks could raise a concern about unequal treatment of banks. For instance, central banks may have diverse policies regarding whether or not they will provide an idiosyncratic LOLR to non-systemic banks.[44] According to Dobler et al., 'time consistency' issues could exacerbate the problem of inequality of treatment to banks. For example, banks which are previously determined as non-systemic could subsequently become systemic due to, for example, their disorderly failures and the panic of depositors.[45]

In the case of ASEAN, the Member States still have not established an ASEAN LOLR mechanism specifically for this sub-region. Hence, central banks in ASEAN have their own policies and comply with their national laws and regulations. These different polices, laws and regulations could result in an inequality of treatment of banks which operate across borders. For example, the MAS has powers under Section 26 of the MASA to provide short-term backstop liquidity, in order to maintain the financial stability and confidence of the population in the financial system. On the one hand, the emergency liquidity assistance (ELA)[46] could be extended to all banks in the form of a 'market-wide ELA' in order to address a system-wide liquidity stress in extraordinary situation. On the other hand, the ELA could be provided in the form of an 'idiosyncratic ELA' addressed to specific D-SIBs which experience a liquidity stress. However, the detailed information regarding the MAS's ELA provision is confidential; it could be released to the public only if 'there are legal or strong public interest' reasons for so doing.[47]

[43] For example, the UK has created policies and provisions for supervising third country branches of international banks in order to reduce uncertainty and increase effectiveness for the supervision of cross-border bank groups.

[44] For instance, Swiss National Bank considers systemic importance as one of the criteria for the eligibility of its assistance. Dobler et al. (n 667) 22.

[45] Ibid.

[46] 'There is no internationally-agreed definition of ELA, as the extent, nature and form of ELA in each jurisdiction depend on the legal powers, objectives and mandate of the respective central bank'. Monetary Authority of Singapore, 'Emergency Liquidity Assistance in Singapore' (June 2019), 3 < https://www.mas.gov.sg/monetary-policy/emergency-liquidity-assistance > accessed 4 June 2025.

[47] In such instance, the MAS will take into consideration the implications on broader financial stability before disclosing the information on a delayed basis. ibid 10.

Meanwhile, Section 32(1)(b) of the Central Bank of Malaysia Act 2009 empowers the Bank Negara Malaysia (BNM) to enter into an arrangement with other central banks, in order to provide liquidity assistance to overseas subsidiaries or branches of banks which are headquartered in Malaysia. The BNM could provide such liquidity assistance by means of financing against a sufficient form of security, purchasing or committing to purchase assets of the bank, lending or exchanging assets of the BNM against those of the bank, and providing guarantees, indemnities or other appropriate arrangements.[48] In the case of an institution which is not supervised by the BNM, it shall propose ELA measures to the Financial Stability Executive Committee (FSEC), which could accept or reject the proposal. Alternatively, the FSCE could require the BNM to prepare another proposal for its consideration.[49]

In addition, differences in the assessment of bank's solvency by central banks could exacerbate the inequality of treatment issues in cross-border cases. According to the Financial Stability Institute of the BIS, the majority of central banks in their survey have different scope and process of solvency assessment. The variation occurs across three dimensions: (1) whether to assess solvency, scope of the assessment, and the assessment method; (2) whether solvency is a requirement for obtaining ELA or other lending facilities and lending conditions; and (3) the role of supervisors and the type of governance arrangements. For example, Thailand uses a forward-looking assessment regarding a bank's viability. Meanwhile, some other surveyed central banks apply a net asset perspective at the time of lending.[50]

Moreover, it would be imprudent to develop other regional bank crisis management mechanisms, as has been argued in previous chapters, while leaves LOLR powers within the complete purview of national authorities. That is, in part, because policy actions regarding these crisis prevention and crisis management tools are highly intertwined in many ways. For example, a deposit insurance system helps minimise the social costs of

[48] S. 34 of the Central Bank of Malaysia Act 2009.

[49] S. 38(1)(b) and s. 38(2) of the Central Bank of Malaysia Act 2009.

[50] Botes et al. (n 374) 21.

bank's insolvency as well as the need for a LOLR intervention.[51] In addition, decisions regarding ELA affects the amount and distribution of loss in resolution.[52] A bank might not enter into a resolution procedure if ELA has solved its liquidity issue before the concern transforms into an insolvency problem.[53] Besides this, a bilateral LOLR may be needed, in limited circumstances, in order to provide a temporary backstop while a plan for creating a bridge bank or implementing recapitalisation measures are carried out.[54] Apart from the aforementioned arguments, a problem of illiquidity could quickly transform into an insolvency issue, when banks have to sell their assets at fire-sale prices in a crisis. Therefore, all mechanisms of the financial safety net have to cooperate closely.[55]

Furthermore, an individual central bank in ASEAN might not have a sufficient capacity to provide LOLR facilities to rescue its banks in a crisis. Such instance could be considered from the AFC where many ASEAN countries experienced a 'twin currency-banking crisis with implications for stock markets'.[56] There were 'double mismatch' problems resulting from both currency speculation, as well as maturity and potential for

[51] Freixas and Parigi (n 645) 4. In addition, the central bank which provides an ELA has to work closely with the fiscal authorities in dealing with a crisis. For example, during the Northern Rock debacle, after the Bank of England had provided an ELA to the Northern Rock, the UK government announced the use of the blanket guarantee as well as underwrote other supports. In addition, in the case of the Royal Bank of Scotland (RBS) and HBOS, the ELA loans were provided by the Bank of England (BOE), while the UK government indemnified the BOE as well as recapitalised RBS and HBOS. Andrew Hauser, 'Lender of Last Resort Operations during the Financial Crisis: Seven Practical Lessons from the United Kingdom' in BIS (n 640) 88.

[52] For instance, Banco Popular and ABLV Bank received ELA before they were declared failing or likely to fail for a resolution. Santiago Fernandez de Lis and Javier Garcia, 'Funding before and in Resolution: A Proposal for a Funding in Resolution Mechanism' Regulation Watch (31 May 2018), 4 < https://www.bbvaresearch.com/en/publicaciones/funding-before-and-in-resolution/ > accessed 4 June 2025.

[53] Thomas F. Huertas, 'Reset Required: The Euro Area Crisis Management and Deposit Insurance Framework' (2021) SAFE White Paper No. 85, 24.

[54] Dobler et al. (n 667) 21.

[55] Sebastian Schich, 'Financial Crisis: Deposit Insurance and Related Financial Safety Net Aspects' (2008) Financial Market Trends, 10.

[56] Gong Cheng, 'Finding Complementarities in IMF and RFA Toolkits' (2020) ESM Discussion Paper Series/8, 22.

bad loans.[57] However, some central banks in ASEAN had limited foreign exchange resources to provide 'foreign currency' LOLR to its domestic banks.[58] For instance, in the case of Thailand, 90 per cent of the Thai foreign reserves were used up by the end of June 1997 in defending Thai baht from currency speculative attacks.[59]

5.3 Guarantees

State guarantees in bank crisis management include two main types of arrangements: (1) deposit insurance; and (2) non-deposit guarantees (i.e., guarantees on other bank liabilities, assets and income streams).[60,61] According to Schich, the 'expansion of existing and introduction of new guarantees for financial institutions has been a key element of the policy response' to the GFC.[62] The role of the governments could be considered as a 'provider of safety net' by acting as a 'guarantor of last resort'.[63]

Those guarantees have a fiscal implication as they create contingent liabilities, rather than impose an immediate fiscal burden on the government. The fiscal cost of government guarantee depends on the robustness

[57] Masahiro Kawai, 'From the Chiang Mai Initiative to an Asian Monetary Fund' (2015) ADBI Working Paper Series No. 527, 4. In other words, banks intermediated 'external short-term funds in foreign currency for long-term domestic investment'.

[58] Foreign currency LOLR is particularly needed in a financial sector which is 'partly-dollarised' or dependent on cross-border foreign exchange funding. Dobler et al. (n 667) 33.

[59] Beomhee Han, 'The CMI and CMIM' in Hoe Ee Khor et al. (eds), *Trauma to Triumph: Rising from the Ashes of the Asian Financial Crisis* (World Scientific Publishing Co. Pte. Ltd. 2022), 713.

[60] Charles Enoch et al., 'Recapitalising Banks with Public Funds: Selected Issues' (1999) IMF working paper WP/99/139, 27 < https://www.imf.org/external/pubs/ft/wp/1999/wp99139.pdf> accessed 4 June 2025. According to Enoch et al., guarantees on liabilities prevent bank runs and the sales of assets at fire-sale prices. Meanwhile, guarantees on assets increase the market value of those assets and capital. Banks might be able to 'recover any provisions that it has previously made against the no longer impaired assets'. As for guarantees on income streams, it enables banks to 'increase capitals through retained earnings'.

[61] Sebastian Schich, 'Expanded Government Guarantees for Bank Liabilities: Selected Issues' (2009) 2009(1) Financial Market Trends, 2.

[62] Sebastian Schich, 'Expanded Guarantees for Banks: Benefits, Costs and Exit Issues' (2009) 2009(2) Financial Market Trends.

[63] Ibid.

of the banking system. In the case that the system is 'severely undercapitalised', the fiscal cost would be the amount needed to recapitalise the system.[64]

Nevertheless, according to Grande et al (2011) and Schich (2009), the actual fiscal cost resulting from a state guarantee on bank bonds being called could be insignificant.[65] In order to gain a thorough understanding of the effects of the introduction of state guarantee, the guarantee scheme introduced by the Australian government during the GFC is a unique and enlightening case study. As Luong et al. state:

> Australia did not previously have any explicit deposit protection, the scheme was voluntary, and unlike other government guarantee offered, there was initially no explicit end date announced for the scheme. This signalled to market participants that the government was prepared to support the banks for 'as long as it takes'.[66]

Australia established the Australian Government Guarantee Scheme for Large Deposits and Wholesale Funding (the Guarantee Scheme) in 2008, to help Australian banks compete against other borrowers for global funding. The guarantee covered only deposits protected under the provision in the Banking Act 1959.[67] In addition, apart from wholesale funding, the deposits eligible for the guarantee must exceed AUD 1 million.[68] When the Guarantee Scheme ended, it did not result in any claims against the government. However, its fees generated the revenue

64 IADI, 'Transitioning from a Blanket Guarantee or Extended Coverage to a Limited Coverage System' (2012) IADI Discussion Paper, 4 < https://ypfs.som.yale.edu/library/document/transitioning-blanket-guarantee-or-extending-coverage-limited-coverage-system > accessed 4 June 2025.

65 Giuseppe Grande et al., 'Public Guarantees on Bank Bonds: Effectiveness and Distortions' (2011) 2011 (2) Financial Market Trends, 56. Schich is of the view that the actual fiscal cost is minimal because there is a political commitment to 'prevent any major institution from failing'. Schich (n 687) 14.

66 Thi Mai Luong et al., 'The Impact of Government Guarantees on Banks' Wholesale Funding Costs and Risk-taking: Evidence from a Natural Experiment' (2020) 61 Pacific-Basin Finance Journal, 2.

67 Trove, 'Global Financial Crisis' (Media Release, 12 October 2008) < https://webarchive.nla.gov.au/awa/20081123235548/http://pandora.nla.gov.au/pan/79983/20081112-0133/www.pm.gov.au/media/Release/2008/media_release_0534.html > accessed 4 June 2025.

68 Luong et al. (n 692) 3.

of 4.4 billion dollars.[69] Therefore, some commentators are of the view that guarantees are suitable for states which have 'limited fiscal space'.[70]

Nonetheless, sovereign guarantees have important downsides; they generate moral hazard and distort competition.[71] As discussed in Chapter 4, deposit insurance and blanket guarantee could create a destabilisation effect as a result of moral hazard. One solution would be to charge a risk-based fee or premium in return for the government guarantee (e.g., the Malaysia Differentiated Premiums System). However, the distortionary effect could still arise in the case that governments price their premiums differently, and/or the fees do not represent the sovereign risk of different states. As a result, weak banks in strong states could obtain a windfall by paying a lower fee, while strong banks in weak states might be disadvantaged by being charged a higher premium.[72] Besides this, it is important to factor in not only the risk of the sovereigns, but also that of the insured banks in creating a pricing mechanism of state guarantees.[73]

Identifying an appropriate premium for state guarantees is not an easy task. Apart from the above-mentioned considerations, there are many factors to be taken into account (e.g., conditions requiring banks to take

[69] Carl Schwartz and Nicholas Tan, 'The Australian Government Guarantee Scheme: 2008–15' (Bulletin, March 2016) < https://www.rba.gov.au/publications/bulletin/2016/mar/pdf/bu-0316-5.pdf > accessed 4 June 2025.

[70] Junkyu Lee et al., 'Strategies for Developing Asia's Nonperforming Loan Markets and Resolution Mechanisms' in John Fell et al. (eds), *Nonperforming Loans in Asia and Europe-Causes, Impacts, and Resolution Strategies* (ADB 2021), 267–268.

[71] Schich (n 688) 1. A research result of Gropp et al (2014) also demonstrates that using state guarantees might result in significant moral hazards of banks. Reint Gropp et al., 'The Impacts of Public Guarantees on Bank Risk-taking: Evidence from a Natural Experiment' (2014) 18(2) Review of Finance, 457.

[72] Aviram Levy and Sebastian Schich, 'The Design of Government Guarantees for Bank Bonds: Lessons from the Recent Financial Crisis (2010) 2010(1) Financial Market Trends, 17.

[73] Grande et al. (n 691) 64. The officials might 'rely on a bank's CDS premium as recorded over an appropriate time period. One caveat when using a bank's CDS premium as a measure of a bank's riskiness is that the CDS does not reflect only the bank's 'standalone' riskiness but it also incorporates the benefit coming from any kind of sovereign guarantee'. *See* Chapter 4 for the discussion regarding the limitation of risk-based premiums.

some specific action, or not to conduct some activities, and market conditions,[74] etc.).[75] The downside of taking too many relevant factors into the calculation is that it will increase the complexity in formulating risk premiums. Complexity, as argued in Chapter 2, would inevitably result in higher administrative costs. In addition, there is no guarantee that a more complex calculation would price the risk more accurately than a simpler one.

Moreover, as Schwartz and Tan have argued, in a systemic crisis, a state might prefer 'to err on the side of supporting the financial system with simple, easy to understand arrangements, than to impose greater control over exposures through features such as limits or institution-specific pricing'.[76] Instead of relying on a complex risk-based pricing mechanism, which is specifically designed for each institution, a country might use other additional safeguards in combination with a simpler risk-based fee. Nevertheless, such auxiliary measures could lead to a bias against foreign banks if they also manifest the willingness of a state to protect its national interest. For example, a state might require banks to be under the supervision of its banking authorities, in order to be eligible for the guarantee.

The aforementioned argument and concern could be considered from the perspective of the Australian Government Guarantee Scheme. Its monthly guarantee fee was priced by using a simpler risk-based method, based on credit rating of the banks and the value of the debts guaranteed.[77] The Guarantee Scheme only provided guarantees with shorter maturities to foreign banks. Its rationale was that those overseas banks were subject to a lesser degree of supervision by the Australian Prudential Regulation Authority. Besides this, the guaranteed liabilities of those foreign banks could not be utilised for supporting 'the foreign branch outside Australia or the obligations of its parent or any related entity'.[78]

[74] The reference prices may be unavailable in an illiquid market. Schich (n 687) 3.

[75] Ibid 23.

[76] Schwartz and Tan (n 695) 45.

[77] Ariel Smith, 'Australian Government Guarantee Scheme for Large Deposits and Wholesale Funding (Australia GFC)' (2020) 2 (3) Journal of Financial Crises, 577 < https://elischolar.library.yale.edu/journal-of-financial-crises/vol2/iss3/28/ > accessed 4 June 2025. The formula for pricing the payable fee was 'Guaranteed liabilities x relevant fee x number of calendar days in month/365'. Smith (n 703) 586.

[78] Schwartz and Tan (n 695) 45.

As ASEAN has become increasingly financially integrated,[79] a Member State which provides guarantees will need to cooperate and coordinate with other relevant states on 'the details of the design, implementation, and exit' of the programmes in those countries in order to minimise distortionary effects.[80] For example, a study by Luong et al. (2017) regarding the impact of the introduction and the exit of the guarantee programme on banks' wholesale debts in Australia found that the state guarantee has an effect beyond its withdrawal from the market,[81] as market participants still perceive that there is implicit government support.[82]

Moreover, according to Walker and Hoontrakul, a state should only consider transitioning from the use of a blanket guarantee to an explicit deposit insurance system when the relevant banking, financial and economic systems are stabilised. Otherwise, the issues regarding 'bank

[79] That is, in part, due to the fact that their deposit bases are highly connected to each other. The capital could flow from a country with low or no protection of bank liabilities to a state which provides a higher level of protection. Cindy Marks and Walter Yao, 'Recent Developments in Asian Deposit Guarantee Programmes' *Asia Focus* (October 2008) < https://www.frbsf.org/banking/publications/asia-focus/2008/october/recent-developments-in-asian-deposit-guarantee-programs/ > accessed 4 June 2025. For example, as a result of the fact that Hong Kong announced the use of a blanket guarantee in 2008, the Singapore government decided to follow suit by utilising a blanket guarantee on 'deposits of individuals and non-bank customers in banks, finance companies and merchant banks in Singapore' which ended in 2010. As a result of a strong connection between the Malaysian and Singaporean banking sectors, the Malaysian government announced that the Malaysia Deposit Insurance Corporation (PIDM) would provide a full protection or blanket guarantee to 'all Ringgit and foreign currency deposits with commercial, Islamic and investment banks regulated by Bank Negara Malaysia'. The guarantee covered 'all domestic and locally incorporated foreign banking institutions'. Marks and Yao (n 739). Concerning Thailand, during the GFC, it decided to remove the cap on its deposit insurance. With respect to Indonesia, the government 'increased the deposit insurance cap from 100 million rupiah to 2 billion rupiah in October 2008'. Kariastanto Bayu, 'Blanket Guarantee, Deposit Insurance, and Risk-shifting Incentive: Evidence from Indonesia' (2011) MPRA Paper No. 35557, 5. As for the Philippines, there were 'pending legislative proposals to double the maximum deposit insurance coverage from P250,000 (US$5,132) to P500,000 (US$10,265)'. Marks and Yao (n 705).

[80] Schich (n 688) 30.

[81] This study focuses upon 'deposit greater than AUD 1 million' and 'wholesale debt funding used by Australian deposit-taking institutions up to maturities of five years'. Luong et al. (n 692) 3.

[82] Ibid 1.

fragility', 'capital flight', 'moral hazards', as well as other 'agency problems' could be exacerbated.[83] Similarly, Gulija et al. are of the view that there should be a 'transition strategy', which is designed for a post- 'containment phase',[84] when the economy has returned to normalcy.[85] The necessity for such strategy could be considered from the economic turmoil in many countries associated with the COVID-19 pandemic. Without sovereign financial support (e.g., public guarantees), a massive number of corporations might have gone bankrupt. Besides this, a sudden removal of those state measures could create a flood of 'corporate defaults' and NPLs. Given the interplay between banks and corporations, a banking crisis could eventually occur.[86]

Hence, ASEAN states might need to create an MOU or a working group to coordinate the exit and transitioning strategies in order to reduce distortionary effects, avoid capital flights, weaken a bank-sovereign 'doom loop' and carefully manage potential contingent liabilities resulting from their state guarantees. For instance, after the GFC, Malaysia, Singapore and Hong Kong formed a tripartite working group when they transitioned from the use of blanket guarantee to a deposit insurance system with limited coverage.[87]

5.4 Recapitalisation

According to Acharya et al (2021), recapitalisation comprises 'all measures involving government-funded capital increases and conversions of existing capital or hybrid instruments into higher-order capital instruments'.[88] In other words, Tier 1 and Tier 2 capital would be levelled up

[83] Walker and Hoontrakul (n 469) 1.

[84] A 'containment phase', according to Gulija et al., is 'the use of extraordinary tools and techniques of last resort to deal with an unexpected systemic crisis that cannot be managed using tools designed for an idiosyncratic crisis in normal times'. Bozena Gulija et al., 'ECB Significant-Bank Risk Profile and Covid-19 Crisis Containment: What Approach in the Transitioning Phase?' (2022) IADI Sponsored Paper Series, 14.

[85] Ibid 9.

[86] Ibid 8.

[87] IADI (n 690) 19.

[88] Acharya et al. (n 635) 4097. 'Banks can be recapitalised using cash, ordinary shares, other Core Tier 1 capital instruments, preferred shares, silent participation, hybrid capital instruments, commitment letters, and rights issues'.

by increasing 'common shares, preferred shares, warrants, subordinated debts, mandatory convertible notes or silent participations'.[89] Recapitalising undercapitalised institutions or 'zombie banks' is an important measure, which enables financial institutions to lend to good borrowers, and thereby enhances economic growth of a country.[90]

In a financial crisis, recapitalisation measures become more important, especially in a severe crisis. That is because crises tend to subside more expeditiously in the case that banks are recapitalised.[91] Besides this, bank recapitalisation could help ameliorate bank runs. For instance, deposit runs on banks in Indonesia, which started in mid-December 1997 and intensified in mid-May 1998,[92] were alleviated in 1999 as a result of the implementation of the joint recapitalisation programme.[93]

Nonetheless, recapitalisation measures may generate negative externalities. For instance, research results by Poczter (2016) show that the recapitalisation scheme implemented in Indonesia in response to the AFC has a long-run effect of increasing risk-taking and lending by banks.[94] Similarly, Beccalli et al. (2018) find that recapitalisation could escalate systemic risk. In their view, regulators might not have taken due consideration regarding this negative externality of recapitalisation into account when designing the Basel III capital requirements, which are more stringent than its predecessors—Basel I and Basel II.[95]

After the AFC had broken out, the authorities in Thailand, Indonesia and Malaysia resorted to use recapitalisation measures.[96] These measures

[89] Fabio Panetta et al., 'An Assessment of Financial Sector Rescue Programmes' (2009) BIS Papers No. 48, 6 < https://www.bis.org/publ/bppdf/bispap48.htm > accessed 4 June 2025.

[90] Willem Pieter de Groen, 'Precautionary Recapitalisations: Time for a Review' (2017) CEPS In-depth Analysis, 5.

[91] Ibid 9.

[92] Lindgren et al. (n 629) 2–3.

[93] Vaasavi Unnava and Ariel Smith, 'Indonesia Joint Recapitalisation of 1999' (2021) 3(3) The Journal of Financial Crises, 187.

[94] Sharon Poczter, 'The Long Term Effects of Bank Recapitalization: Evidence from an Emerging Market (2016) 25 Journal of Financial Intermediation.

[95] Elena Beccalli et al., 'Hidden Effects of Bank Recapitalisations' (2018) 94 Journal of Banking and Finance, 1.

[96] Thailand announced a plan for bank recapitalisation on 14 August 1998. Meanwhile, Malaysia announced a recapitalisation programme for commercial banks on 25

were pursued mainly by using government bonds to inject capital into ailing but viable banks. For example, in the case of Indonesia, the joint recapitalisation programme was utilised. Eligible banks which shareholders chose to participate in the recapitalisation programme had to provide 20 per cent of the capital shortfall. Meanwhile, the Indonesian government, through the Indonesian Bank Restructuring Agency (IBRA), injected the remaining 80 per cent of the capital shortfall. The contributions from the problem bank's shareholders and the government together comprise the four per cent minimum requirement of the capital adequacy ratio at that time.[97]

As for Thailand, private investor contribution was matched with the amount of the capital injected by the government subject to some conditions. First, the problem banks had to completely implement loan classification and provisioning rules by 2000. Secondly, the new equity injected received a preferred status. Thirdly, the government and the new investors possessed the right to change management. Lastly, the banks in trouble had to present a restructuring plan to the authorities.[98]

Nevertheless, some countries, especially fiscally-constrained states, might be unwilling to use recapitalisation measures to assist their domestic and foreign banks. This issue would be exacerbated during a crisis where the government's fiscal capacity becomes more limited.[99] With respect to this concern, Acharya et al. conducted a study regarding the relationship between the fiscal constraint of the governments in the Eurozone countries and their willingness to recapitalise banks. Acharya et al. find that the fiscal capacity of the sovereign determines the likelihood of the utilisation of recapitalisation measures. In other words, a more fiscally constrained sovereign could restrain or delay its assistance in recapitalising problem banks by, instead, using guarantees to assist those institutions.[100] The delay could, in turn, result in the vulnerability in the distressed banking sector to future economic shocks. In addition, it could lead to

March 1998. As for Indonesia, it revealed the plans for a joint recapitalisation programme of private banks on 30 September 1998. However, it was in March 1999 when the Indonesian programme began to recapitalise eligible banks. Lindgren et al. (n 629), 2–4.

[97] Unnava and Smith (n 719) 170.

[98] Lindgren et al. (n 629) 33.

[99] De Groen (n 716) 16.

[100] Acharya et al. (n 635) 4090.

the bank's poor practice of lending to low-quality borrowers and holding risky government bonds.[101]

In the case of ASEAN, countries such as Cambodia, Lao PDR, Vietnam and Myanmar might already have limited fiscal space.[102] Therefore, overseas branches and subsidiaries in these countries would be likely to have to seek a recapitalisation support from their home states. However, if the home state also experiences a systemic crisis, overseas branches and subsidiaries might not be able to secure any recapitalisation assistance from both the home and host states. For example, Saigon Thuong Tin Commercial Joint-Stock Bank (Sacombank), which is headquartered in Vietnam, has one subsidiary and nine branches located in Cambodia. In a systemic crisis which affects both Vietnam and Cambodia, the bank would be less likely to be recaptalised by those states.

Moreover, recapitalisation programmes implemented by each ASEAN state might lead to the problem of the inequality of treatment among banks and their creditors in a systemic crisis. That is because a state might have a discriminatory policy, which excludes foreign banks from its recapitalisation programme. For example, the joint recapitalisation programme of 1999 in Indonesia denied foreign and joint venture banks from gaining an equity support by the state.[103] Considering Fig. 1.1 in Chapter 1, in Indonesia there are 259 branches and/or subsidiaries of Singaporean banks, 920 branches and/or subsidiaries of banks headquartered in Malaysia, and three branches and/or subsidiaries of Thai banks. It is questionable whether or not these home states would be willing and able to rescue their banks located in Indonesia.

In order to consider the magnitude of potential issues, which could arise from national recapitalisation policies on foreign banks, Fig. 5.1 summarises the number of overseas branches and subsidiaries of banks

[101] Ibid 4124–4125.

[102] For example, Lao PDR experienced a fiscal crisis in 2022 as the government was unable to service its external debts. Souknilanh Keola, 'Averting fiscal crisis in Laos' (*EASTASIAFORUM*, 2 April 2022) < https://www.eastasiaforum.org/2022/04/02/averting-fiscal-crisis-in-laos/ > accessed 4 June 2025. Meanwhile, according to the World Bank's Press Release, Myanmar's economy has still contracted. World Bank, 'Myanmar Economy Remains Fragile, with Reform Reversal Weakening the Outlook' (*Press Release*, 21 July 2022) < https://www.worldbank.org/en/news/press-release/2022/07/21/myanmar-economy-remains-fragile-with-reform-reversals-further-weakening-the-outlook > accessed 4 June 2025.

[103] Unnava and Smith (n 719) 184.

headquartered in other ASEAN states in accordance with Fig. 1.1 in Chapter 1. Figure 5.1 shows that many ASEAN countries are the host states of more than 50 foreign bank branches (i.e., Indonesia, Thailand, Cambodia and the Philippines). According to Fig. 5.1, in the case that Indonesia chooses to pursue the same recapitalisation policy in the next crisis, the significant number of 1176 foreign branches of banks headquartered in other ASEAN states would not receive a recapitalisation support from the Indonesian government. Those foreign branches would have to rely on recapitalisation aids of their home states.

In addition, Fig. 5.2 illustrates the number of foreign bank branches and subsidiaries that ASEAN countries are the home states, in accordance with Fig. 1.1 in Chapter 1. Banks headquartered in Malaysia and Singapore have the largest numbers of branches and subsidiaries located in other ASEAN countries. In other words, these two countries are systemically important for the ASEAN sub-region. In the case that Malaysia and Singapore do not provide a recapitalisation assistance to their overseas branches located in other ASEAN countries, this could increase a systemic risk within this sub-region.

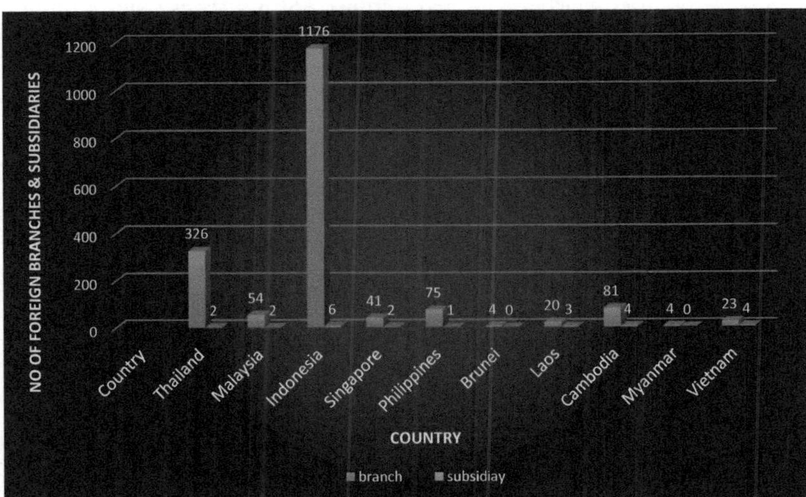

Fig. 5.1 Number of branches and subsidiaries of banks headquartered in other ASEAN states (*Source* Author's calculations based on Orbis Bank Focus and commercial banks' websites)

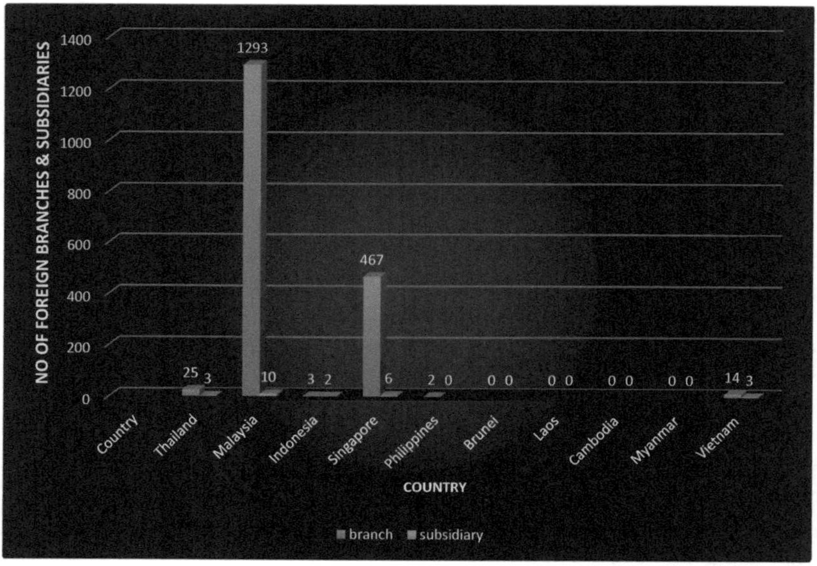

Fig. 5.2 Number of foreign branches and subsidiaries of banks headquartered in ASEAN countries which are located in other ASEAN states (*Source* Author's calculations based on Orbis Bank Focus and commercial banks' websites)

5.5 Troubled Asset Relief: Public Asset Management Companies

One of the most important tools to pursue a troubled asset relief programme is a 'bad bank' or asset management company (AMC).[104] A 'bad bank' or AMC is established in order to deal with non-performing assets (NPAs), which include NPLs.[105] A 'bad bank' differs from an AMC in that the former could be created for managing assets of a particular

[104] AMCs are suitable for managing commercial real estate loans rather than assets such as household mortgages, which could involve higher administrative costs. Lee et al. (n 696) 268.

[105] There is no universally accepted definition of the term NPLs; banks have a discretion to define the term as well as change it overtime. Nevertheless, the Basel Committee on Banking Supervision has defined NPLs as loans which are 'more than 90 days past due'. Rodrigo Olivares-Caminal and Andrea Miglionico, 'Non-performing Loans: Challenges and Options for Banks and Corporations' in Platon Monokroussos and Christos Gortsos

financial institution. Meanwhile, the latter should be established when the concerned problems have systemic impacts, which could jeopardise the public funds.[106] This part will focus upon an AMC rather than a 'bad bank'.

There are three main purposes of establishing an AMC: (1) to facilitate a bank resolution[107]; (2) to remove NPLs from the balance sheet of a still viable bank[108]; and (3) to enable the privatisation of state-owned institutions.[109,110] For the purposes of this chapter, the second function will be emphasised. According to the European Commission, a top-down centralised AMC should be set up if the NPL problem is prevalent in a large part of the national banking system. Moreover, the NPL problem should mainly concern 'loans secured by commercial real estate and large corporate exposures' rather than impaired assets which are markedly heterogeneous (e.g., retail customer loans).[111]

According to Ingves et al., during a crisis, it would be challenging to find investors who are willing to own an AMC without the government providing a guarantee for its operation.[112] Hence, from the perspective of the government, it would be more efficient to establish a public

(eds), *Non-performing Loans and Resolving Private Sector Insolvency: Experiences from the EU Periphery and the Case of Greece* (Springer Nature 2017), 18.

106 Caroline Cerruti and Ruth Neyens, *Public Asset Management Companies: A Toolkit* (World Bank 2016), 8–9.

107 Eg, Resolution Trust Corporation (RTC) in the US and the Thai Financial Sector Restructuring Agency (FRA). Stephen Ingves et al., 'Issues in the Establishment of Asset Management Companies' (2004) IMF Policy Discussion Paper, 5.

108 The functions of KAMCO of Korea and Danaharta of Malaysia spanned over both the first and the second groups. ibid.

109 Eg, the Financial Institutions Development Fund, which is part of the Bank of Thailand, owned an AMC which was responsible for the sale of Radanasin Bank. In the case of the IBRA, its functions cover all three groups. ibid.

110 Christos Gortsos, 'Non-performing Loans—New Risks and Policies: What Factors Drive the Performance of National Asset Management Companies? (2021) European Parliament, 14.

111 European Commission, 'AMC Blueprint' (2018) Commission Staff Working Document, 22.

112 In addition, 'NPL markets are not well developed or do not even exist in some countries in Asia and the Pacific. And even when they do, they are not liquid enough to be of significant help in resolving NPLs.' Lee et al. (n 696) 248. '...active NPL markets allow AMCs to raise funds by disposing of the NPLs acquired from banks with which AMCs can acquire more NPLs from banks'. Lee et al. (n 696) 268.

AMC, which might generate the profits from selling assets, rather than to seek a private AMC.[113] In addition, a study by Lee et al. demonstrates that a centralised public AMC is 'the most effective policy for reducing NPLs' in Asian countries when compared with other measures (i.e., government bank bailout or capital injections, and macro-prudential tightening).[114]Similarly, by analysing the effects of the AFC, Arner et al (2020) find that the combining use of 'state-backed AMCs' and balance sheet restructuring is the 'optimal approach' in managing NPLs.[115]

Furthermore, a public AMC has many advantages over an internal restructuring unit of the problem bank in mitigating a crisis. For example, public AMCs acquire assets at 'long-term economic values' instead of 'market prices'.[116] Hence, they help avoid imposing large losses on the bank balance sheets. Besides this, government-backed AMCs provide supports which reduce the need for a 'forced workout of NPLs'. This, in turn, decreases the necessity for banks to liquidate their assets at fire-sale prices—a practice which could exacerbate the crisis.[117]

Nevertheless, in the context of the European Union, the use of a national AMC has some limitations. It must be in compliance with the EU legal framework, especially the BRRD, the SRMR, and the state aid rules. This is irrespective of whether a resolution, national insolvency proceeding or precautionary recapitalisation[118] is utilised.[119] For instance, an impaired asset aid granted in transferring NPLs from a bank to a public AMC, which is at above 'estimated market value' (EMV) but below 'real economic value' (REV), could constitute a state aid or

[113] Ingves et al. (n 733) 7.

[114] Junkyu Lee et al., 'Countries Case Studies on Resolving Problem Loans in Asia: Crises, Policies, and Institutions' in John Fell et al. (n 696) 163. The country case studies include Thailand, Indonesia, Vietnam, Indonesia, Malaysia, and the Philippines among other Asian countries.

[115] Douglas W. Arner et al., 'Financial Stability, Resolution of Systemic Banking Crises and COVID-19: Toward an Appropriate Role for Public Support and Bailouts' (2020) University of Hong Kong Faculty of Law Research Paper No. 2020/044, 1.

[116] The IBRA of Indonesia is an exception. It acquired assets at the price of 0 as the payment was in the form of capital injection by the government. Lee et al. (n 740) 145.

[117] Lee et al. (n 696) 272.

[118] Precautionary recaptalisation could be utilised to facilitate a transfer of impaired assets to an AMC in the case that it effectively performs the same function as a capital injection measure. European Commission (n 737) 8.

[119] Ibid 7.

extraordinary public financial support.[120] In such circumstances, resolution or insolvency proceedings could be triggered. However, a bank could avoid being declared failing or likely to fail if such state support is considered a precautionary recapitalisation,[121] which is 'to remedy a serious disturbance in the economy of a Member State and to preserve financial stability'.[122]

In practice, an AMC is typically used in combination with recapitalisation measures. This can be considered from the practice of some ASEAN countries, which made use of both AMC and recapitalisation measures during the AFC. For instance, Danaharta of Malaysia, a centralised public AMC, required banks which were recapitalised by Danamodal, a bank recapitalisation company, to sell NPLs to it.[123] Besides this, in Indonesia, banks which were recapitalised had to transfer all bad loans to the IBRA.[124] The dual use of both AMC and recapitalisation strategies could be explained by the fact that these two measures are closely related to each other. On the one hand, in the case that impaired bank assets are purchased at above-market prices or more than their REV, this could, in effect, constitute an indirect recapitalisation. That is because the measure would reduce the need for recapitalising the transferring bank.[125] On the other hand, if the AMC buys assets at below-market prices or less than REV, this would result in losses on the transferring bank.[126]

In addition, the utilisation of an AMC needs to be combined with recapitalisation for both programmes to be effective. According to McNamara et al. (2021) and Brei et al. (2020), removing NPAs alone neither

[120] According to the Impaired Asset Communication of 2009, the transfer price must not be higher than the REV. Ibid 29.

[121] 'The precautionary recapitalisation budget can be used for any combination of recapitalisation aid (injected into the bank to recapitalise it) and impaired asset aid (as a contribution to a higher price at which the bank transfers impaired assets to the AMC to help bank avoid bearing full extent of losses that would stem from sale of the impaired assets in market). The sum of recapitalization aid and the impaired asset aid cannot exceed the precautionary recapitalisation budget'. Ibid 37.

[122] Article 32(4)(d) BRRD I. Ibid 7.

[123] Fung et al. (n 663) 30.

[124] Ibid 8.

[125] Christian M. McNamara et al., 'Broad-based Asset Management Programs' (2021) 3(2) The Journal of Financial Crises, 68.

[126] Ibid 49.

increased loan growth nor lowered the level of NPAs in the future. Similarly, using a recapitalisation measure without separating good from bad assets did not enhance the prospect of loan growth, although the level of NPAs was reduced.[127]

Apart from the need to use an AMC together with recapitalisation measures, the effectiveness of a state-owned AMC hinges, to a large extent, on the legal system and context in which it operates. For example, a research by the EBA regarding bank loan recovery finds that 'different legal cultures influencing the efficiency of different legal systems in providing timely resolution of NPLs'.[128] Besides this, the operation of a state-backed AMC could be subject to the risks of forbearance and susceptible to governance issues.[129] According to Cerruti and Neyens (2016), it is not suitable for countries which have weak rule of law and governance to establish a public AMC.[130] Cerruti and Neyens do not define what they mean by weak 'rule of law'. In my view, the meaning of the 'rule of law' used by Cerruti and Neyens is that which is vaguely utilised by the IFIs (e.g., the World Bank).

With respect to the view regarding the rule of law of the World Bank, the World Development Report 2002 states that the rule of law prevails where there are 'transparent legislation, fair laws, predictable enforcement, and accountable governments to maintain order, promote private sector growth, fight poverty, and have legitimacy'.[131] This interpretation of the meaning of the rule of law would be consistent with other commentators' views with respect to the necessary legal environment for

[127] Ibid. According to Brei et al., 'asset segregation is more effective when: (i) asset purchases are funded privately; (ii) smaller shares of the originating bank's assets are segregated; and (iii) asset segregation occurs in countries with more efficient legal systems'. Michael Brei et al., 'Bad Bank Resolutions and Bank Lending' (2020) BIS Working Paper No. 837, 1.

[128] In addition, the absence of options for out-of-court settlement and long moratoria are identified by the EBA as factors which prolong recovery time and affect the recovered amount. Gulija et al. (n 710) 20.

[129] Moritz Schularick et al., 'Bank Capital and the European Recovery from the COVID-19 Crisis' (2020) CEPR Discussion Paper No. DP14927, 3. In addition, a centralised public AMC is susceptible to the risk of political interference. Lindgren et al. (n 629) 39.

[130] Cerruti and Neyens (2016) (n 732) 10.

[131] World Bank, 'World Development Report 2002: Building Institutions for Markets' (Oxford University Press 2002), 3.

a government-driven AMC. For instance, McNamara et al. state that there should be a good legal system and enforcement of creditors' rights, as well as strong corporate governance and transparency for a 'broad-based asset management programme' to be successful.[132]

In the case of ASEAN, some states used public AMCs in order to cope with the mounting NPLs of their banks (i.e., Indonesia, Malaysia, Thailand and Vietnam).[133] The experience of these countries in using AMCs demonstrates the necessity of a well-functioning rule of law for the success of a public AMC. For instance, the struggle of the IBRA,[134] a centralised public AMC, provides a lesson about how 'weak rule of law' in the sense of the rule-of-law conception used by the IFIs, could act as an impediment to the functioning of a state-owned AMC.[135]

According to Enoch et al (2001), the lack of effective legal provisions in Indonesia at that time caused a delay in recovering the values of impaired bank assets, as the IBRA did not possess necessary powers

[132] McNamara et al. (n 751) 75.

[133] According to Lindgren et al., Indonesia and Malaysia chose to use a centralised public AMC. Meanwhile, Thailand's AMC originally dealt with only 'residual assets of closed finance companies'. Lindgren et al. (n 629) 6. At that time, Thailand preferred establishing bank-specific AMCs under the Emergency Decree on Asset Management Company (1998). In 2001, the Thai Asset Management Company (TAMC) was established under another Emergency Decree to deal with NPLs of financial institutions. Lee et al. (n 740) 147. With regard to Vietnam, the Debt and Assets Trading Company, which managed distressed assets from state-owned commercial banks, was established in 2003. Vietnam also established the Vietnam Asset Management Company, which copes with NPLs of credit institutions in 2013. Lee et al. (n 740) 148. As for the Philippines, it utilised private AMCs by passing the Special Purpose Vehicle (SPV) Act of 2002 (Republic Act No. 9182 (December 23, 2002) An act granting tax exemptions and fee privileges to special purpose vehicles which acquire or invest in non-performing assets, setting the regulatory framework therefor, and for other purposes). Lee et al. (n 740) 149.

[134] The IBRA's mandates were excessively broad when considering its capacity. The IBRA comprised three main units, which might be within separate organisations in other countries: 1) Asset management credit (AMC); 2) Asset management investment (AMI); and 3) Bank restructuring unit. Fung et al. (n 663) 9. These multiple tasks could have contributed to the IBRA's lower level of performance when compared with other AMCs in ASEAN, as it would be more difficult for the IBRA to focus on asset management. McNamara et al. (n 751) 49.

[135] After dissolution of IBRA, 'PT Perusahaan Pengelola Aset was established as a state-owned AMC in charge of managing the assets of IBRA, restructuring state-owned enterprises and managing state-owned assets. Indonesian banks rely on private, in-house methods. Foreign banks establish asset management units as nonperforming loan (NPL) warehousing entities'. Lee et al. (n 696) 253.

to secure those assets.[136] This situation continued until late 1998 when Section 37A of the Act No. 10 of 1998 amended the Act No. 7 of 1992.[137] Section 37A(3)(c) enables the IBRA to take control and manage the assets of the troubled institutions without the borrowers or owners' consent. Section 37A(3)(e) also allows the IBRA to sell the bank's assets located in or outside Indonesia without using a public auction. Besides this, the IBRA could 'threaten owners of failed banks with seizure of their assets for violation of prudential obligations'.[138]

In addition, the IBRA faced a credibility crisis in the eyes of the public as they had authorised the controversial 'payment of the interbank claims' to a problem bank—Bank Bali. There was a scandal that the owners of Bank Bali made payments to the politically powerful in Indonesia, in order to facilitate the payment of eligible outstanding interbank claims on the failed banks. As a consequence, those involved in the payments, including the IBRA, were subject to a full investigation.[139] Moreover, there were issues with respect to the lack of transparency of the IBRA's operation and its sufferance from political pressure. For instance, President Soeharto ordered that the work of the IBRA officials should not be made public. Besides this, 'the first head of IBRA was removed within a month of the agency's operation, under the reasoning that he was doing his job too diligently'.[140] Furthermore, the IBRA officials were 'unwilling to go after politically connected debtors' despite the fact that they 'possessed powerful enforcement mechanisms'.[141]

In contrast, Danaharta of Malaysia illustrates a successful story of a publicly funded AMC. Its main mission was to remove NPAs from the

[136] Charles Enoch et al., 'Indonesia: Anatomy of a Nanking Crisis: Two Years Living Dangerously 1997–99' (2001) IMF Working Paper WP/01/52, 77 < https://www.imf.org/en/Publications/WP/Issues/2016/12/30/Indonesia-Anatomy-of-a-Banking-Crisis-Two-Years-of-Living-Dangerously-199799-4074 > accessed 4 June 2025.

[137] Act of the Republic of Indonesia Number 7 of 1992 concerning banking as amended by Act Number 10 of 1998. < https://www.icj.org/wp-content/uploads/2013/01/Indonesia-Banking-Act-1992-1998-eng.pdf > accessed 4 June 2025.

[138] Enoch et al. (n 762) 77–78.

[139] Ibid 80.

[140] Unnava and Smith (n 719) 173.

[141] McNamara et al. states further that the officials of IBRA were 'often prevented from utilising' those enforcement mechanisms by Indonesian courts. McNamara et al. (n 751) 53.

bank balance sheets and maximise the recovery rates of the assets.[142] In addition, Danaharta embraced Malaysia's Code on Corporate Governance (2002) in it. Hence, its operation was conducted in a way which was consistent with international best practice (e.g., in term of transparency).[143] This soft law approach, in turn, provided a safeguard against the political interference in the functioning of Danaharta. Moreover, Danaharta could appoint Special Administrators, subject to an Oversight Committee's approval, to oversee the borrower in the case of non-viable loans. The Special Administrators could propose a workout plan, which Danaharta and a majority of secured creditors had to approve it.[144] Besides this, Danaharta could 'foreclose on real estate or equity shares pledged as collateral'.[145]

Furthermore, the existing laws equipped Danaharta with special legal powers, which allowed it to transfer assets from a failed bank quickly, without the need to obtain the borrowers' consent.[146] In other words, Danaharta could acquire a NPL through statutory vesting by issuing a vesting certificate, which gave it the same charge over the land possessed by the transferring bank.[147] The Malaysian government, then, provided a guarantee on zero coupon bonds to replace the transferred assets on the bank balance sheet.[148]

With respect to a sovereign guarantee facilitating the functioning of an AMC, it could generate a negative effect on financial stability by strengthening the sovereign-bank nexus and creating a doom-loop. As Buchheit and Gulati have stated, a sovereign will eventually need to restructure its debts, including contingent liabilities resulting from guarantees on third-party debts.[149] A state guarantee similar to that of the Malaysian

[142] Fung et al. (n 663) 30.

[143] Ibid 32.

[144] John Hawkins, 'Bank Restructuring in South-East Asia' (1997) BIS, 207.

[145] Fung et al. (n 663) 34.

[146] Ibid.

[147] Hawkins (n 770) 206–207.

[148] Fung et al. (n 663) 32.

[149] There are three possible ways to manage contingent liabilities of the sovereign in a debt restructuring. First, the contingent liabilities could be left intact, as they are not called by the beneficiaries or creditors. However, this strategy would pose a risk to the sovereign and its creditors in the future. Second, the sovereign could force the beneficiaries or creditors to call on the guarantees, and bring the liabilities into a debt restructuring.

government would bring an advantage to an AMC, which receives the government guarantee.

In the context of the EU, such state guarantee has to be in compliance with the EU state aid rules and bank resolution framework. Otherwise, it would be incompatible with the common market.[150] Nevertheless, a Member State could avoid a situation in which its guarantee is considered as a state aid by requiring an AMC to pay a market-conform guarantee fee in accordance with the Commission Notice (2008).[151]

Alternatively, an EU Member State could provide an aid-free guarantee by utilising NPL securitisation. In doing so, SPVs which securitise NPLs need to pay a market-oriented guarantee fee to the state.[152] In addition, two conditions must be satisfied for the state to be able to do so: (1) a credit rating agency approved by the ECB must confirm that the SPV's senior notes is of investment grade; and (2) not less than 50 per cent of junior and mezzanine tranches of the SPV's notes are sold to private investors.[153]

Apart from strengthening the link between the sovereign and its banks, the sovereign guarantee could impose costs on depositors as in the case of Cyprus. Most of the sovereign debts of Cyprus during the crisis in 2013 were governed by English law; they could not be restructured. Hence,

Third, the sovereign may honour the guarantees regardless of when the beneficiaries or creditors call on them. Lee C Buchheit and Mitu Gulati, 'The Treatment of Contingent Liabilities in a Sovereign Debt Restructuring' in John R LaBrosse et al. (eds), *Financial Crisis Containment and Government Guarantees* (Edward Elgar Publishing 2013), 208.

[150] European Commission (n 737) 16.

[151] 3.2 (d) of the Commission Notice on the application of Article 87 and 88 of the EC Treaty to state aid in the form of guarantee (2008/C 155/02).

[152] For instance, the Italian government set up the Guarantee on Securitisation of Non-Performing Loans (Garanzia sulla cartolarizzazione delle sofferenze (GACS)) facilitating the securitisation of NPLs, which were transferred to SPVs. According to the Commission Decision regarding the Guarantee Scheme for the securitisation of NPLs in Italy, in the case that the transferring entity of NPLs to a SPV is a bank, the transfer price must not be below the NPLs' net book value (NBV). However, there is no such requirement for the transfer to be aid-free if the transferring entity is a state-owned AMC. European Commission, 'Letter to the Member State' (SA 48,416), 4–5 < https://ec.europa.eu/competition/elojade/isef/case_details.cfm?proc_code=3_SA_48416 > accessed 4 June 2025.

[153] European Commission (n 737), 79–80.

the Cypriot government had to require uninsured depositors to take a haircut—a practice which effectively amounted to a co-insurance.[154]

In the case of cross-border banking, various levels of the strength of the rule of law in each ASEAN countries could raise a concern regarding the enabling legal environment for enforcing creditor's rights, and for the functioning of AMCs in mitigating the impact of bank failures. For example, assets of a banking group might locate across countries, which might not have a well-functioning or strong rule of law. The ineffectiveness of the AMCs due to the weaknesses of the legal environment in those countries could affect the financial position of the banking group as a whole.

The functioning of an AMC of a country in which a parent entity is established has an implication for the level of NPLs of its overseas subsidiaries. According to empirical research by Plekhanov and Skrzypinska (2022), the connection between the level of NPLs of a parent bank and that of its overseas subsidiaries is not negligible. Plekhanov and Skrzypinska find that a reduction of one per cent of NPLs of parent banks 'is associated with an approximately 0.25 per cent reduction in NPLs of their overseas subsidiaries.[155] Moreover, there are significant cross-border spillovers as a result of the establishment of an AMC in a country in which a parent bank is located. In other words, NPLs of the bank's overseas subsidiary reduce by 15 per cent per annum faster than those of domestic banks located in the same jurisdiction.[156]

The research results could be explained, in part, by the fact that an NPL shock at the level of the parent bank is 'likely to propagate to its subsidiary through the funding substitution effect. This weakens the ability of the subsidiary to deal with NPLs through timely provisioning and write-offs'.[157] In addition, the resolution of NPLs at the level of

[154] Asli Demirguc-Kunt, 'Cyprus Bank Bailout—Should Depositors Pay the Bills?' (*World Bank Blogs*, 25 March 2013) < https://blogs.worldbank.org/allaboutfinance/cyprus-bank-bailout-should-depositors-pay-the-bill > accessed 4 June 2025. The original plan to impose a haircut on all depositors was not pursued due to the fear of contagion, which could spread to other European countries. Marcus Miller and Dania Thomas, 'Eurozone Sovereign Debt Restructuring: Keeping the Vultures at Bay' (2013) 29 (4) Oxford Review of Economic Policy, 749.

[155] Alexander Plekhanov and Marta Skrzypinska, 'Cross-border Spillovers from Reducing Non-performing Loans' (2022) EBRD Working Paper No. 265, 11.

[156] Ibid 2.

[157] Ibid 5.

the parent entity might allow more resources to be allocated for the performance of its subsidiaries. In other words, the sale of the parent bank's NPLs to AMCs can release funds, which could be reallocated to its subsidiaries through 'internal capital markets'. As a consequence, the subsidiaries' ability to manage NPLs would be enhanced.[158]

Hence, it is crucially important that an AMC, which manages the assets of a parent bank, is efficient. Nevertheless, in some ASEAN countries, debt and collateral enforcement is an obstacle in resolving the NPLs of banks. For instance, according to the World Bank Doing Business 2020, the recovery rate and the time taken in Cambodia and Vietnam in resolving insolvency lagged far behind those of other ASEAN states. Resolution time in Cambodia took six years with the recovery rate of 14.6 cents on one US dollar while resolving insolvency in Vietnam took 5 years with the recovery rate of 21.3 cents on a US dollar. In contrast, it took only 0.8 years in Singapore to resolve insolvency with the recovery rate of 88.7 cents on a US dollar.[159]

However, it could be argued that Vietnam has already promulgated new laws and regulations which has helped improve the enabling legal environment for the functioning of an AMC and debt enforcement. For instance, Article 8 of Regulation No. 42[160] introduced in 2017 a fast-track court proceedings, as prescribed in the Civil Procedure Code to resolve disputes regarding collaterals.[161] Article 8 also enables the

[158] Ibid.

[159] Lee et al. (n 696) 255. The authors use World Bank Doing Business 2020 database. Lee et al. are of the view that there is a need to create a special legal framework in order to increase the efficiency of debt enforcement. Lee et al. (n 696) 259.

[160] Regulation No. 42/2017/QH14 Resolution on Pilot Settlement of bad debts of credit institutions.

[161] Lee et al. (n 696) 265. The fast-track court proceedings includes a 'hearing with one judge and only one conciliation attempt'. The new rules lessen resolution time around three to six months. Karry Lai, 'Vietnamese NPLs: New Right to Seize Secured Assets is Major Improvement' (*IFLR*, 4 April 2018) < https://www.iflr.com/article/2a63bc7p3g45ktam307b4/vietnamese-npls-new-right-to-seize-secured-assets-is-major-improvement> accessed 4 June 2025. Nevertheless, it is only a pilot scheme which was originally intended to last for five years. Later on, the Vietnamese government has approved an extension of the scheme until 15 August 2025. 'Gov't Approves Extension on Bad Debt Settlement Scheme' *VietnamPlus* (Hanoi, 30 March 2022). < https://en.vietnamplus.vn/govt-approves-extension-on-bad-debt-settlement-scheme/224271.vnp > accessed 4 June 2025. Meanwhile, the bad debt trading floor of the VAMC was created on 15 October 2021 in order to trade NPLs in the long run. 'Bad

Vietnam Asset Management Company (VAMC)[162] to sell distressed assets, including NPLs, to the public.[163] Besides this, Article 7(1) of Regulation No. 42 empowers the VAMC to seize secured assets without the need to initiate a Vietnamese court process.

Nonetheless, Article 7(2) of Regulation No. 42 makes the right of seizure of secured assets subject to some conditions. For example, according to Article 7(2)(d), the collaterals concerned must not be in dispute. In addition, Article 7(3) states that the creditor has to publish the information regarding when and where to seize the collateral, as well as the reasons for so doing at least 15 days before the seizure. According to Lai, a collateral holder or grantor could utilise these conditions to circumvent the creditor's right of seizure by taking a legal action during the 15-day period after the publication of the notice and before the seizure. Moreover, there is a legal uncertainty resulting from the fact that different enforcement agencies could interpret the condition of non-existence of disputes in different ways.[164]

This issue could affect the NPL resolution of the parent banks in Vietnam as well as the level of NPLs and the performance of their overseas affiliates. According to Fig. 1.1 of Chapter 1, there are 10 branches and/or subsidiaries of a Vietnamese bank in Cambodia (i.e., Sacombank) and seven branches and/or subsidiaries of Sacombank and Joint Stock Commercial Bank for Foreign Trade of Vietnam (Vietcombank) in Lao PDR.[165] Sacombank is the parent entity of most of those foreign branches and subsidiaries. Therefore, in the case that Sacombank fails and the VAMC cannot seize collaterals of the bank, the level of NPLs and the performance of the bank's 16 branches and subsidiaries in Lao PDR and Cambodia would be affected.

debt trading platform to start operation', *Viet Nam News* (Hanoi, 15 October 2021) < https://vietnamnews.vn/economy/1059268/bad-debt-trading-platform-to-start-operation.html > 19 April 2023.

162 The State Bank of Vietnam, a central bank, has established the VAMC in 2013. The VAMC has been established under Decree No. 53/2013/ND-CP of May 18, 2013, on the establishment, organization and operation of the Asset Management Company for Vietnamese credit institutions. According to Article 3 of the Decree No. 53/2013/ND-CP, the VAMC is intended to tackle NPLs and boost economic growth of the country. The VAMC only deals with NPLs of the parent banks. Lee et al. (n 696) 264.

163 Ibid 265.

164 Lai (n 787).

165 Vietcombank has one subsidiary in Lao PDR.

5.6 The Chiang Mai Initiative Multilateralisation and its Role as a Regional Financing Arrangement

In minimising the financial trilemma, there is a need to increase cooperation and coordination among ASEAN states in the areas of public assistance and fiscal backstop. Currently, there is no operative mechanism at the ASEAN level.[166] Nevertheless, the horizontal government network comprising central banks and finance ministries of ASEAN states and East Asian countries (i.e., Japan, Korea, China and Hong Kong) has created a regional financing arrangement (RFA) called the Chiang Mai Initiative Multilateralisation (CMIM). According to the IMF, a RFA is[167]:

> a financing mechanism through which a group of countries in a region pledges financial support to members that are experiencing, or might experience, a liquidity shortage or balance of payments difficulties. Resources are provided either through drawing from a pool of contributed or borrowed resources or through a swap of financial assets.

I argue that the CMIM has a prospect of contributing to the minimisation of the financial trilemma. Nonetheless, the CMIM needs some improvements in order to eliminate its weaknesses.

The CMIM arrangement, which was founded on its predecessor—the Chiang Mai Initiative (CMI) (2000–2009)—is an intergovernmental agreement initiated at the Annual Meeting of the Board of Governors of Asian Development Bank (ADB) in a northern province of Thailand—Chiang Mai.[168] The CMI (and the CMIM) were created as a 'self-help

[166] The ASEAN Swap Arrangement, which was established in 1977 to provide short-term liquidity support among participating ASEAN member countries, expired in 2021 due to the failure to sign the 8th Supplemental MOU. Bangko Sentral ng Pilipinas, 'Updates on the ASEAN Swap Arrangement' (24th SLC meeting, 18 October 2022).

[167] IMF, 'Stocktaking the Fund's Engagement with Regional Financing Arrangements' (2013) Policy Paper, 10 < https://www.imf.org/en/Publications/Policy-Papers/Issues/2016/12/31/Stocktaking-the-Funds-Engagement-with-Regional-Financing-Arrangements-PP4781 > accessed 4 June 2025.

[168] C. Randall Henning, *East Asian Financial Cooperation* (Columbia University Press 2002), 12.

mechanism' for Asian countries in response to the unsatisfactory assistance from the IMF and other IFIs in the aftermaths of the AFC.[169] The CMIM is based on currency swap agreements.[170] Currency swaps are a derivative contract based on a series of forwards,[171] in which contracting parties exchange income streams denominated in different currencies.[172] According to Duran, the increasing use of swaps is 'a symptom of an important change in international monetary politics and institutional design' of international lenders of last resort (ILOLRs).[173] In other words, it is a product of the unwillingness of emerging economies to seek an assistance from the IMF, which has acted as a 'de facto' ILOLR.[174] In addition, this institutional structure of the CMIM has manifested a lack of trust among Asian countries. These states prefer keeping their foreign reserves with their national central banks, rather than pooling those resources in the form of an Asian Monetary Fund.[175]

The Mechanism was set up outside the system of ASEAN institutions. It is also distinct from other ASEAN-related mechanisms in that it is a rules-based regime, which functions differently from the 'ASEAN Way'. The characteristics of the 'ASEAN Way' are that ASEAN's operations and

[169] IMF (n 793) 13–14. In addition, the CMI was intended to expand and enhance the ASEAN Swap Agreement, as well as form a regional network of bilateral swap arrangements. Hoe Ee Khor et al., 'ASEAN+3 Regional Financial Cooperation in Retrospect' in Khor et al. (n 685) 861.

[170] Camila Villard Duran, 'The International Lender of Last Resort for Emerging Countries: A Bilateral Currency Swap?' (2015) GE.G., Working Paper 2015/108, 7 < https://www.geg.ox.ac.uk/publication/geg-wp-2015108-international-lender-last-resort-emerging-countries-bilateral-currency > accessed 4 June 2025.

[171] 'A forward contract is an agreement to buy or sell a specified quantity of a specified type of asset (the reference asset) at a specified future date for a specified price'. Benjamin (n 425) 66.

[172] Ibid 67.

[173] Duran (n 796) 10.

[174] Lastra (n 641) 539. Stanley Fischer is also of the view that the IMF has acted as a LOLR despite the fact that it is not an international central bank. Fischer (n 628).

[175] Duran (796) 7. Concerning the issue of establishing an Asian Monetary Fund, according to Park et al., the proposal of Japan to do so was objected strongly by the IMF and the US. The objection was on the basis that it would result in a duplication of the IMF's functions, as well as increase the moral hazard arising from potentially more lenient conditionalities. Cyn-Young Park et al., 'Strengthening Asia's Financial Safety Net' (2019) Asian Development Bank, 1 < https://www.adb.org/publications/strengthening-asia-financial-safety-net > accessed 4 June 2025.

decision-making are based on non-binding decisions, consensus-driven processes, and informal institutional frameworks.[176] In contrast, the CMIM has a legal basis stemming from contractual agreements among central banks and finance ministries of the member countries. The rules regarding the CMIM's decision-making processes depend on the importance of the issue concerned. As for fundamental issues (e.g., the CMIM's total size[177] and the contribution of each party, etc.), the Ministerial Level Decision Making Body (MLDMB) comprising ASEAN+3 Finance Ministers and the governors of central banks must give an approval on a consensus basis.[178] However, executive level issues (e.g., renewal of drawing and events of default etc.) are not decided by a consensus-based approach. Instead, a two-thirds majority vote of the Executive Level Decision Making Body (ELDMB) is sufficient. The ELDMB consists of the deputy-level representatives of ASEAN+3 Finance Ministries and central banks, as well as that of the Monetary Authority of Hong Kong.[179]

In addition, in 2011, ASEAN+3 Macroeconomic Research Office (AMRO), which acts as the CMIM's surveillance unit, was founded. It was previously a company limited by guarantee in Singapore. Since 2016, AMRO has transformed into an international organisation established under public international law by a treaty with its own staff and budget.[180] According to Article 3 of the AMRO Agreement, AMRO has focused on four main areas: (1) monitoring, assessing and reporting to members regarding their 'macroeconomic status and financial soundness'; (2) identifying 'macroeconomic and financial risks and vulnerabilities in the region' as well as assisting members; (3) supporting the implementation of the CMIM; and (4) performing other activities as determined by the Executive Committee of AMRO.[181] In achieving these objectives, AMRO has carried out assessments of the member states quarterly

[176] Dorsh (n 89).

[177] The size of the CMIM is currently USD 240 billion.

[178] Plus-3 countries are China, Japan and Korea.

[179] Annex I of the Joint Ministerial Statement of the 13th ASEAN+3 Finance Ministers' Meeting, Tashkent, Uzbekistan (2 May 2010).

[180] Khor et al. (n 685), 864.

[181] Agreement Establishing ASEAN+3 Macroeconomic Research Office ('AMRO').

and biannually, as well as maintained close contact with regional policy-makers.[182]

In principle, the CMIM could help minimise the financial trilemma by increasing cooperation and coordination among member parties. For example, it could reduce the inequality of access to financial assistance of member economies in a crisis, by providing a regional fiscal backstop to those countries. In a circumstance in which there is no existing agreement, which promotes coordination, a bilateral swap arrangement could take a long time to coordinate.[183] Moreover, the success of a bilateral swap agreement depends heavily upon a political strength or diplomatic power of the seeking country against the providing state.[184] For instance, during the GFC, both Indonesia and Singapore sought to have a bilateral swap agreement with the US. However, the latter refused to provide an assistance to Indonesia, which was experiencing a sharp depreciation in its currency.[185]

Meanwhile, the US accepted the request for a swap agreement with Singapore. This was despite the fact that the financial standing of Singapore at that time did not actually require currency swap lines with the US. The US's practice could be explained by the fact that it has an amicable political relationship with Singapore rather than Indonesia.[186] In my view, it is unlikely that other ASEAN states would obtain a favourable position as in the case of Singapore for a bilateral currency swap with the

[182] Masahiro Kawai, 'Asia's Financial Stability as a Regional and Global Public Good' in Antoni Estevadeordal and Louis Goodman (eds), *21st Century Cooperation: Regional Public Goods, Global Governance, and Sustainable Development* (1st edn, Routledge 2017), 329.

[183] In the case of Thailand during the AFC, Thailand 'secretly sought financial assistance from China and Japan' after the devaluation of Thai baht on 2 July 1997. Freddy Orchard and Guani.e.,Lim, 'Thailand' in Khor et al. (eds) (n 685), 59. However, it was not until 11 August 1997 when the rescue package for Thailand was agree upon. More than 60 per cent of the package were supported by East Asian economies and Australia in the form of bilateral arrangements. Han (n 685) 713.

[184] Chalongphob Sussangkarn, 'Managing Economic Stability under Volatile Capital Flows: East Asia Perspectives' (2017) 16(1) Asian Economic Paper, 188.

[185] Kawai (n 683) 7. Indonesia 'secured $5.5 billion in 'standby loan facility,' or 'deferred drawdown options' from the World Bank ($2 billion), the ADB ($1.5 billion), Australia ($1 billion), and Japan ($1 billion)'.

[186] As a consequence of the failure to secure a bilateral swap agreement with the USA, Indonesia had to request a financial assistance from Japan, Australia, the World Bank and the ADB in order to raise funds for fiscal purposes. ibid.

US.[187] Besides this, according to Han, unlike Malaysia, the Philippines, Indonesia, Thailand and Singapore, non-ASEAN-5 states are normally not within the network of bilateral swap agreements.[188]

Nevertheless, it could be argued that, in practice, the CMIM might not be able to fully provide those benefits to the member parties and minimise the financial trilemma effectively. That is because the mere existence of the CMIM Agreement might not yield an adequate credibility in providing a fiscal backstop to a country suffering from a crisis for some reasons. First, it is questionable whether the CMIM could support a requesting party swiftly in a crisis, since the activation procedures of its facilities have not been concretised.[189] In addition, a disbursement of funds might take some time to administer, as there is no real fund contributed to the reserved pool of the CMIM. Instead, the member parties will only do so when there is a lending programme.[190] The funding structure

[187] These states need to seek a bilateral agreement with other Asian countries. Two states which are major providers of bilateral currency swaps in Asia are Japan and China. In the case of Japan, it has so far established bilateral currency swaps with Indonesia (swap commitment from Japan to Indonesia $22.76 billion) and the Philippines (from Japan to the Philippines ($6 billion); from the Philippines to Japan $0.5 billion) between US dollar versus domestic currency. Ibid 22. However, it is still uncertain whether other ASEAN states would be able to obtain bilateral currency swaps with Japan. Meanwhile, China has allowed some bilateral currency swaps; nevertheless, those swap lines are provided in renminbi. ibid 22. Therefore, it is doubtful whether those swap lines would be sufficient in a crisis since a seeking state might only need US dollars rather than other currencies.

[188] Han (n 685) 751.

[189] The CMIM Agreement mentions about the activation procedures that 'two countries will be appointed to coordinate the swap activation process when a request for drawing is made. Two Coordinating Countries shall be the two co-chairs of the ASEAN+3 Finance Minister Process, one Coordinating Country from ASEAN member countries and the other from China, Japan and Korea'. Annex I of the Joint Ministerial Statement of the 13th ASEAN+3 Finance Ministers' Meeting (n 805).

[190] Sussangkarn (n 810) 189. However, the prevailing view has evolved, as reflected in the Joint Statement of the 27th ASEAN+3 Finance Ministers' and Central Bank Governors' Meeting (2024), in which the policymakers expressed the view that the CMIM should be supported by a new paid-in capital structure. ASEAN Plus Three, *'Joint Statement of the 27th ASEAN+3 Finance Ministers' and Central Bank Governors' Meeting'* (Georgia, 3 May 2024) < https://aseanplusthree.asean.org/27th-afmgm3/ > accessed 4 June 2025. In addition, in 2025, ASEAN+3 policymakers agreed to focus on the IMF-type model for establishing the CMIM's paid-in capital structure. ASEAN Secretariat, *'Joint Statement of the 28th ASEAN+3 Finance Ministers' and Central Bank Governors' Meeting'* (Italy, 4 May 2025), 5 < https://asean.org/joint-statement-of-the-28th-asean3-finance-ministers-and-central-bank-governors-meeting/ > accessed 4 June 2025.

of the CMIM is based upon commitments by its members, which have declared their willingness to support the CMIM to perform its function as a 'regional financial safety net'.[191] However, there is no guarantee that in a systemic crisis in which many countries experience liquidity shortages or shocks in a similar scale simultaneously, those commitments will be honoured.

Moreover, according to the CMIM Agreement,[192] it is possible for the CMIM party to refuse to contribute to a swap request by securing an approval from a two-thirds majority of the ELDMB.[193] The number of votes allocated to each state is based upon its financial contribution to the CMIM. Hence, in the case that East Asian countries, which possess together around 80 per cent of the total number of votes, are not in favour of providing a swap line to ASEAN states, the latter are unlikely to obtain an assistance from the CMIM. Besides this, in exceptional circumstances (i.e., extraordinary or force majeure events, and domestic legal limitations), a member party could escape its commitment to provide funding by bypassing an approval of the ELDMB.[194] It is not clear whether a systemic crisis, which affects a contributing country severely, could constitute an 'exceptional circumstance'. If this is the case, the CMIM's financial assistance would be very unreliable during a crisis when it is most needed.

Secondly, the CMIM might not have adequate mandates and capacity to mitigate a systemic crisis in ASEAN. This is especially the case where there are no other sub-regional financial safety net mechanisms in place (e.g., an ASEAN deposit insurance regime). For instance, the CMIM focuses mainly on addressing balance of payments difficulties and mitigating a liquidity shortage; it does not aim to facilitate a recapitalisation of regional SIFIs.[195] In the case that there are bank runs in the sub-region, ASEAN states could not rely on the CMIM to recapitalise their banks.

[191] AMRO, 'Overview of the CMIM' < https://www.amro-asia.org/about-amro/amro-and-the-cmim/#:~:text=The%20amended%20Chiang%20Mai%20Initiative,effect%20on%2031%20March%202021 > accessed 4 June 2025.

[192] The CMIM Agreements are confidential documents which are not available to the public.

[193] Annex I of the Joint Ministerial Statement of the 13th ASEAN+3 Finance Ministers' Meeting (n 805).

[194] Ibid.

[195] Park et al. (n 801) 28.

In such instance, it is debatable whether some ASEAN states would be fiscally allowed to support foreign banks and mitigate the crisis. Besides this, a bank with cross-border operation might find itself in a situation in which neither the home state nor the host country is willing and able to provide a recapitalisation assistance.

In addition, the CMIM has equipped the member parties with only a few main lending instruments: (1) 'crisis prevention facility' called 'the CMIM Precautionary Line (CMIM-PL)' and (2) 'crisis resolution facility' or 'the CMIM Stability Facility (CMIM-SF)', and the newly launched Rapid Financing Facility (RFF). With regard to the CMIM-PL, it is intended to be used for precautionary purposes (e.g., temporary liquidity shortage and 'near-crisis situations'). According to Kawai, only the CMIM programme member economies which meet the prequalification requirements can gain access to it. Requesting countries will be assessed against five major criteria: (1) external position and market access; (2) fiscal policy; (3) monetary policy; (4) financial sector soundness and supervision and (5) data adequacy.[196]

In my view, the possibility that a member party is eligible to borrow the CMIM-PL would depend on how rigorous these five criteria are applied in practice. Countries which do not have a sufficiently strong financial standing to satisfy these criteria are also unlikely to meet the requirements in accessing other sources of financial assistance. For instance, the ADB's instruments also have access criteria for crisis support, which could disadvantage small low-income economies. In other words, these countries might not be 'ordinary capital resource-eligible'.[197] Typically, only countries which have achieved a higher level of economic development would be eligible for ordinary capital resources (OCR) loans.

In 2023, the ADB classifies developing member countries (DMCs) into regular OCR-only countries (e.g., Malaysia, Thailand, Indonesia, the Philippines and Vietnam) and concessional assistance countries. Within the latter category, there are two sub-categories: (1) OCR Blend countries (e.g., Timor-Leste) and (2) concessional assistance-only countries (e.g., Myanmar, Cambodia and Lao PDR).[198] As a result of being classified as

[196] Kawai (n 808) 320.

[197] Park et al. (n 801) 30.

[198] Asian Development Bank, 'Lending Policies and Rates' < https://www.adb.org/what-we-do/public-sector-financing/lending-policies-rates > accessed 4 June 2025.

concessional assistance-only countries, lower income ASEAN states could be excluded from emergency assistance of the ADB.[199]

Meanwhile, the CMIM-SF is expected to be utilised as a crisis response measure. It is only accessible to a member party which is facing a temporary balance of payments problem.[200] A member party can request the activation of swap transactions; however, the maximum arrangement amount or the swap quotas is capped to the amount of the contribution of each member multiplied by its purchasing multiple. For instance, Thailand has contributed for an amount of USD 9.104 billion and its purchasing multiple is 2.5. Therefore, the swap quota of Thailand is USD 22.76 billion.[201] It is doubtful whether this maximum arrangement amount will be sufficient to rescue Thailand in a crisis. For example, during the AFC, Thailand borrowed over THB 1 trillion (around USD 27.77 billion in 2022)[202] under three emergency decrees.[203]

Neither CMIM-PL nor CMIM-SF has ever been utilised since their inceptions. Duran (2015) has argued that during the GFC Korean and Indonesia did not seek an assistance from the CMI,[204] because they have taken a 'unilateral action (reserve accumulation) as their main international monetary policy' since the AFC. The accumulation of foreign reserves enabled these countries to utilise 'ad hoc' bilateral currency agreements, rather than relying on an aid of the CMI.[205] In addition, according to Hoe Ee Khor et al., there are various opinions as to the reasons why the CMI and CMIM facilities have never been used. Some commentators are of the view that there are stronger external buffers and improved capital flow management measures in ASEAN+3

199 Park et al. (n 801) 30.

200 Khor et al. (n 685) 862.

201 Han (n 685) 739.

202 1 USD is approximately 36 THB as of 13 July 2022. According to the data regarding public financing during the AFC, Thailand secured a rescue package for the total amount of USD 17.2 billion from multiple sources (e.g., the IMF, World Bank, ADB, Japan, US, Singapore etc.). ibid 714.

203 Thitima Chucherd, 'Financial Assistance of the State: How Much is Needed?' (*in Thai*) < https://www.bot.or.th/Thai/ResearchAndPublications/articles/Pages/Article_20Apr2020.aspx > accessed 4 June 2025.

204 The CMIM was established in 2009.

205 Duran (n 796) 21.

region, which render the CMIM assistance redundant. Other commentators such as Kawai and Morgan (2014) opine that the IMF stigma and the CMIM's nebulous process to draw funds deter the member economies from seeking its assistance.[206] The potential stigma is attributable to the fact that the IMF-delinked portion is only 40 per cent of the maximum swap quota of each member party—the level which might not be adequate to cope with a liquidity crisis.[207]

In my view, the IMF stigma could raise a grave concern to ASEAN countries, as some of them still have a painful memory about the IMF programmes operating in their countries during the AFC. In addition, the IMF stigma manifests the conflicting conceptions of the rule of law. The IMF's practice and its conception of the rule of law is that of neoliberalism stemming from the Washington Consensus.[208] Meanwhile, I argue that the national interest and economy are some of the most important factors determining the conceptions of the rule of law in ASEAN states.

In the aftermath of the AFC, the conception of the rule of law utilised by the IFIs, including the IMF, wrestled with those of ASEAN countries, which sought the IMF's assistance. For instance, the IMF's conditionality of a law reform created tensions on the rule of law in Thailand. According to the fifth Letter of Intent (LOI) (25 August 1998), Thailand must pass 11 economic laws in order to facilitate economic recovery.[209] These laws concerned, for example, foreign ownership of property, bankruptcy procedure and privatisation of state-owned enterprises.[210] The senate requested the LOI to be considered by the Parliament. However, the request was rejected by the government on the ground that the LOI is not a treaty as required in Section 224 of the Constitution of Thailand, B.E. 2540 (1997) to be approved by the National Assembly. The issue of the status

[206] Khor et al. (n 685) 870.

[207] Kawai (n 808) 328. This is despite the fact that the IMF-delinked portion was raised to 40 per cent in 2021 from the previous level of 30 per cent.

[208] See Chapter 1 for the discussion regarding the Washington Consensus.

[209] Frank Flatters, 'Thailand, the IMF and the Economic Crisis: First in, Fast Out?' (Conference on the Asian Financial Crisis and Taiwan's Role in the Region, Washington, D.C., April 1999), 19 < http://qed.econ.queensu.ca/faculty/flatters/main/writings.html > accessed 4 June 2025.

[210] Ibid.

of the LOI was later challenged in the Constitutional Court (Decision 11/2542).[211]

In addition, the 11 economic laws shifted the balance of power to the executive without providing any check-and-balance mechanism. For example, the most controversial piece of legislation among them was the Capital of State Enterprise Act of 1999 (often referred to as the Corporatisation Act). The Corporatisation Act 'provides a regulatory framework for the conversion of state enterprises to either private limited companies or public limited companies' (i.e., corporatisation).[212] After being corporatised, the company will be sold on the stock market (i.e., privatisation). The Act was criticised heavily as undemocratic.[213] The cabinet and the State Enterprise Capital Policy Committee, of which members were appointed by the executive,[214] monopolised the decision-making power.

The Act allowed the cabinet to dissolve state enterprises by a Royal Decree—a legal tool devoid of any participation from the legislative branch.[215] This is despite the fact that state enterprises are normally

[211] The decision was divided into three groups. The majority comprising six judges held that the LOI was not a contractual agreement. The minority of two judges dissented. The rest of five judges held that it was not for the Constitutional Court to decide this issue. They were of the view that this case should have been decided by the National Counter Corruption Commission.

[212] Chandler and Thong-Ek Law Offices Limited, 'Thai Power Sector' (2011), 3 < https://www.yumpu.com/en/document/read/41284531/thai-power-sector-chandler-and-thong-ek > accessed 4 June 2025.

[213] In 1982, when the Thai government, led by General Prem Tinsulanonda, signed an agreement with the IMF for its financial assistance, the IMF required Thailand to privatise its state enterprises. However, at that time there were strong trade unions. Therefore, the government did not follow the IMF-dictated privatisation programme. The IMF did not reduce or withdraw the financial support. However, in 1997, trade unions were not as strong as in 1982. This time the government decided to follow the IMF's conditionality strictly.

[214] The Committee is comprised of the Prime Minister (President of the Committee), not more than 15 ministers appointed by the Prime Minister, the President of the Bureau of the Budget, the Secretary General of the Office of the Council of the State, the Secretary General of the Office of the National Economic and Social Development Board, not more than 6 experts appointed by the cabinets to be committee members, the Permanent Under-Secretary of the Ministry of Finance to be the secretary and a committee member, a representative from the Ministry of Finance to be the vice-secretary and a committee member.

[215] A Royal Decree is a legal order approved by the king upon the recommendation of the cabinet. According to the Thai legal hierarchy, a Royal Decree is subordinated to

created by an Act of Parliament—a higher legal order.[216] It is not surprising that the 11 economic laws were considered by the public as being passed to benefit the powerful in the society, as well as foreigners whose ownership restrictions on Thai corporations and properties were relaxed.[217] As a result, the laws were turned into a political battlefield with diverse groups of people protesting against the government (e.g., non-governmental organisations (NGOs), academics, labour unions, civil rights activists etc.).[218]

Concerning the newest facility, ASEAN+3 members endorsed the establishment of the RFF at the 28th ASEAN+3 Finance Ministers' and Central Bank Governors' Meeting in May 2025. The RFF aims to provide rapid assistance to member parties affected by exogenous shocks (e.g., natural disasters and pandemics). It allows the use of certain currencies other than the USD (e.g. the Chinese renminbi) as the preferred medium of financing.[219] According to Yu and Lim, eligible member parties must demonstrate to the CMIM that they possess adequate capacity and a firm

the Constitution, an Act of Parliament and an Emergency Decree. A Royal Decree must not be contradictory to any related higher legal order.

[216] However, the Constitutional Court held on 4 December 1999 that the Corporatisation Act was legal and not contradictory to the Thai Constitution in Decision number 50/2542.

[217] Some critics called the 11 economic laws 'the eleven slavery laws'.

[218] The Foundation for Consumers, a NGO, and five individuals filed lawsuits in the Administrative Court arguing against the Royal Decrees enabling the privatisation of the Petroleum Authority of Thailand (PTT) and the Electricity Generating Authority of Thailand (EGAT). The Supreme Administrative Court delivered a decision against two Royal Decrees privatising the EGAT. The Court found that the SECP Committee, which was responsible for preparing the establishment of the corporation, had a conflict of interest. In addition, public hearings, which were required before corporatisation was conducted, were not held properly. However, the Royal Decrees of PTT were upheld as valid. 'Failure of Thaksin Regime: The Court Reversed the Corporatisation of EGAT' *Manager Online* (Bangkok, 23 March 2006) (*in Thai*) < https://mgronline.com/daily/detail/9490000039785 > accessed 4 June 2025.

[219] Zhou Lanxu, 'New Financing Facility Set Up to Bolster Stability' (*Chinadaily*, 6 May 2025) < https://www.chinadailyhk.com/hk/article/611045 > accessed 4 June 2025.

commitment to pursuing sound policy measures in order to receive assistance.[220] Currently, specific eligibility criteria for the RFF have not yet been made publicly available. In addition, it remains to be seen whether the member parties will ultimately choose to utilise this instrument.

Furthermore, the CMIM might not be able to help resolve some of the home-host issues by coordinating all aspects of bank crisis management. That is because it does not possess an adequate level of expertise, sufficient capacity, permanent staff members, and its own financial resources. In order to solve these institutional issues of the CMIM, Kawai has argued that AMRO needs to enhance its analytical capacity in order to assist the CMIM in performing its centralised functions (e.g., assessing whether a requesting member party has satisfied the prequalification criteria).[221] Besides this, the CMIM has to be able to discern whether a country is experiencing a liquidity shortage, or it is on the brink of a crisis. This capacity would, in turn, allow the CMIM to provide a right facility, since the CMIM-PL and CMIM-SF cannot be drawn by the same member party simultaneously.[222]

5.7 Conclusion

This chapter demonstrates that the financial trilemma exists when national governments seek to provide public assistance and/or fiscal backstop to their banks. An ASEAN state might treat banks differently depending on whether those entities are local or foreign banks. A state is likely to have a policy which protects its national interest and banks over those of other states. This is despite the fact that such a policy could jeopardise the common good of financial stability. Therefore, banks within the same banking group could receive an unequal treatment when they operate in different ASEAN countries. For example, the host state might not grant a financial assistance to foreign bank branches located in the country. Those overseas branches would, therefore, have to rely on the willingness and capacity of their home states to support them. Besides this, the issue of

[220] Jiangyan Yu and Justin Lim, 'Everything Everywhere All at Once: Revamping the ASEAN+3 RFA's Lending Toolkit' (*AMRO Blogs,* 9 January 2024) < https://amro-asia.org/everything-everywhere-all-at-once-revamping-the-asean3-rfas-lending-toolkit/ > accessed 4 June 2025.

[221] Kawai (n 683) 22.

[222] Kawai (n 808) 320.

inequality of treatment could be exacerbated in a systemic crisis when states are more fiscally constrained simultaneously.

Currently, ASEAN still lacks a comprehensive and coherent framework and tools for public assistance and fiscal backstop in cross-border cases. In my view, increasing financial integration and centralisation of power in this sub-region could help develop the necessary cooperation and coordination in minimising the financial trilemma. I argue that government networks such as the CMIM and AMRO could play an important role in so doing. Nevertheless, the functioning of these institutions is still subject to the willingness of the parties to contribute in a crisis. Moreover, the CMIM and AMRO need to improve as there are some major weaknesses in their operation (e.g., no prompt activation procedures to support a requesting party, and insufficient powers and resources to manage a systemic crisis).

References

Acharya V et al, 'Kicking the Can Down the Road: Government Interventions in the European Banking Sector' (2021) The Review of Financial Studies 34

AMRO, 'Overview of the CMIM'

Arner DW et al, 'Financial Stability, Resolution of Systemic Banking Crises and COVID-19: Toward an Appropriate Role for Public Support and Bailouts' (2020) University of Hong Kong Faculty of Law Research Paper No. 2020/044

ASEAN Plus Three, 'Joint Statement of the 27th ASEAN+3 Finance Ministers' and Central Bank Governors' Meeting' (Georgia, 3 May 2024)

ASEAN Secretariat, 'Joint Statement of the 28th ASEAN+3 Finance Ministers' and Central Bank Governors' Meeting' (Italy, 4 May 2025)

Asian Development Bank, 'Lending Policies and Rates'

Bangko Sentral ng Pilipinas, 'Updates on the ASEAN Swap Arrangement' (24th SLC meeting, 18 October 2022)

Bayu K., 'Blanket Guarantee, Deposit Insurance, and Risk-shifting Incentive: Evidence from Indonesia' (2011) MPRA Paper No. 35557

Beccalli E. et al, 'Hidden Effects of Bank Recapitalisations' (2018) 94 Journal of Banking and Finance

Benjamin J, Financial Law (Oxford University Press 2007)

Botes J. et al., 'Managing Banking Crises in Emerging Market Economies' (December 2021) FSI Insights on Policy Implementation No. 38

Brei M. et al, 'Bad Bank Resolutions and Bank Lending' (2020) BIS Working Paper No. 837

Briault C., 'Recovery Planning' (2020) Toronto Centre Note

Buchheit L.C. and Gulati M., 'The Treatment of Contingent Liabilities in a Sovereign Debt Restructuring' in John R LaBrosse et al (eds), *Financial Crisis Containment and Government Guarantees* (Edward Elgar Publishing 2013)

'Bad debt trading platform to start operation', *Viet Nam News* (Hanoi, 15 October 2021)

Cerruti C. and Neyens R., Public Asset Management Companies: A Toolkit (World Bank 2016)

Chandler and Thong-Ek Law Offices Limited, 'Thai Power Sector' (2011)

Cheng G., 'Finding Complementarities in IMF and RFA Toolkits' (2020) ESM Discussion Paper Series/8

Chucherd T., 'Financial Assistance of the State: How Much is Needed?' (*in Thai*)

Demirguc-Kunt A., 'Cyprus Bank Bailout—Should Depositors Pay the Bills?' (*World Bank Blogs*, 25 March 2013)

de Groen W.P., 'Precautionary Recapitalisations: Time for a Review' (2017) CEPS In-depth Analysis

de Lis S.F. and Garcia J., 'Funding before and in Resolution: A Proposal for a Funding in Resolution Mechanism' Regulation Watch (31 May 2018)

Dietz S.E., 'The ECB as Lender of Last Resort in the Eurozone? An Analysis of an Optimal Institutional Design of Emergency Liquidity Assistance Competence within the Context of the Banking Union' (2019) 26(5) Maastricht Journal of European and Comparative Law

Dobler M et al, 'The Lender of Last Resort Function after the Global Financial Crisis' (2016) IMF Working Paper WP/16/10

Domanski D. and Sushko V., 'Re-thinking the Lender of Last Resort: Workshop Summary', in *Re-thinking the Lender of Last Resort*, BIS Papers No 79 (September 2014)

Dorsh J, 'Regional Answers to the Global Crisis? Asia-Pacific Multilateral Organisations and the Economic Downturn' in Jorn Dosch and Christopher Dent (eds), The Asia-Pacific, Regionalism and the Global System (Cheltenham: Edward Elgar 2012)

Duran C.V., 'The International Lender of Last Resort for Emerging Countries: A Bilateral Currency Swap?' (2015) GE.G., Working Paper 2015/108

D'Hulster K, 'Cross-border Banking Supervision: Incentive Conflicts in Supervisory Information Sharing between Home and Host Supervisors' (2011) Journal of Banking Regulation 13 (4)

EBA, 'EBA Final Draft Regulatory Technical Standards on the Content of Recovery Plans under Article 5(10) of Directive 2014/59/EU Establishing a Framework for the Recovery and Resolution of Credit Institutions and Investment Firms' EBA/RTS/2014/11 (2014)

EBA, 'Guidelines on the Range of Scenarios to be Used in Recovery Plans' EBA/GL/2014/06 (2014)

Enoch C. et al, 'Indonesia: Anatomy of a Nanking Crisis: Two Years Living Dangerously 1997–99' (2001) IMF Working Paper WP/01/52

Enoch C. et al, 'Recapitalising Banks with Public Funds: Selected Issues' (1999) IMF working paper WP/99/139

European Central Bank, 'Recovery and Resolution: Banks Need to be Prepared'

European Commission, 'AMC Blueprint' (2018) Commission Staff Working Document

European Commission, 'Letter to the Member State' (SA 48416)

Farina M.R. and Scipione L., 'Recovery and Resolution Planning' in Mario P. Chiti and Vittorio Santoro (eds), The Palgrave Handbook of European Banking Union Law (Palgrave Macmillan Cham 2019)

Financial Stability Coordination Council, 'Systemic Risk Crisis Management Framework' (2022)

Fischer S., 'On the Need for an International Lender of Last Resort' (*IMF*, 3 January 1999)

Flatters F., 'Thailand, the IMF and the Economic Crisis: First in, Fast Out?' (Conference on the Asian Financial Crisis and Taiwan's Role in the Region, Washington, D.C., April 1999)

Freixas X. and Parigi B.M., 'Lender of Last Resort: A New Role for the Old Instrument' in Allen N. Berger et al, The Oxford Handbook of Banking (3rd edn, OUP 2019)

Fung B. et al, 'Public Asset Management Companies in East Asia—Case Studies', BIS (2005)

'Failure of Thaksin Regime: The Court Reversed the Corporatisation of EGAT' *Manager Online* (Bangkok, 23 March 2006) (*in Thai*)

Giannini C., ''Enemy of None but a Common Friend of All'? An International Perspective on the Lender-of-Last-Resort Function' (1999) IMF Working Paper

Gortsos C., 'Non-performing Loans—New Risks and Policies: What Factors Drive the Performance of National Asset Management Companies? (2021) European Parliament

Grande G. et al, 'Public Guarantees on Bank Bonds: Effectiveness and Distortions' (2011) 2011 (2) Financial Market Trends

Gropp R. et al, 'The Impacts of Public Guarantees on Bank Risk-taking: Evidence from a Natural Experiment' (2014) 18(2) Review of Finance

Gulija B. et al, 'ECB Significant-Bank Risk Profile and Covid-19 Crisis Containment: What Approach in the Transitioning Phase?' (2022) IADI Sponsored Paper Series

'Gov't Approves Extension on Bad Debt Settlement Scheme' *VietnamPlus* (Hanoi, 30 March 2022)

IADI, 'Transitioning from a Blanket Guarantee or Extended Coverage to a Limited Coverage System' (2012) IADI Discussion Paper

IMF, 'Stocktaking the Fund's Engagement with Regional Financing Arrangements' (2013) Policy Paper

Ingves S. et al, 'Issues in the Establishment of Asset Management Companies' (2004) IMF Policy Discussion Paper

Kawai M, 'Asia's Financial Stability as a Regional and Global Public Good' in Antoni Estevadeordal and Louis Goodman (eds), 21st Century Cooperation: Regional Public Goods, Global Governance, and Sustainable Development (1st edn, Routledge 2017)

Han B., 'The CMI and CMIM' in Hoe Ee Khor et al (eds), Trauma to Triumph: Rising from the Ashes of the Asian Financial Crisis (World Scientific Publishing Co. Pte. Ltd. 2022)

Hauser A., 'Lender of Last Resort Operations during the Financial Crisis: Seven Practical Lessons from the United Kingdom' in *Re-thinking the Lender of Last Resort*, BIS Papers No 79 (September 2014)

Hawkins J., 'Bank Restructuring in South-East Asia' (1997) BIS

Henning C.R., *East Asian Financial Cooperation* (Columbia University Press 2002)

Huertas T.F., 'Reset Required: The Euro Area Crisis Management and Deposit Insurance Framework' (2021) SAFE White Paper No. 85

Kawai M., 'From the Chiang Mai Initiative to an Asian Monetary Fund' (2015) ADBI Working Paper Series No. 527

Keola S., 'Averting fiscal crisis in Laos' (*EASTASIAFORUM*, 2 April 2022)

Khor H.E. et al, 'ASEAN+3 Regional Financial Cooperation in Retrospect' in Hoe Ee Khor et al (eds), Trauma to Triumph: Rising from the Ashes of the Asian Financial Crisis (World Scientific Publishing Co. Pte. Ltd. 2022)

Laeven L and Valencia F, 'Systemic Banking Crises: A New Database' (2008) IMF Working Paper WP/08/224

Lai K., 'Vietnamese NPLs: New Right to Seize Secured Assets is Major Improvement' (*IFLR*, 4 April 2018)

Lanxu Z, 'New Financing Facility Set Up to Bolster Stability' (*Chinadaily*, 6 May 2025)

Lastra RM, 'Emergency Liquidity Assistance and Systemic Risk' in Anita Anand, Systemic Risk, Institutional Design, and the Regulation of Financial Markets (OUP 2016)

Lastra RM, International Financial and Monetary Law (2nd edn, OUP 2015)

Lee J. et al, 'Countries Case Studies on Resolving Problem Loans in Asia: Crises, Policies, and Institutions' in John Fell et al (eds), Nonperforming Loans in Asia and Europe-Causes, Impacts, and Resolution Strategies (ADB 2021)

Lee J. et al, 'Strategies for Developing Asia's Nonperforming Loan Markets and Resolution Mechanisms' in John Fell et al (eds), Nonperforming Loans in Asia and Europe-Causes, Impacts, and Resolution Strategies (ADB 2021)

Levy A. and Schich S., 'The Design of Government Guarantees for Bank Bonds: Lessons from the Recent Financial Crisis (2010) 2010(1) Financial Market Trends

Lindgren C-J. et al, 'Financial Sector Crisis and Restructuring: Lessons from Asia' (1999) IMF Occasional Paper 188

Luong T.M. et al, 'The Impact of Government Guarantees on Banks' Wholesale Funding Costs and Risk-taking: Evidence from a Natural Experiment' (2020) 61 Pacific-Basin Finance Journal

Marks C. and Yao W., 'Recent Developments in Asian Deposit Guarantee Programmes' *Asia Focus* (October 2008)

McNamara CM et al, 'Broad-based Asset Management Programs' (2021) 3(2) The Journal of Financial Crises

Miller M. and Thomas D., 'Eurozone Sovereign Debt Restructuring: Keeping the Vultures at Bay' (2013) 29 (4) Oxford Review of Economic Policy

Monetary Authority of Singapore, 'Emergency Liquidity Assistance in Singapore' (June 2019)

Olivares-Caminal R. and Miglionico A., 'Non-performing Loans: Challenges and Options for Banks and Corporations' in Platon Monokroussos and Christos Gortsos (eds), Non-performing Loans and Resolving Private Sector Insolvency: Experiences from the EU Periphery and the Case of Greece (Springer Nature 2017)

Orchard F. and Lim G., 'Thailand' in Hoe Ee Khor et al (eds), Trauma to Triumph: Rising from the Ashes of the Asian Financial Crisis (World Scientific Publishing Co. Pte. Ltd. 2022)

Panetta F. et al., 'An Assessment of Financial Sector Rescue Programmes' (2009) BIS Papers No. 48

Park C-Y. et al, 'Strengthening Asia's Financial Safety Net' (2019) Asian Development Bank

Plekhanov A. and Skrzypinska M., 'Cross-border Spillovers from Reducing Non-performing Loans' (2022) EBRD Working Paper No. 265

Poczter S., 'The Long Term Effects of Bank Recapitalization: Evidence from an Emerging Market (2016) 25 Journal of Financial Intermediation

Schoenmaker D., 'Is Burden Sharing Needed for International Financial Stability? in Philipp Hartmann et al, *The Changing Fortunes of Central Banking* (Cambridge University Press 2018)

Schich S., 'Expanded Government Guarantees for Bank Liabilities: Selected Issues' (2009) 2009(1) Financial Market Trends

Schich S., 'Expanded Guarantees for Banks: Benefits, Costs and Exit Issues' (2009) 2009(2) Financial Market Trends

Schich S., 'Financial Crisis: Deposit Insurance and Related Financial Safety Net Aspects' (2008) Financial Market Trends

Schinasi G.J. and Teixeira P.G., 'The Lender of Last Resort in the European Single Financial Market' (2006) IMF working paper WP/06/127

Schoenmaker D., 'The Financial Trilemma' (2011) 111(1) Economics Letters 57

Schularick M. et al, 'Bank Capital and the European Recovery from the COVID-19 Crisis' (2020) CEPR Discussion Paper No. DP14927

Schwartz C. and Tan N., 'The Australian Government Guarantee Scheme: 2008–15' (Bulletin, March 2016)

Singh D and LaBrosse JR, 'Developing a Framework for Effective Crisis Management' (2012) (2) OECD Journal: Financial Market Trends 2011

Smith A., 'Australian Government Guarantee Scheme for Large Deposits and Wholesale Funding (Australia GFC)' (2020) 2 (3) Journal of Financial Crises

Sussangkarn C., 'Managing Economic Stability under Volatile Capital Flows: East Asia Perspectives' (2017) 16(1) Asian Economic Paper

Trove, 'Global Financial Crisis' Media Release (12 October 2008)

Tucker P., 'The Lender of Last Resort and Modern Central Banking: Principles and Reconstruction' in Re-thinking the Lender of Last Resort, BIS Papers No 79 (September 2014)

Unnava V. and Smith A., 'Indonesia Joint Recapitalisation of 1999' (2021) 3(3) The Journal of Financial Crises

Walker D and Hoontrakul P, 'Transitioning from Blanket to Limited Deposit Guarantees: Thailand Policy Considerations' (2001) SSRN Paper

World Bank Group, 'Evaluation of the World Bank Group's Early Response in Addressing the Economic Implications of COVID-19' (2021) Approach Paper

World Bank, 'Myanmar Economy Remains Fragile, with Reform Reversal Weakening the Outlook' (*Press Release*, 21 July 2022)

World Bank, 'World Development Report 2002: Building Institutions for Markets' (Oxford University Press 2002)

Yu J and Lim J, 'Everything Everywhere All at Once: Revamping the ASEAN+3 RFA's Lending Toolkit' (*AMRO Blogs*, 9 January 2024)

CHAPTER 6

Conclusion

Schoenmaker's model suggests that there are three objectives which cannot be pursued simultaneously: financial stability, financial integration, and national sovereignty. Only two out of the three goals could go hand in hand. It is likely that states would favour policies which protect their national interest in a crisis. In such circumstances, financial stability or financial integration could be jeopardised. Nevertheless, Schoenmaker argues that integration forces, which enable a centralisation of power and decision-making by using legal instruments, could allow the three main objectives to be achieved simultaneously. The monograph analyses this proposition in the context of cross-border bank crisis management in ASEAN.

The monograph begins with Chapter 1, which uses data from various sources (e.g., BIS, Orbis Bank Focus, and commercial banks' websites) to demonstrate that there are alarming concerns as financial integration in ASEAN has increased. For example, ASEAN states share some common lenders (e.g., US, UK and Japan). In the case that those lenders experience a crisis simultaneously, ASEAN states which financially expose to those countries would inevitably be adversely affected. In addition, Singapore and Malaysia are systemically important states in this sub-region, according to the number of foreign branches and subsidiaries that their banks have established in other ASEAN states. In the case that these two

© The Author(s), under exclusive license to Springer Nature Singapore Pte Ltd. 2025

W. Kun-amornpong, *The Financial Trilemma and Cross-border Bank Crisis Management in ASEAN*,
https://doi.org/10.1007/978-981-95-0512-8_6

countries are affected by a banking crisis occurring outside ASEAN sub-region, they could transmit a shock into Southeast Asia. Moreover, given the expansion of QABs under the ABIF, systemic risk in this sub-region could be intensified.

Schoenmaker has developed model-based solutions for the financial trilemma, by arguing that a greater level of integration by means of legal tools is key to an effective cooperation and coordination among countries during a crisis (e.g., integrated deposit insurance and bank resolution systems). In his view, soft laws and voluntary measures would not provide sufficient incentives for national authorities to follow them when a crisis exacerbates. The monograph then discusses how soft laws would, nevertheless, be an effective means in strengthening cooperation and coordination among national authorities. For example, soft laws could result in a social or reputational sanction for non-cooperative actors in a close-knit community of regulators.

In addition, various actors have been involved in using the law to pursue their objectives related to the financial trilemma. These actors employ different legal conceptions and tools, particularly the rule of law, in doing so. However, the rule of law has multiple meanings or conceptions; it might be understood differently by international actors (e.g., the IFIs and governance networks) and ASEAN states. In order to understand the rule of law in ASEAN, unique characteristics of this sub-region (in terms of history, political ideology, social norms, cultural values, and level of economic development) should be factored in.

Historically, the rule of law in ASEAN is under-developed. The functioning of ASEAN institutions relies on the diplomatic norms called the 'ASEAN Way'. The ASEAN Way is based on a consensus-based and non-confrontational approach. One of the drawbacks of the ASEAN Way is the fact that when national interests of the Member States are in conflict with each other, it is challenging, if not impossible, for ASEAN to propose a hard legal measure to solve the problem by consensus.

ASEAN might decide to utilise soft legal measures in order to minimise the financial trilemma in this sub-region. Soft legal instruments have been used extensively by government networks in many areas (e.g., bank supervision). According to Slaughter, government networks could reduce problems associated with the centralisation of power in many ways. For example, by engaging state authorities to work closely with other participants of the network, states would be less likely to consider that their national sovereignty has been infringed. In addition, national laws and practices of different countries could be harmonised as a result of the network providing information and trainings to the national actors.

Thus, the monograph argues in Chapter 2 that government networks could help minimise the financial trilemma as demonstrated by cross-border bank supervision. Those networks could be in the form of either a horizontal or vertical network. In the case of ASEAN, the horizontal government network of the BCBS has played an important role. This network utilises soft laws (e.g., BCPs) which are incorporated into national regulatory frameworks of ASEAN states. This is despite the fact that only Indonesia and Singapore are the Basel Committee members in this sub-region.

Nonetheless, the monograph argues that the effectiveness of soft laws and horizontal network of the BCBS has been reduced due to three main reasons: (1) the complexity of the risk model; (2) the unavailability of widely accepted rationale and measurement of its liquidity requirements; and (3) the inappropriateness of its design for developing countries and emerging markets. As for the risk model, its complexity and sophistication might not yield the best regulatory result. There is no guarantee that a complex risk model can create risk predictions which are more accurate than those produced by a simpler model. In addition, it is costly and burdensome for a state to administer and collect the information held by banks in order to use a complex risk model.

With regard to the liquidity requirements, they could act as a second-best solution to the LOLR intervention. Nevertheless, it is still uncertain whether those requirements could increase systemic risk. Besides this, the effects of liquidity requirements on banks' profitability and financial development are not conclusive. With respect to the inappropriateness of the design of Basel standards, low-income countries might have goals (e.g., financial inclusion and financial development) which are not consistent with those of the standards. Moreover, some developing countries might pursue policies of 'policy-directed credit', which are incompatible with a market-based allocation of credit assumed by the Basel standards. In the former case, states play an active role in allocating credits, while the latter allows the government to intervene in the market only when there is a market failure. Further, developing countries might not have infrastructure, resources, capacity and expertise to implement complex tools in accordance with the Basel standards.

Due to the weaknesses of the horizontal network of the BCBS, the monograph suggests that ASEAN might consider creating a vertical government network for bank supervision. In doing so, ASEAN could learn from the experience of the EU. Within the Banking Union, there is a vertical government network of national authorities and EU institutions (i.e., the SSM). The SSM ensures that relevant supervisory authorities behave in a similar manner. The EU Member States have delegated their power and authorities to a supranational organisation – the ECB. By supervising all significant financial institutions, the ECB can reduce home-host conflicts among the authorities of different Member States.

Nonetheless, the vertical government network of the SSM has some weaknesses. For example, the NCAs still have a large discretion in supervising their banks, because the Single Rulebook does not fully harmonise the SSM regulation. In addition, the ECB has to rely on the enforcement power and information from the NCAs. As a result, there could be enforcement arbitrages as well as agency problems. Moreover, the EBA – which issues draft technical standards and acts as a dispute mediator – might be subject to political influence of the national authorities.

In the case that ASEAN would like to follow the EU's path by creating a vertical government network, the monograph proposes three main steps for so doing:

(1) First, ASEAN should strengthen its capacity-building and training programmes, which would enable the non-ASEAN-5 countries to catch up with financial development of the ASEAN-5 states. It would also help the BCLMV countries in creating regulations which are in line with international standards.
(2) Secondly, ASEAN might need to empower its institutions which could take a role to minimise the financial trilemma, while a supranational authority for banking supervision has not been created. In doing so, rule-based norms would need to be strengthened.
(3) Lastly, ASEAN should create a supranational authority for banking supervision when the Member States are ready to do so.

Another area in which soft laws and government networks could play an important role for ASEAN, in centralising power as well as increasing cooperation and coordination, is bank resolution. The experience of the EU has demonstrated that a hard-law bank resolution regime might manifest some weaknesses if the whole system is not well-designed. For example, the BRRD regime has caused an inequality of treatment among creditors of banks. The EU has created a two-tier framework of bank resolution and insolvency in which the latter is a default option. Therefore, creditors of banks in cross-border cases could be treated differently, depending on whether the authorities in their jurisdictions decide that their banks should be resolved in resolution under the BRRD framework or be liquidated under NIPs.

In addition, the BRRD has merely provided a minimum harmonisation of rules. Therefore, the EU also utilises the vertical network of the SRM, which comprises NRAs and its supranational authorities—the SRB. The SRM was established under the SRMR in order to increase centralisation of decision-making power in resolution. In performing its tasks, the SRB has resorted to soft laws created by the governance network (i.e., the FSB). For instance, the SRB developed a common approach for assessing critical functions by creating the Critical Functions Template in accordance with the FSB assessments.

Moreover, soft laws developed by ISDA help enhance the effectiveness of hard laws, such as the BRRD. For example, in cases involving a temporary stay of contracts governed by non-EU law, market participants often prefer to use standard clauses provided by ISDA. Users of the ISDA MA are automatically subject to ISDA Protocols. The Protocols would help ensure consistent understanding and practice among their users. However, soft laws such as those of ISDA still need to be recognised by a domestic court in order to have a binding effect. According to Hugh Collins, when there are conflicts between ISDA MA and national laws, national courts are still unlikely to uphold a decision in favour of the former.

In the case of ASEAN, there are no common rules and regulations for ASEAN bank resolution. Cross-border resolution still relies on the horizontal government network of supervisory college and home-host supervision. The monograph argues that the existing horizontal network might not be sufficient for managing bank failures, as it could still create legal uncertainty in ASEAN. For example, it is uncertain whether the home or host rules would govern in a cross-border case, since ASEAN countries might have different policies, laws or rules in this area.

Moreover, the lack of common rules and regulations means that ASEAN Member States might use different criteria to differentiate banks which should be resolved in resolution from those which should be liquidated under NIPs. Besides this, some ASEAN countries have not established a bank resolution regime; therefore, those states have to rely on their NIPs in order to deal with bank failures. In the case that insolvency laws of the Member States are in conflict with each other, there would be no ASEAN conflict-of-law rule to resolve a dispute.

The strong effects of soft laws are further elaborated in Chapter 4, which uses deposit insurance as an illustration. The Core Principles of BCBS-IADI can produce robust effects in securing compliance of a particular state in several ways. For example, the IADI norms could be disseminated through a deposit insurer, which participates in the IADI forums, to other state authorities in the country. In addition, governance networks and IFIs might utilise the IADI Core Principles as a benchmark for international best practice. Hence, implementing agencies of a recipient state might be under an obligation to follow the IADI Core Principles in order to comply with the IFIs' financing agreement.

In contrast, the use of hard laws by the EU DGSD regime has revealed some soft aspects of hard legal measures. The monograph discusses those weaknesses from the perspectives of the synchronisation of the DGSD regime with other safety-net systems, as well as the incompleteness of the EU vertical government network. As for the synchronisation of the EU financial safety net regimes, the weaknesses could be considered from the non-traditional roles of the DGSs:

(1) financing a resolution to preserve continuous access to deposits;
(2) failure prevention; and
(3) preserving the access of depositors to covered deposits in insolvency proceedings.

With respect to the first function, the DGSD does not state that the DGS funds are the primary source for financing a resolution. However, the fact that the BRRD sets insolvency as a default option, as well as limits the use of the NRFAs and the SRF effectively renders the DGS funds to be potentially utilised in a wide range of cases. This would, in turn, raise a question regarding the adequacy and role of the DGS funds. Concerning failure prevention function, it is an NOD which the Member States can choose whether or not to transpose it. When using this function of the DGS, there are some inherent legal risks. For example, different structures of national DGSs could lead to different decisions regarding the compatibility of the measures concerned with state aid rules. With regards to the last function, the combination of the financial cap with the super-preference rule limits the amount of the DGS funds for alternative measures to the extent that it might cause financial instability concerns.

Apart from hard laws, the EU DGSD system utilises the vertical network of EU authorities and national DGS officials. Nevertheless, the incompleteness of the network makes it cumbersome for controlling and mitigating a systemic risk. For instance, there is no European deposit guarantee scheme; most of the tasks regarding DGSs are performed at the national level. Supranational organisations (e.g., the EBA) play a very limited role. In addition, the home DGSs do not have sufficient power to assume a greater role in supervising foreign branches of their banks, in spite of the fact that they are responsible for funding the liquidation of those entities.

Hence, the monograph argues that in the case of ASEAN, factors to be taken into account in order to improve the DISs in this sub-region should not be restricted to a consideration about legal form. That is because soft laws could be an effective measure in securing compliance from the Member States. In addition, there should be a well-functioning rule of law acting in the background in ASEAN, regardless of whether ASEAN decides to utilise soft or hard laws for an ASEAN DIS. For instance, there should be a well-designed legal framework to help safeguard the independence of deposit insurers, by preventing undue interference from other entities or political actors. Moreover, there should be a legal framework enabling insurers to have a sufficient power to obtain adequate and up-to-date information from the banking industry. Further, a harmonised ASEAN DIS regime would need support from strong bank supervision, as well as efficient resolution and liquidation proceedings.

Apart from bank supervision, resolution and deposit insurance, bank crisis management measures (e.g., state financial supports and fiscal backstop) are discussed in Chapter 5 as important tools in dealing with a systemic crisis. Such state support could lead to the financial trilemma, because national authorities are likely to protect their own interest, rather than take into account the effects of their policies on or problems of other states. The monograph categorises those state measures into four main groups:

(1) LOLR;
(2) guarantees;
(3) recapitalisation; and

(4) troubled asset relief or AMCs.

In the case of ASEAN, during the AFC, the Member States had policies regarding government supports provided to banks which manifested a willingness to protect their national interest. For example, Indonesia recaptalised only its local banks. Therefore, overseas branches of banks headquartered in other ASEAN states had to rely on the assistance of their home states, which might not always be available in a crisis. The monograph, then, highlights the fact that Malaysia and Singapore are systemically important home states in ASEAN due to their large numbers of overseas bank branches. Hence, policies regarding state support of these two countries are crucially important in the case that there is a banking crisis in this sub-region.

Chapter 5 also examined the importance of the rule of law regarding bank crisis management. For instance, the rule-of-law conception used by the IFIs is necessary for the success of public AMCs as in the case of the IBRA of Indonesia. However, ASEAN states might also need a rule-of-law concept which goes beyond institutional attributes, to focus on the ends of the rule of law. This necessity is demonstrated by the conflict between the rule-of-law conception of the IMF and that of Thailand in the aftermaths of the AFC.

The IMF mandated Thailand to conduct a law reform programme, which concentrated merely on reforming its legal institutions. The law reform programme overlooked some important aspects in the Thai society, including a strong willingness of the citizens to protect their national interest. As a consequence, the IMF's law reform programme and its rule of law, which emphasised only institutional attributes, resulted in tensions as well as widened the divide in the Thai society.

Furthermore, Chapter 5 discusses the importance of government networks for bank crisis management. The monograph argues that the horizontal government network of the CMIM, which comprises central banks and finance ministries of ASEAN + 3 countries, has a prospect to minimise the financial trilemma. The CMIM is a rule-based regime, which functions differently from the 'ASEAN Way'. It could, in principle, provide an equal access to financial supports to the parties. In addition, the centralisation of decision-making power at the regional level could, ideally, help reduce home-host conflicts. Besides this, AMRO, which acts as a surveillance unit of the CMIM, could increase information sharing among the parties by monitoring and identifying macroeconomic and financial risks in the region.

Nonetheless, the CMIM and AMRO should be equipped with more power, resources and capacity, in order to be able to mitigate a systemic risk in ASEAN. For instance, the CMIM does not aim to facilitate a recapitalisation of regional SIFIs, which might be necessary in coping with a systemic crisis. It merely focuses on addressing balance of payments difficulties and mitigating a liquidity shortage. The CMIM would be able to help pre-empt and mitigate a crisis more effectively if it had more facilities and tools which dovetail precisely with the needs of this sub-region. For example, the CMIM might provide a recapitalisation support to systemically important banks in ASEAN, in the case that such banks do not receive an assistance from both the home and host states. Such support would help prevent an associated risk of bank runs which might happen to ailing banks.

In addition, the IMF-delinked portion of the CMIM funds is far below the level of financial assistance which a country would need in a crisis. Increasing the IMF-delinked portion would help reduce the IMF stigma. This would, in turn, provide an incentive for the parties to use the CMIM funds. Besides this, AMRO should be allocated more resources so that it could enhance its organisational capacity to provide more timely policy advice and proactive assistance to members, as well as to support the decision-making of the CMIM.

Given the issues discussed throughout the monograph as well as the inadequacy of power, resources and capacity of the CMIM and AMRO, ASEAN states might consider using MOUs or other mechanisms to promote cooperation and coordination in cross-border bank crisis management beyond information-sharing. In addition, in the case that ASEAN decides to create an ASEAN bank crisis management framework, such framework should take into account the following recommendations:

- There should be a clear division of supervisory responsibility (e.g., whether the home or host state rules would be applied) among national supervisors in ASEAN regarding foreign bank branches and subsidiaries.
- ASEAN states' resolution triggers and identification criteria for distinguishing banks which should be resolved in resolution from

those which should be restructured or liquidated by NIPs should be harmonised.

- Bank resolution and/or (bank) insolvency regimes in ASEAN countries should provide a power for their national resolution authority or other competent authorities to enforce and recognise foreign resolution measures.
- National deposit insurance systems of ASEAN states should guarantee deposits in the accounts of overseas branches and subsidiaries of banks which are headquartered in their territories.
- National preference rules should be eliminated.
- ASEAN countries should use the same method for levying deposit insurance premiums (e.g., risk-based premiums).
- There should be an arrangement among the central banks of ASEAN states to provide liquidity assistance to overseas branches and subsidiaries of banks which are headquartered in their countries.

FSC
www.fsc.org
MIX
Papier | Fördert gute Waldnutzung
FSC® C083411

Kolibri 360 GmbH
Ferdinand-Jühlke-Straße 7
99095 Erfurt, Deutschland
produktsicherheit@kolibri360.de